D1097691

JAPANESE MAPLES

MOMIJI AND KAEDE

JAPANESE MAPLES

MOMIJI AND KAEDE

J. D. Vertrees

Timber Press   Forest Grove, Oregon

© Copyright Timber Press, 1978

Library of Congress Cataloging in Publication Data
Vertrees, J   D
    Japanese maples.
    Bibliography: p.
    Includes index.
    1. Japanese maple.   2. Fullmoon maple.   3. Maple
—Japan.   I. Title.
SB413.J34V47   634.9′722′7   77-18737
ISBN 0-917304-09-8

PRINTED IN THE UNITED STATES OF AMERICA

Timber Press
P.O. Box 92
Forest Grove, Oregon 97116

(ALL PHOTOGRAPHS BY THE AUTHOR)

Dedication

To Roseann—
Without her unselfish
encouragement, wisdom,
and devotion,
none of this would have
been possible.

Acer palmatum in the native forests of Japan.

(photo by Hideo Suzuki)

FOREWORD

The history of horticulture in Japan cannot be told without mentioning maples. For hundreds of years, the maple has penetrated into the hearts and gardens of the Japanese people from all walks of life. As far back as the seventh century they admired and appreciated its beauty in a romantic way as shown by a book of poems, *Man-Yoshu*, published in 614 A.D.

During the peaceful Edo era (1603–1867) the zeal and enthusiasm for cultivating this beautiful plant reached its height. People not only went out into the wild to enjoy it, holding maple-viewing parties, but also brought it into their places as a garden plant or as a bonsai. New varieties and new forms were especially sought after and poetic names given them as cultivars. A record shows that as many as two hundred named cultivars existed in those days.

However, to our regret, many of them were lost or disappeared during the recent war years. As peace was restored both to the country and to the minds of the people, interest has revived and the popularity of the plant increased. Today our nurserymen are trying to select new cultivars to compensate for what we have lost, although it seems that the number of cultivars is still far from reaching that of old days. Growers now propagate them on a larger scale, and with the increasing popularity overseas, also ship them to other countries.

A maple is a must in every Japanese garden, large or small—planted in the ground or potted as bonsai. Maples are cherished in the gardens because of their brilliant crimson new Spring growth, bright green leaves in Summer, red or gold foliage in Autumn, or the shapely appearance of branches in the Winter. A maple never fails to grasp the hearts of people when they recognize the ever-changing beauty. Thus, for hundreds of years in Japan the maple has been the subject of poems, novels, dramas, paintings, and other art forms. It has played an important role in developing the culture of the country.

An old writing, *Chikinsho* Supplement, published in 1710, illustrates thirty-six cultivars. Associated with the name of each cultivar is an old, famous poem. For instance, beside the precise drawing of the leaf of an old cultivar called 'Shigitatsu sawa', is a poem printed in artistic calligraphy:

"Kokoronaki minimo
Aware wa shirarekeri
Shigitatsu sawa no
Akino yugure"

'Shigitatsu sawa' means "near a swamp where solitary snipes start out." (Snipes, or woodcocks, flying up from a swamp.) In the poem, it is the name of a place called Shigitatsu sawa where snipes often stay. The gist of the poem is that even an insensitive person will deeply appreciate the charm of the scenery when standing by the maple cultivar 'Shigitatsu sawa' in the dusk of an Autumn evening, as when standing by the swamp of that name at the close of the day.

I have known the author of this book for many years. He was so fascinated with the beauty of these plants that he has devoted all his effort to intensive study of *A. palmatum* and other maple species and their cultivars for more than ten years. He has also accumulated one of the most complete collections of cultivars to be grown in one place. Although all were grown in Japan, some of them have become extremely rare, and some no longer exist in Japan to my knowledge.

I recognize that not a few cultivars are in trade under mistaken names in countries where Kanji characters are not used but are supposed to be intriguing poetic names in Japanese. Also, many synonyms seem to be confused. The author of this book is dedicated to clarifying the nomenclature and describing all of the cultivars, based on careful examination of his extensive collection.

This is the first book to be published on the subject in the English language. It will certainly be found useful around the world by gardeners, nurserymen, arboreta, and horticulturists.

May 1977
Hideo Suzuki
Saitama-ken, Japan

INTRODUCTION

 For more than 300 years Japanese Maples have been developed and selected for their beauty and variation of form and color. Japanese plantsmen have contributed to the world a heritage of beauty from this group of plants which are indigenous to their country.

The native Japanese Maple has the tendency to produce great variations within the species. By selection and cross pollination over 250 cultivars have been developed. Plants to fit every need in landscaping can be found, from the extremely dwarf forms with minute leaves to the bold upright types with large leaves. There are variations of color in foliage in Spring growth which are not found in other types of trees. Fall coloration among these cultivars becomes a second period of color explosion. There are variations of leaf shape from tiny, crinkled, strap-like, and lace-like to the bold, broad, large leaves of 'Ōsakazuki.' As time has passed these beautiful ornamental plants have found their way around the world in horticulture. Discerning plantsmen in many countries have recognized the beauty available in the use of these plants. They fit well with other genera as companion plants or make outstanding specimen plants.

A great many people associate the name Japanese Maple principally with the dissected form known in horticulture as "Red Laceleafed Maple" but desire information about other forms. Further confusion exists because other species of *Acers* growing in Japan are included with the *A. palmatum* in commerce. Nurserymen, collectors, propagators, and maple enthusiasts have indicated a need for a guide to the determination of the numerous forms of these maples.

There are small books, now in print in Japan, which give good descriptions of many of the cultivars presently grown. However, they are printed in Japanese and therefore are largely inaccessible to English-speaking horticulturists. In the English-speaking world there have been occasional writings in horticultural publications and magazines, together with annotated lists and taxonomic arrangements. Early nursery catalogs have given descriptions of some of the major cultivars. There has not been, however, a comprehensive work on the Japanese Maples which provides the English-speaking world a reference tool by which these maples may be understood.

This book has therefore been prepared to provide such a comprehensive source of information on and description of this general group of plants. "Typical" color leaf identification prints of the majority of the cultivars are presented to aid in determination of the cultivars. The difference between some cultivars is so slight that verbal descriptions may not be clear. Therefore, this is in part a book intended for identification.

The second purpose of the book is to clarify and simplify the nomenclature of these plants. Over many decades these plants spread from Japan to all parts of the world. In the course of this dispersion names have been confused, duplicated, lost, or new names substituted. The differences in languages, dialects, writing, spelling, pronunciation, and the neglect of detail in many countries have created nomenclature difficulties and confusion.

I have spent many years collecting information, having documents translated, viewing cultivars in several countries, and collecting specimen plant material. In many cases by growing plants of various "names" side by side I have been able to demonstrate and clarify synonyms or mis-nomers. In other cases we have studied original descriptions in the literature or received propagating material from verified stock plants for comparisons. The generous assistance of arboreta, collectors, nurseries, propagators, and research stations from many countries has added greatly to the availability of plant material and information for these comparative studies.

My third purpose in writing this book has been to provide guidance to gardeners, landscapers, nurserymen, etc. with an authoritative guide to propagation, cultivation and horticultural characteristics of this extraordinarily useful group of plants.

This book is designed to meet the needs of four types of readers: the amateur gardener, the avid plant enthusiast, the commercial nurseryman, and the serious dendrologist. I hope that it will assist all readers in enjoying and understanding Japanese Maples.

ACKNOWLEDGEMENTS

There will perhaps be some surprise that a comprehensive book on Japanese Maples should come out of the little town of Roseburg, Oregon, U.S.A. It is the result of a desire to learn as much as possible about these maples and to grow in one location for comparative purposes as many cultivars as we could find.

During the early years the progress in getting information and plant material was extremely slow. There were the readily-available eight or ten cultivars produced commercially throughout the United States. There were also a very few short and general-subject articles and references in the English language. The only books which dealt in any depth with the subject were written in Kanji (mainly illustrated with black and white pictures) and were of little use to me since I could not read Japanese.

Gradually through correspondence and personal visits, we became acquainted with people who had segments of information on the subject. With the complete cooperation of an understanding wife, the collection of cultivars began to grow in numbers—slowly at first, but more rapidly in later years. We obtained plant material from cooperative people around the world. Also, the collection of information began to grow: old books, publications in Japanese and Chinese, descriptive material from other countries, paintings in rare publications, copies of old Japanese nursery catalogs, and a few rare Japanese horticultural publications. In addition, the files of helpful, friendly, and informative correspondence grew rapidly.

It is to all the people who have helped in so many ways that I wish to express my sincere appreciation. In listing those who have been so helpful I do so with the fear that I may inadvertently omit someone who should be remembered. If I commit this error, I beg to be forgiven; it is not intentional.

Mr. Hideo Suzuki has been of immeasurable assistance in the entire production of this book. He is an outstanding authority in horticulture, particularly in azaleas and rhododendrons of Japan. As a life member of the American Rhododendron Society, President of the Japanese Rhododendron Society, and a frequent writer of horticulture articles, his authoritative assistance has been valuable. Hideo searched out obscure cultivars in the many islands of Japan and supplied descriptions and history of rare types. He also obtained books (some very rare) for my nomenclature and descriptive work. His ability and willingness to translate great amounts of Japanese writings into English gave authenticity to many cultivar descriptions and nomenclature. The countless hours and his tireless efforts on my behalf are gratefully acknowledged. This volume would have been less authentic without his assistance.

Mr. D. M. Van Gelderen has also contributed greatly to this book. His unselfish assistance in obtaining plant material and furnishing information has made the descriptions of cultivars and species much more complete. Dick and his wife, Hildi, devoted several days' time personally conducting us around Holland, giving us an opportunity to see old plants of many cultivars which we do not see in the United States. The Van Gelderens have an excellent nursery at Boskoop, Holland, the Firma C. Esveld, where they specialize in rhododendrons, conifers, Japanese Maples, and other high quality plant material. Dick supplied a large amount of information in several years of correspondence with the author. This included information on descriptions, nomenclature and history. His article in "Dendriflora", 1969, was one of the more descriptive articles to come from Europe in recent years. We are indeed indebted to the Van Gelderens.

J. G. S. Harris of Wiveliscombe, England, contributed greatly to the interest in other species of *Acer* (besides *A. palmatum* and *A. japonicum*), particularly those from Japan. Gordon is a well-recognized authority on *Acers*, widely traveled, and an excellent writer of many articles on *Acers* and their propagation. Following his visit to Maplewood, we had the pleasure of spending a few days at The Cottage, in Somerset. Many obscure Asiatic species have been grown and added to our collection from seed supplied by Mr. Harris. His assistance rounded out our entire study of maples, and we are grateful to him.

I would also like to express my gratitude to Mr. Harold G. Hillier for the several hours he spent with us "talking maples". Going with him through Hillier Gardens & Arboretum at Jermyns, (Ampfield, near Romsey) was most educational. This aided greatly in our search for clarification and verification of many cultivars, descriptions, and nomenclature.

Many individuals in arboreta have contributed greatly to this study. Plant material, information, and encouragement have all been unselfishly given over the years. At times, I well imagine I might have been of considerable bother to some of them. It would take many pages to list in detail all the assistance given me, and my gratitude is no less as I list them in a group:

Academiae Scientarium Hortus Botanicus Principalis, USSR. Vice-director, P. Lapin

The Arnold Arboretum, Jamaica Plain, Mass. Messrs. Alfred J. Fordham, Richard E. Weaver, Jr., Gary L. Koller, Stephen A. Spongberg, and Jack Alexander.

Botanischer Garten and Botanisches Museum, Berlin-Dahlem. Herr Kraft

Knightshayes Garden Trust, The Cottage Garden, Tiverton, Devon, England. Michael Hickson

Loth Lorien, Wadhurst, Sussex, England. Mr. Dan E. Mayers

The Morton Arboretum, Lisle, Illinois. Mr. Walter E. Eickhorst

The New York Botanical Gardens, Bronx, New York. Mr. Thomas Delendick

The Proefstation voor de Boomkwekerij, Boskoop, Holland

The Trompenburg Arboretum, Rotterdam, Holland. Mr. J. R. P. Van Hoey Smith

The University of Washington Arboretum, Seattle, Washington. Mr. Joe Witt, Director, and Mr. Brian O. Mulligan, Director-Emeritus.

The United States National Arboretum, Washington, D.C. Mr. Sylvester G. March, Horticulturist, and Mrs. Judith Shirley, Plant Propagator.

The Willowwood Arboretum, Gladstone, New Jersey. Dr. Benjamin Blackburn Zuiderpark, The Hague, Netherlands.

Many people in nurseries as well as other horticultural enthusiasts have been cooperative in supplying information, history, and plant material. I would like to thank the following friends:

Mr. Fred W. Bergman, Raraflora, Feasterville, Pennsylvania

Mr. William Curtis, Wil-Chris Acres, Sherwood, Oregon

Mr. Toichi Domoto, Domoto's Nursery, Hayward, California

Mr. Herman J. Grootendorst, F. J. Grootendorst & Sons, Ltd., Boskoop

Mrs. John Henny, Henny & Wennekamp, Inc., Salem, Oregon

Mr. Henry Hohman (posthumously) Kingsville Nursery, Kingsville, Md.

Mr. Boyd Kline, Siskiyou Rare Plant Nursery, Medford, Oregon

Mr. Jiro Kobayashi, Kobayashi Nursery, (and author) Japan

Mr. Michael Kristick, Wellsville, Pennsylvania

Mr. Roy Lancaster, Curator, The Hillier Arboretum collection, Jermyns, Ampfield

Mr. John Mitsch, Mitsch Nursery, Aurora, Oregon

Mr. Ken Ogata, Forest Experiment Station, Meguro, Tokyo

The Don Smiths, Watnong Nursery, Morris Plains, New Jersey

Mr. Joel Spingarn, Dwarf and Rare Plants, Baldwin, New York

Mr. Arnold Teese, Yamina Rare Plants, Victoria, Australia

Dr. Robert Ticknor, Professor, North Willamette Exper. Station, Oregon State University, Aurora, Oregon

Dr. Y. Tsukamoto, Professor, College of Agriculture, Kyoto Univ., Kyoto, Japan

Mr. Richard P. Wolff, Red Maple Nursery, Media, Pennsylvania

Mr. Arthur Wright, Jr., Wright's Nursery, Canby, Oregon

In every large undertaking there is one outstanding factor that makes the entire procedure possible. In my case, it is my wife, Roseann. Her contribution was of prime importance and consisted of: grammatical reconstruction, editing, guidance, encouragement, patience, and countless hours of typing and re-typing.

My eternal gratitude!

CONTENTS

I

CHARACTER AND HISTORY

―――――――――――――――

What Is A Japanese Maple?

The term "Japanese Maple" has two meanings. One is applied in the nursery industry to a group of small ornamental trees. For the serious dendrologist the second meaning indicates all the species of the genus *Acer* which are endemic to Japan and portions of neighboring regions.

The ornamental nursery industry in the United States has often grouped all the cultivars of a few species of *Acers* into this general term of Japanese Maples. Included are all the cultivars and forms of *A. palmatum*. However, we also find listed the cultivars of *A. japonicum*, *A. Sieboldianum*, *A. pseudo-sieboldianum*, *and A. shirasawanum*, and in some cases the extraordinary forms of *A. mono*, *A. truncatum*, *A. buergerianum*, *A. crataegifolium*, and even *A. rufinerve*.

The primary group centers around the more than 250 cultivars of *A. palmatum* and those of *A. japonicum*. The cultivars and variations of these two species have been bred, selected, and propagated for over 300 years by the Japanese. In their love of beauty and their infinite patience, they have been most discerning in their selection of these cultivars since at least the early 1600's. This, like many other aspects of their horticulture, forms a great part of their heritage and has been shared with horticulturists around the world. During the last 200 years these cultivars have found their way into horticultural collections, arboreta, and the nursery industry.

The second connotation of the term indicates the scientific difference of being "Maples from Japan." This includes more than 23 species of the genus *Acer* which occur in nature on the islands of Japan and adjacent territories. In some cases, writers group the species into the Asiatic species and include China and Korea. In that general area there are more species of the genus *Acer* than in the rest of the world area combined.

Many of these other species from Japan have interesting forms, horticultural cultivars, and varieties which are becoming popular in ornamental horticulture. There are magnificent forms, long neglected, which should be more widely used for landscaping.

In this book, however, I regard "Japanese Maples" as the term for the cultivars of *A. palmatum* and *A. japonicum*. All others become "Maples from Japan."

A. palmatum 'Red Pygmy'. In Fall color, the linearilobed cultivar, 'Red Pygmy', presents an entirely different appearance. Spring foliage is a rich maroon. The delicate leaves give the plants in this group a special appeal in landscaping.

Japanese Maples

To show the relationship of the "Japanese Maples" of horticulture and the other *Acers* which are closely related, I present the following taxonomic outline. This indicates the close relationship of *A. palmatum* and *A. japonicum* to certain other *Acers*.

Family *ACERACEAE*
　　Genus *Dipteronia*
　　Genus *Acer*
　　　　Subgenus *Acer*
　　　　　　Section *Palmata*
　　　　　　Series *Palmata*
　　　　　　　　Species:
　　　　　　　　　　A. anhweiense
　　　　　　　　　　A. ceriferum
　　　　　　　　　　A. pauciflorum
　　　　　　　　　　A. pubipalmatum
　　　　　　　　　　A. robustum
　　　　　　　　　　A. tenuifolium
　　　　　　　　　　A. shirasawanum — includes one noteable cultivar
　　　　　　　　　　A. pseudo-sieboldianum
　　　　　　　　　　A.Sieboldianum — includes a few cultivars in horticulture
　　　　　　　　　　A. circinatum. The "Vine Maple" of the N.W. United States.
　　　　　　　　　　　　The only species of Series *Palmata* outside of Asia
　　　　　　　　　　A. japonicum — many cultivars in horticultural cultivation
　　　　　　　　　　A. palmatum. — numerous cultivars in horticulture
　　　　　　　　　　　　Sub species, or varieties, (depending upon the author)
　　　　　　　　　　　　　　Var. *amoenum* — many horticultrual cultivars
　　　　　　　　　　　　　　Var. *Matsumurae* — many horticultural cultivars

The latter two species, and their subspecies and varieties, along with the numerous cultivars, comprise the "Japanese Maples" of the nursery industry.

Momiji and Kaede

These words are both used by the Japanese to indicate the species and cultivars of *Acer*. Academically, the word "Kaede" is more correctly applied. However, in horticultural use both "Momiji" and "Kaede" are used. There seems to be no distinct separation in the use, although most often "Momiji" is applied to those maples such as *A. palmatum* and its cultivars which have leaves with deeply separated lobes. Most other maples are termed "Kaede."

"Kaede" stems from the ancient language term "Kaerude"—(Kaeru = frog, de = hand). The lobed leaves of maples brought to mind the webbed hand of a frog. As the centuries passed, this was shortened to "Kaede."

"Momiji" may literally be translated "baby's hands", but it is not correct in this case to apply the meaning directly. Instead, one may apply it as "Little baby extends his tiny hands which are like the leaves of momiji (maple)."

On the other hand, in ancient times there was a verb "momizu", meaning "becomes crimson leaves." In more modern times the word changed to "Momiji" which is in use today.　　　　　　　　　(Courtesy Hideo Suzuki)

The Character of Japanese Maples

I admit prejudice, but I feel this group of plants has one of the greatest ranges of use and beauty of any of the horticultural plants in use today. The diversity of size, color, form, shape, and utility is so great that when selected wisely they will fit almost any need.

We do not think of them as blooming shrubs. Even though the maples have most interesting blossoms, some quite colorful, they are not a predominant characteristic. Many people do not even realize that they bloom. Blossoms of many cultivars such as *A. japonicum aconitifolium* are quite striking, though not large, and perhaps of interest only to the more discerning gardener.

However, the lack of bold blossoms is more than offset by the great variation of leaf color and shape which these plants can add to the color tone of the landscape. Spring foliage among the cultivars offers a wide choice in plant selection. In the larger forms there are the bold greens with rust or tangerine tones in the new foliage. The brilliant reds, orange-reds, maroons of many of the upright palmatums will lend accent to plantings. Wide choices also are possible with the variegated white-pink-green leaves such as 'Asahi zuru', 'Orido nishiki' 'Kasen nishiki', and many others. Nothing could look more like blooming shrubs than the extraordinary shell-pinks found in 'Corallinum', 'Matsugae', and 'Karasugawa'. The eye can never pass lightly over the flare of color which is presented by the brilliant flaming foliage of 'Shindeshōjō,' 'Shishio', 'Seigai', or 'Beni komachi', to name only a few. These brilliant fire-reds, crimsons, and tangerine-reds are so intense at times as to be almost fluorescent. All these color combinations occur in the larger, more upright forms. The same choices occur in the cultivars which are more dwarf and lend themselves to small companion plantings or container growing.

Unusual types such as 'Higasayama' have a "bloom" quality as the new buds unfold. They open much like pop-corn with irregular unfolding leaves colored in yellows and reds. 'Tsuma gaki' has new foliage which approaches a floral dispaly. These stages last for several weeks, thus giving a long "bloom" period. All the colored foliage will retain its brilliance for at least one or two months which is longer than most of our flowering shrubs will perform.

The dissectum group offers unusual brilliance and delicacy. Combinations of lace-like tracery of form, plus crimson, maroon, green-red, or variegated white-pink-green tones blend in the most pleasing way with the delicate cascading of the plant form. These make breathtaking specimen plants. They are even more striking when group-planted in the proper setting.

A second color display occurs each Fall, which is surely an added bonus when compared to most flowering shrubs. This show of Fall foliage color is absolutely spectacular. The bold green plant 'Ōsakazuki', for example, adds a strong green accent all season. Then in the Fall it bursts forth with the most vivid crimson flame display imaginable. Even in early morning light, or late evening dusk, the tones carry a fluorescent quality which demands attention. Equally vivid, but of a different crimson tonality, is the display of 'Maiku jaku', the Fern-leaf japonicum. I hesitate to list specific cultivars, fearing the reader will limit his thinking to just these few, when the possiblities are almost limitless. The several cultivars in the heptalobum group all present vivid yellows, orange, and orange-red foliage. Most of the japonicum selections are outstanding for Fall color. The delicate Golden Full Moon maple, *A. japonicum aureum*, 'Kinkakure' follows the Spring display of chartreuse yellow-green with a Fall display of gold, crimson, and orange, blended at times with purple overtones. One must see to believe.

Fall colors are an inherent characteristic of the plant. However, this can be suppressed or enhanced somewhat by conditions. Therefore, the landscaper who is aware of this malleability can aid in bringing about an excellent Fall display. As late Summer approaches and the late season growth is hardening off, it is best when possible to reduce the supply of moisture. Hardening for Fall will intensify the coloration as the season advances and colder temperatures begin to occur. A plant which has a continued supply of water will retain the leaves in greenish condition well into the Fall and may never color brilliantly. Eventually they will just turn brown with the early Winter temperatures and fall off. Slight stress, and we emphasize SLIGHT, will intensify the coloration of most of the Japanese Maples. Too much stress (or neglect as I mention elsewhere) and the leaves will rapidly turn brown and fall off. The discerning gardener will find the best level of culture under his own conditions.

In addition to the two "bloom" periods or seasons of striking coloration every year, these plants present such a wide range of size possiblities that there can be "a plant for every occasion." Some cultivars and selections of the species type will form tall, upright-growing trees. We can expect these plants to form a small tree of up to 9 to 10 meters (30-35 ft.) They will fit in landscaping in many ways: accent plants, shade for smaller understory plants, outline plantings along driveways and walks, interplanting with other similar size plants for "naturalizing" landscapes, or an outstanding specimen plant holding forth with its own importance.

Then there are the endless possibilities of the medium size selections. These include all those uses listed above but in addition they can be interplanted with rhododendrons and other flowering shrubs to provide variety and color. The magnificent cascading group which would include all the "laceleafs" or dissectum cultivars work well in mixed planting. There are numerous forms of lower-growing plants of great interest like the 'Shishigashira,' 'Tsuchigumo,' 'Katsura,' and the linear foliage groups as represented by that outstanding form 'Red Pygmy.' They naturally shape themselves into room-conserving plants and with additional shaping and pruning can be established in limited spaces. Again I point out that the beautiful Fall colors in these plants will brighten the otherwise dull Fall garden. Even the "red" forms of the lace-leaf, or threadleaf, cultivars take on an entirely different appearance in the Fall. Changing from their normal red, maroon, or greenish red tones of Summer, they flame out in a glory of crimson or gold tones which dominate a planting in late Fall and early Winter.

Dwarfs constitute another entire group which offers endless possibilities for use. Tucked in among alpine plants they will develop a blend of texture which cannot be attained with other genera. They make splendid companion plants with some of the smaller rhododendrons and other low-growing shrubs and perennials. They excel as accent plants in secluded nooks or bold sites in an informal landscape.

A wide range of dwarf material is available. The tangerine-colored 'Katsura,' the delicate foliage of 'Koto ito komachi,' the many forms of the yatsubusa group with tiny leaves, and the magnificent miniature growth and foliage of 'Goshiki kotohime' all illustrate choices for container growing as well as for small landscape plantings. In discussing container growing I include the range of size from large patio containers down to small bonsai pots. By using the dwarf forms for bonsai some of the problems of early training and establishment are overcome. However, we hasten to say that any of the *A. palmatum* and *A. japonicum* adapt quite well to bonsai formation. All of the cultivars as well as the species type and its varieties have been used in bonsai. Japanese Maples respond so well to pruning and shaping that they are an excellent choice for bonsai work.

In all descriptions of the range or size of plant, the extremes in size of leaves, the color range available, and the texture and form of the plants, I hesitate to name in this writing any particular cultivar names. I fear that in so doing I might cause a reader to choose something that is written and thereby overlook some outstanding cultivar unmentioned in this section. Suffice to say that there is such a great variation in leaf size, form, color, and texture, as well as plant size, shape, and vigor that one may find a plant or group of similar plants to fill almost any need in the garden landscape or containerized patio collection. Browsing through the section on cultivar descriptions will help you find just the plants you are seeking.

Variegation

The Japanese people have long been attracted to plants with variegated foliage. The selection and breeding of such plants has been going on for centuries, and they still regard these plants with special fondness.

The following story was told to me to illustrate the Japanese love of variegation. A rhododendron (*Rhododendron degronianum* f. *variegatum*) was exhibited a few years ago at an Ornamental Plant Fair. It was priced at 20,000,000 Yen, which at the time was equal to $66,000. (I wonder if business was booming!)

Variegation ranges from the extremes of total lack of chlorophyll to a very subtle marking on a few leaves. 'Nusitoriyama' has a total lack of green, and the leaves first emerge with a pink tone, soon changing to a pure white. Not quite so totally lacking in chlorophyll, 'Karasugawa' will have predominately pink and white foliage, irregularly marked with small amounts of normal green. White and pink variegations also occur in a few cultivars of dissectums. The other extreme is 'Iijima sunago' which has foliage of strong red-green tones, minutely flecked with darker spots. 'Kasen nishiki' has very subtle minute white flecks almost overshadowed by the basic green leaf color. A search through the cultivar section of this book will uncover numerous variegated cultivars with their descriptions.

Technically, these belong in a physiological group called Chimeras. Reference to technical books on the subject (such as Hartman and Kester) will give the reader a more thorough description of the genetic and cellular origin of these Chimeras. The term indicates that on a single plant, a tissue, in this case the foliage, may have two or more distinctly different types of tissue growing adjacent to each other. The white and pink variegations are totally devoid of plastids in those cells and lack the capacity to produce chlorophyll. The normal cells have the green colors. The mixture of these two types of cells within the leaf produces the pattern of variegation.

Some cultivars of Japanese Maples derive their names and were selected because of the color variation which occurs only with the production of Fall colors. I consider this a different origin of "variegation" than that described above.

Quite often the young stems producing variegated foliage also have a streaking of color tones in the bark. Some, like 'Orido nishiki' have pink stripes in the green bark, often rather subdued.

It is sometimes claimed that the plants "grow out" of their variegation. Perhaps as trees reach maturity, there is a tendency for the variegated character to become suppressed. I have taken wood from old plants of 'Versicolor', for example, which had "lost" the variegation. By taking young terminals from healthy side branches, the new grafts produced marked young plants.

I have observed in the nursery, and in older plantings, that culture may have a large influence on the retention of variegation. Plants that are over-fed and produce exceptionally long shoots of new growth may have the variegation suppressed in that wood. Markings may also be masked, or overcome, with excessive nitrogen feeding in the absence of sufficient phosphate and potash. This can be observed in container growing of young grafts.

Conversely, trees grown in totally unfavorable conditions may produce wood so lacking in vigor that the tendency toward variegation is masked. I have received scions from such types of plants and grafted well-marked plants. Summer foliage of the parent plant showed almost a total lack of marking.

Occasionally I have had a variegated cultivar produce a shoot which lacked all markings of the cultivar. I intentionally grafted from these shoots. The majority of the grafts resumed the characteristic variegation. The remainder developed typical palmatum foliage.

In view of this fact, I usually try to mark the best variegated young growth on a cultivar during the foliage season. Then, when collecting scions for grafting during the dormant season, I am able to cut the best-marked wood. This does not apply to all cultivars but only those that produce strong unmarked shoots.

There are other causes for variation in leaf markings: certain viruses, excessive soil pH condition, or a lack of one of the minor elements necessary for total nutrition. Such variations are all so different in appearance from variegation that they are immediately apparent. If in doubt, plant disease experts can usually give a prompt determination.

Variegated cultivars can only be perpetuated true to form through vegetative propagation. The seed from variegated cultivars will not produce the true form of the parent tree. There are occasionally exceptions. I have planted large amounts of seed, for example, from 'Shigitatsu sawa' ('Reticulatum').Most of the seed will produce the normal green palmatum type. Occasionally, however, a seedling will show the characteristic yellow leaf with green veining of the parent. One must not distribute these as the cultivar 'Shigitatsu sawa' but only as "seedlings from . . .". This is true with seedlings from all other named cultivars of any type when the seedling is similar to the parent. Named cultivars must be propagated vegetatively to prevent dilution of the true cultivar.

In Regard to Fu

The variegated group of cultivars in the Japanese Maples is increasing due to selection and cross breeding. New and beautiful cultivars continue to arise from these efforts. The Japanese reference to variegation is termed Fu. In a Japanese-American dictionary one might find at least 20 interpretations for the word Fu and undoubtedly there are more. However, when applied to the horticultural usage, it refers to dots, mottles, specks, and marks on a leaf of different background.

This, then is Fu.

To help the reader better understand the terms and names used in Japan to identify variegation I offer the following:

Fukurin Fu (Fuku=cover, Rin=ring or circle) Denotes the type of variegation which appears as a different color or tone along the outer margin of the leaf lobe. Used usually for a rather uniform marking.

Shin Fukurin Fu (Shin=deep) Indicates a deep variegated marking around the edge of the lobe.

Ito Fukurin Fu (Ito=thread, Hoso=slender) Contrasts with Shin Fukurin Fu to describe a very narrow margin around the lobe. It may also be written as Hoso Fukurin Fu.

Fukurin Kuzure (Kuzure=irregular) Indicates an irregular margin of variegation around the edge of the lobe.

Sunago Fukurin (Sunago=sand) Refers to a very fine speckling or dotting in the margins only.

Tsuma Fukurin Fu (Tsuma=nail) Describes a margin which is stronger near the point of the lobe—not an even margin of variegation all around the lobe. Leaves with white tips on the lobes are indicated by 'Tsuma jiro' (Tsuma shiro) which indicates "white nail." Of course, the counterpart, 'Tsuma beni,' indicates "red nail" as in the cultivar of that name. It has a light green leaf with the tip of the sharp lobe contrasting red.

Ubu Fu (Ubu=naive or virgin) Denotes instances where the variegation covers almost the entire leaf, or a pure white leaf, such as is found in the cultivar of *A. buergerianum* 'Nusitoriyama.'

Kiri Fu (Kiri=cut) Describes leaves with half the leaf variegated to the center vein with the other half normal.

Haki Homi Fu (Haki homi=brushed in) Describes the type of variegation which appears to be created by brushing in the white or yellow color on the base tone of the leaf.

Hoshi Fu (Hoshi=star or stars)Denotes the delicate "star-dust" variegations which appear on the background of green. *A. mono* 'Hoshiyadori' derives its name from this term.

Sunago Fu (Sunago-sand) Indicates dots or tiny markings (smaller than Hoshi) which cover most or all the surface of the leaf, often indistinctly. 'Iijima sunago', and 'Usu gumo' exemplify this form. Synonymous with this is Shimo Furi Fu (Shimo=frost, Furi=scattered). Fukiwake is a similar term but used very little.

Goma Fu (Goma=sesame seed) Indicates green blotching when it appears on pure white leaves (Ubu Fu) usually as quite small markings.

History of Japanese Cultivars

The Japanese have long been famous and admired for their intense and sensitive work in horticultural science. Their work with azaleas, bonsai, chrysanthemums, and maples has contributed much to the pleasure of the rest of the world. The native species, *Acer palmatum,* was found to adapt to the specialized types of horticulture which became a significant part of the Japanese heritage. From very early times the Japanese people revered, selected, propagated and increased the number of types.

The species *Acer palmatum* and its varieties is endemic almost wholly to Japan. A few geographical varieties occur in Korea and parts of China . The species occurs in a wide range of soil conditions, on most of the islands of Japan, and in a variety of exposures. It is found from 100 to 1300 meters above sea level. In its wide range it is like the North American native "Vine Maple", *A. circinatum*, which is indeed closely related to the Japanese Maple.

The species displays many variations in its native habitat, and these are designated subspecies, varieties, and forms. "New" types developed in the confines of domestic horticulture give rise to the term "cultivar" in its present day sense. Viz: "a variety from cultivation".

I have to conclude that this species has a strong genetic tendency to proliferate into many variations, mutations, and sports. In the very early days of horticulture, the Japanese collected the outstanding and beautiful forms of the palmatums from the native stands. These consisted of seedling sports and variants. In addition, as bud mutations were discovered, they were propagated vegetatively and introduced into cultivation. As the number of these plant materials increased, they were planted in close proximity and cross-pollination occurred. The various parents of unusual form, therefore, gave rise to additional hybrid variants. This process expanded, and the genetic potential for new and interesting seedlings and sports proliferated. Over a 300-year period of intensive culture, this process has yielded a great number of selections and cultivars.

During the Edo Era (1603 to 1867) horticulture flourished and reached a high level of development in selection, breeding, culture, and specialization. Many of the cultivars of the native Japanese trees and shrubs were brought into intensive development—notably azaleas and maples.

The Japanese Maples reached a peak of popularity from the middle of the 17th Century to the late 18th Century. It became fashionable to select, cultivate, and nurture as many different types as possible. Collectors and gardeners searched for mutations and sports among the native stands as well as through gardens and large landscape plantings.

A standard garden book published in 1710 mentions 36 named varieties of *A. palmatum*. By 1733, 28 additional names were listed. An *Acer* list of 1882 numbered 202 varieties or cultivars. This rapid increase is spectacular, and yet undoubtedly did not include all the named types due to extent of cultivation, lack of communication, and the large number of gardeners pursuing the vogue. Combining lists from older literature we can safely assume that there were more than 250 cultivars at the height of this period.

In the early 1900's, interest waned and some of the less spectacular cultivars were dropped from wide propagation. Even during this period, however, outstanding new cultivars were being named. As late as 1930 the Angyo Maple Nursery listed 219 named cultivars and types in propagation.

A sad period occurred in the 1940's. During the war years economic conditions caused many cultivars to be destroyed and lost to cultivation. Areas previously devoted to ornamental horticulture were used for food production. Old maples were cut to alleviate shortages of fuel and wood. One nurseryman tells of his ancestors having put together a very large collection of cultivars over the generations only to have many of them burned as fire wood.

In the past decade, interest in Japanese Maples has been re-kindled. Once again observant selection and careful development of additional cultivars is going forward. Increased propagation of some of the older cultivars has allowed the wider distribution of many choice types to the rest of the world.

While the list of names referred to in this book will total several hundred, the presence of synonyms, alternate names, misnomers, and misapplications will reduce the valid number of cultivars.

As interest spreads and observant fanciers work with this group of plants, we can expect outstanding cultivars to be "discovered" and introduced. The magnificent new dissectum 'Red Filigree Lace' just being introduced exemplifies this point.

Old Literature on Japanese Maples

There were many other ancient Japanese writings on the maple group. These listed represent the more typical and useful compilations.

One of the earliest known books dealing with descriptions of Japanese Maples was published in 1695. It was titled *Kadan Chikinshō* and was written by Mr. San-nojō Hanado. It must have been a major work on horticulture as it extended to six volumes and covered the entire range of ornamental trees and shrubs.

Following this was a publication in 1710 titled *Zōho Chikinshō* written by Mr. Ibei Itō. Ibei Itō is said to have been the son of San-nojō Hanado, although their family names are different. This was a revision of the former book covering the range of ornamental trees and shrubs of Japan and comprised eight volumes. Volume 4 dealt with the maples.

Kōeki Chikinshō was another revision by Mr. Ibei Itō done in 1719 as an eight-volume set with maples described in volume 3. In 1733 he put out *Chikinshō Furoku*, "Furoku" meaning supplement.

In 1882 the *Kaede Binran* was published by Seigorō Oka, Isaburō Itō, and Gosaburō Itō. Probably Isaburō and Gosaburō were descendants of Ibei Itō who wrote the earlier publications. The title literally means "Maple List."

The last book I mention is *Kaede Rui Zukō* which was a rather complete work of three volumes. The title means "Maples with Illustrations." This set described most of the maple cultivars existing at that time, many of which have since been lost to cultivation.

In 1898 the Yokohama Nursery Company issued a catalog of maples for export under the title *Maples of Japan.* Illustrations were included and created much early interest in the United States. Subsequent issues of the Yokohama Nursery catalogs included additional descriptions and illustrations.

References after 1900 are listed in the bibliography.

II

TAXONOMY AND NOMENCLATURE

Taxonomy

I present here in tabulated form the genetic and taxonomic relationship between the species of *Acers* dealt with in this book including some species from China and Korea.

This book has not been designed as a definitive technical reference or taxonomic key for identification by the serious dendrologist. The means of determining species status in taxonomy is still changing as research functions expand. Taxonomists are turning to the chemistry of plant parts; similarity of floral components; cellular arrangement in the woody portions; and other methods for better determination of species and the taxonomic inter-relationship within the Series and Sections. P. C. DeJong's excellent work in 1976, a biosystemic study, is especially noteworthy.

The taxonomy of this group of plants varies considerably from one author to the next. We find some authors recognize only the species *A. palmatum* with appropriate subspecies and varieties. (Koidzumi, Rehder, Mulligan, and others.) In contrast, we find *Acer amoenum* raised to full species status, equal to *Acer palmatuum*. *A. amoenum*, with its subspecies, then becomes the species in which a great number of the cultivars originate. (Ogata and others) Other references place *A. amoenum* in the subspecies category equal to Ssp. *Matsumurae* under the full species of *A. palmatum*. (Murray and others)

So at the outset, I admit to the "sin" of being a "lumper" in my taxonomy of *Acer palmatum*. For purposes of clarity and simplification I have not attempted to delineate in every case the species, subspecies, variety, form or cultivar which would apply taxonomically. At least in the United States, the group in its entirety has been referred to as "palmatums" in horticultural circles. Since this book deals primarily with the horticultural forms, I have used this simple designation.

The interrelationship of the species of *Acer* within the Series, and to some extent between the Sections, has been important to the author in propagation. I am usually most successful in grafting and cross-hybridizing species within the specific Series. There are notable exceptions to this rule, but in the majority of cases it is a useful guide in choosing a more common understock on which to graft a rare specimen. An obvious example is the use of *Acer palmatum* for understock in grafting an unusual form of *Acer circinatum*, even though the species occur as

A. palmatum 'Kamagata'. An example of the cultivars called "yatsubusa", the Japanese designation of "dwarf."

natives in different sections of the world. The reverse is also equally possible although we have found that palmatums grafted on understock of *Acer circinatum* are less successful.

To exemplify further, one would not normally choose *Acer pseudoplatanus* as an understock for a variegated form of *Acer rufinerve*. One would choose understock in the same Series. An example of total contrast has been experience with the species *Acer pentaphyllum.* Most authorities agree that this maple is quite unrelated to most other species. However, I have successfully grafted on such totally unrelated understocks as *A. saccharinum, A. Davidii, A. pseudo platanus,* and *A. rubrum.*

This explanation is used to emphasize the need to understand the taxonomic position of each species in the true interrelationship with other *Acers.*

SIMPLIFIED SYSTEMATIC TREATMENT OF THE FAMILY *Aceraceae*
(As it relates to species in Japan and neighboring territories)

Family *Aceraceae*
  Genus *Dipteronia*
      Species *D. Dyerana* Henry. 1903
              D. sinensis Oliver. 1889
  Genus *Acer*
      Series *Arguta*
          Species *A. argutum* Maxim. 1867
                  A. stachyophyllum Hiern. 1875
      Series *Carpinifolia*
          Species *A. carpinifolium* S & Z 1845
      Series *Cissifolia*
          Species *A. cissifolium* Koch. 1864
      Series *Crataegifolia*
          Species *A. caudatifolium* Hyata. 1911
                  A. crataegifolium S & Z 1845
                  A. Davidii Franchet. 1885
                  A. Morrisonense Hyata. 1911
      Series *Campestre*
          Species *A. Miyabei* Maxim. 1898
      Series *Distyla*
          Species *A. distylum* S & Z. 1845
      Series **Grisea**
          Species *A. griseum* Pax. 1902
                  A. triflorum Komarov. 1901
                  A. Maximowiczianum (A. Nikoense) Miquel.
                  1867
      Series *Lithocarpa*
          Species *A. diabolicum* Blume. 1864
      Series *Micrantha*
          Species *A. Maximowiczii* Pax. 1889
                  A. micranthum S & Z. 1845
                  A. Tschonoskii Maxim. 1886

top—*Acer palmatum*
lower left—*A. palmatum* ssp. *amoenum,*
lower right—*A. palmatum* ssp. *Matsumurae.*
The three basic divisions of the species *A. palmatum.*

Series *Palmata*

 Species *A. amoenum* (some authors) Hu & Cheng.
  1948

  A. japonicum Thunb. 1784

  A. palmatum Thunb. 1783

  A. pseudo-sieboldianum Komarov. 1904

  A. pubipalmatum Fang. 1932

  A. robustum Pax 1902

  A. shirasawanum Koidz. 1911

  A. Sieboldianum Miquel. 1865

  A. tenuifolium Koidz. 1916

Series *Parviflora*

 Species *A. nipponicum* Hara. 1938

Series *Pentaphylla*

 Species *A. pentaphyllum* Diels. 1931

Series *Platanoidea*

 Species *A. fulvescens* Rehder. 1911

  A. mono Maxim 1857

  A. truncatum Bunge. 1833

Series *Rubra*

 Species *A. pycnanthum* Koch. 1864

Series *Sinensia*

 Species *A. erianthum* Schwerin. 1901

Series *Spicata*

 Species *A. caudatum* Wallich. 1830

  A. ukurunduense Traut & Meyer. 1856

Series *Tatarica*

 Species *A. ginnala* Maxim. 1857

  A. Seminovii R & H. 1866

  A. tataricum Linn. 1753

Series *Tegmentosa*

 Species *A. capillipes* Maxim. 1867

  A. rufinerve S & Z. 1845

  A. tegmentosum Maxim. 1857

  A. pectinatum Wall. 1881

Series *Trifidia*

 Species *A. Buergerianum* Miquel. 1865

  A. Paxii Franchet. 1886

Nomenclature, Difficulties and Confusion

There is much confusion in the nomenclature of Japanese Maples, particularly in the United States. One of the purposes of this book is to identify and rectify this unhappy situation. Considering Japanese variations in names, Latinized taxonomic nomenclature, localized names originating in Europe and America, and all the opportunities for error in the 200 or more years, it is not surprising that some cultivars are known by several names.

Prior to the time when Karl von Linne proposed the bi-nomial nomenclature system of classification in 1735, there was no uniform guide or set of rules for naming such things as "new" plants. Many of the names in Japan arose from common usage in a limited and perhaps isolated area.

In Japan linguistic dialects result in spelling or pronunciation variations. For example, a plant name may have a different spelling or pronunciation when coming from the northern islands than from other parts of Japan.

Serious study of the old literature reveals that in some instances the same Japanese name has been applied to several different cultivars. The Japanese and Chinese horticulturists of several centuries ago were located throughout a widespread territory including many islands and lacked adequate communication. Therefore, similar names were applied to entirely different species or selections without any knowledge of the duplication.

To illustrate the multi-use of certain names, "Itaya" and combinations thereof are listed below:

'Itaya' is the name of a popular cultivar of *A. japonicum*.

"Itaya" is the "common" name for *A. japonicum*.

"Itaya" and "Tokiwa" are both used for *A. truncatum* (which some authors equate with *A. mono* or *A. pictum*).

"Itaya kaede" is the horticultural name for *A. japonicum*.

"Itaya kaede" is the academic name for *A. mono* which is horticulturally called "Tokiwa kaede".

"Itaya meigetsu" or "Hauchiwa kaede" is the academic name for *A. japonicum*.

"Itaya meigetsu" is the synonym for "Kohauchiwa kaede" which is *A. mono*.

"Itaya meigetsu" is the academic name for *A. Sieboldianum*.

"Meigetsu kaede" is also a horticultral term for *A. japonicum*.

"Ō itaya meigetsu" is the Japanese name for *A. shirasawanum*.

The system of transliteration into the Roman alphabet has been changed three times by the Japanese government. Many Japanese cannot read a large number of the Japanese characters used 50 years ago since the government in recent years reduced the number of characters from tens of thousands to about 2000. This adds to modern-day confusion with cultivar names which originated perhaps 200 years ago.

A further difficulty occurs when changing certain Japanese sounds into English. Very few Japanese pronunciations have a direct English equivalent. For example, the sound "Ch" (like a sneeze) may be spelled in a name as "Shi", "Chi", "Tsu", etc., as for example in 'Tsukushigata','Chikushigata', 'Shikushigata', and 'Shukushigata'. 'Chishio' and 'Shishio' are often interchanged. When used in names, "g" and "k" are often interchangeable. One of the the tones of "o" is interpreted several ways when Japanese write the English name equivalent: Ō, Oo, Oh, and even Ooh. We find the cultivar 'Shōjō' spelled many ways in different countries.

Confusion results from the difficulties of translation from one language to another. There is often more than one valid name for the same plant. Most Japanese Maple names are written in Japanese Kanji characters which were adapted from Chinese characters several centuries ago. In addition, minute differences in the structure of some of these Japanese characters contributed to the nomenclatural variations when translated into English.

Further, there are different ways of transliterating the same Kanji characters into English. For instance, the synonyms 'Ōsakazuki' and 'Taihai' are read from the same character. 'Daimyo nishiki' and 'Taimin nishiki' are valid interpretations of the same Kanji. The characters for "tsuma" and "uri" are quite similar. 'Beni uri' is easily confused with 'Beni tsuma'. When properly written, 'Tsuma beni' denotes a cultivar of *A. palmatum*. 'Beni uri' is a cultivar of *A. rufinerve.*

We must also consider the circuitous route some of these plants have travelled as they were dispersed around the world. We might take as a theoretical case a cultivar going from Japan into Europe. The translation from Japanese into any of these languages was difficult. Later, the plant found its way into early English collections. Again a language exchange in spelling occurred. When the cultivar was sent to a nurseryman in the United States, there was another possibility of spelling change. We have traced maple names which have gone through these many sea changes.

Another problem arises from the unwillingness of some nurserymen to cope with Japanese names, especially in the United States. There have been cases where cultivars were brought from Europe or Japan and given popular names in the United States for the ease of the nursery trade. I am of the opinion that 'Roscoe Red' and diss. 'Ever Red' are examples of this practice. Another example is the name "Crispa", which I have found applied to four different cultivars. It is assumed easier to put "Crispa" on a nursery label than 'Okushimo'. (also occasionally written 'Okushima') To further exemplify, 'Okushimo' is found in texts (Koidzumi) taxonomically as *Acer palmatum*, subsp. *genuinum*, subvar. *crispum*. Andre, in 1870, shows it as *Acer palmatum Thunbergi*, subvar. *eupalmatum*, f. *crispum*. United States nurseries call it "Crispa" while designating the entirely different cultivar 'Shishigashira' as "Crispum". I have gone into much detail here to show the difficulties which can arise when we are not meticulous about names. One further example: the cultivar 'Higasayama' (also spelled 'Hikasayama') is sold under several popularized names. On the East coast of the United States it is sold by a different name than on the West coast. We find it in collections and nurseries under the following names: Roseo marginatum, Roseo variegatum, Cristata variegatum, and Aureo variegatum. Unfortunately, some of these popular names rightfully belong to other cultivars, so even more confusion. The true *Acer palmatum Matsumurae*, form *roseo marginatum* bears the Japanese name of 'Kagiri' or 'Kagiri nishiki'. This has an entirely different appearance from 'Higasayama' for which the term "Roseo marginatum" should be discontinued. The similarity of spelling lends further confusion between 'Kageori nishiki' and 'Kagiri nishiki' which are two different cultivars.

In reverse, I find the cultivar 'Shishigashira' under at least five different names around the world: 'Crispa', 'Crispum', 'Cristata', 'Minus', and ribescifolium. (The latter has some valid status.)

We also have to consider penmanship, haste in writing labels, and (later) hitting the wrong key on a typewriter. If someone along the line writes as poorly as the author, a "u" can become an "o" or an "r" is read as an "n". This undoubtedly happened. Transposing letters results in printed differences on such cultivars as 'Hōgyoku' and 'Hōgyuko'. When printed often enough in one of the countries involved, the wrong name becomes established.

All this may not be considered important to the reader who wants a few maples in his landscape. However, to the nurseryman and the serious collector it is vital. If someone requested a plant from me under the name 'Crispa', or 'Roseo marginatum', I would not be sure just which of several cultivars he desired.

I have a strong personal preference for adhering to the Japanese nomenclature for the cultivars whenever possible and valid. Since this group of plants originated and has been developed in the main by discerning and devoted Japanese horticulturists and is an important part of their horticultural heritage, I consider such practice appropriate. This is not to say that some of the new cultivars from Europe and the United States should not carry Anglicized names. We refer mainly to the older cultivars originating in Japan which have experienced dilution in their usage because of name alteration in other countries.

Throughout the text of the book I have attempted to list all the nomenclature variances under each cultivar and therefore will not list them here.

Taxonomic Subdivisions of *Acer Palmatum*

The three major taxonomic subdivisions of the palmatums separate the cultivars and varieties into basic groups. Based on leaf structure, seed type, or bud scales, they are placed in *A. palmatum*, subsp. (or sp.) *amoenum*, or subsp. *Matsumurae*. The following cultivars are listed in the appropriate divisions, based upon the composite data contained in several taxonomic references. This gives a representative sampling of the many cultivars existing today.

PALMATUM

Akaji nishiki	Higasayama	Okushimo
Aocha nishiki	Iso chidori	Orido nishiki
Aoyagi	Issai nishiki momiji	Pine bark maple
Asahi zuru	Kagero	Ryuzu
Aureo variegatum	Kagiri nishiki	Sango kaku
Aureum	Kamagata	Sazanami
Beni komachi	Karasugawa	Seigai
Beni maiko	Kasen nishiki	Seigen
Beni schichihenge	Kashima	Sekka yatsubusa
Bonfire	Katsura	Shindeshōjō
Butterfly	Kiyo hime	Shishio improved
Chirimen nishiki	Komon nishiki	Takao
Chishio	Koreanum	Tama hime
Chizome	Koshibori nishiki	Tsuchi gumo
Coonara Pygmy	Koto hime	Tsukomo
Corallinum	Kurui jishi	Ueno homare
Deshōjō	Mama	Ukegumo
Goshiki kotohime	Monzukushi	Versicolor
Hanami nishiki	Murakumo	Yatsubusa
Hanazono nishiki	Nishiki momiji	

AMOENUM

Aratama
Ariake nomura
Atrolineare
Benino tsukasa
Daimyō nishiki
Elegans
Filifera purpurea
Hamaotome
Harusame
Heptalobum
Hessei
Hichigosan
Hōgyoku
Ichigyōji
Iijima sunago
Karaori nishiki
Kinran
Koto ito komachi

Koto no ito
Linearilobum
Lutescens
Mikawa yatsubusa
Miyagino
Musashino
Nomura
Novum
O jishi
Ogon sarasa
Omato
Ōsakazuki
Red Pygmy
Rubrum
Rufescens
Samidare
Saoshika

Scolopendrifolium
Shigarami
Shikageori nishiki
Shime no uchi
Shino buga oka
Shishigashira
Shōjō
Taimin nishiki
Tana
Tana bata
Tatsuta gawa
Tsukushigata
Tsuma beni
Tsuma gaki
Tsuri nishiki
Utsu semi
Villa Taranto
Yūgure

MATSUMURAE

Aka shigitatsu sawa
Akegarasu
Ao shidare
Aoba
Azuma murasaki
Atropurpureum
Atropurpureum diss.
Beni kagami
Beni shidare
Beni shidare variegated
Bloodgood
Brocade
Burgundy Lace
Chitoseyama
Crimson Queen
Ever Red
Filigree
Flavescens diss.
Garnet
Garyū
Goshiki shidare
Hageromo
Hazeroino
Hibari
Inaba shidare
Inazuma
Jirō shidare

Kageori nishiki
Kasagiyama
Ki hachijō
Kiri nishiki
Komurasaki
Koshimino
Masu murasaki
Matsugae
Matsukaze
Mizu kuguri
Momenshide
Moonfire
Muragumo
Murasaki hime
Mure hibari
Murogawa
Nana segawa
Nicholsonii
Nigrum diss.
Nishiki gasane
Nomura nishiki
Nuresagi
O ginagashi
Ō kagami
Omurayama
Ornatum
Ōshū beni

Ōshū shidare
Palmatifidium
Pendulum Julian
Red Filigree Lace
Sagara nishiki
Saotome
Seiryū
Sekimori
Sherwood Flame
Shigitatsu sawa
Shigure bato
Shigure zome
Shinonome
Shiranami
Shōjō shidare
Suminagashi
Tamukeyama
Toyama nishiki
Trompenburg
Ukon
Umegae
Viridis
Volubile
Wabito
Washi no ō
Wou nishiki

A. palmatum 'Versicolor'. Exemplifies the fascinating group of variegated cultivars. Fall coloration usually intensifies the base color of the leaf into reds and oranges.

III

CULTURE

Culture in the Garden

Gardeners and hobbyists will probably want a little more discussion on the care and culture of Japanese Maples in this writing. Commercial nurseries already will have worked out their own methods of handling these plants in production.

These trees are remarkably adaptable to soil and climatic conditions. As a native plant, the *Acer palmatum* and its natural varieties have adapted to a wide range of environments on the islands of Japan. The plants thrive in the soils and climates ranging from the rain-forest type of the Pacific Northwest to the very warm climate of Southern California; from up-state New York down the Atlantic seaboard to the Southeastern states and through the Mid-West; from the almost-pure peat soils of Boskoop, Holland, to the varied soils in central and southern England. Thus we begin to understand the versatility of these plants as ornamentals throughout the world.

LOCATIONS

Japanese Maples are widely used as specimen plants and companion plants. Since they rarely attain great height, they are not classed in the shade tree category. The largest *Acer palmatum* we have seen personally was at The Ford, Wiveliscombe, near Taunton, in Somerset, England. It is more than 11 meters (37 ft.) tall and over 12 meters (40ft.) in spread of canopy. This magnificent specimen of the species was planted about 1850 or before. The species was first described by Thunberg in 1783 and was introduced into England in 1832 by J. R. Reeves. There are probably larger trees under cultivation, but this grand specimen is worthy of note.

Most upright cultivars of *A. palmatum* and *A. japonicum* attain the height of 8 to 9 meters (25 to 30 ft.) in 50 years, depending upon site and soils. Many cultivars, especially from the dissectum group, mature at 5 m (15 ft.) or less. This places them in the large shrub category.

The green varieties and cultivars will take full sun very well. In extremely hot conditions, the green forms may sunburn slightly under late Summer conditions. Afternoon shade will aid in preventing this.

Variegated leaf forms need semi-shade or at least protection from the blistering afternoon sun in hot climates. Cultivars such as 'Sagara nishiki' do best with afternoon protection to keep the golden variegations in the leaves from crisping brown. Other white and pink variegated forms should also have afternoon shade. Variegates such as 'Versicolor' and 'Waka momiji', however, are more tolerant, and we grow them in full sun without serious sunburn.

The red cultivars of the dissectums appreciate some shade. However, they will not develop their typical deep red colors without benefit of strong sunlight for at least part of the day. We have a fine specimen of *diss*. 'Garnet' growing under *Calocedrus decurrans*, but it does not develop the true color for which it is known. Instead of the strong orange-red of 'Garnet' it remains a greenish red although in fine condition and leaf form.

Such extreme forms as the variegated dissectums must have ample shade or they will sunburn seriously.

PLANTING

Japanese Maples are easy to plant. Their root system is not a deep tap-root type of structure but is predominantly a fibrous root network that will stay in the upper level of the soil. Naturally, with age the roots will be found rather deep, but they do not go to an excessive depth. This is especially true in irrigated landscapes where the roots do not need to search for sustaining moisture. Regularly-supplied irrigation will maintain the roots in the upper levels of the soil.

This fact, however, does not make them serious competitors with companion shrubs such as the rhododendron group or similar ornamentals. They are not overly competitive but co-exist well with practically all landscape material.

The nature of rooting in the upper surface allows planting in soils which may have a hard stratum or bedrock close to the surface. With adequate root coverage and attention to uniform moisture supply these plants do an excellent job of beautifying difficult areas. This also is a reason they will do so well in containers of all sizes. The fibrous roots will utilize the limited area without root-binding and choking themselves. The uniform level of moisture supply, whether great or small, must be emphasized. We cannot stress the uniformity of watering too much; we do not imply the need for large amounts, but rather, constant amounts.

The newly-purchased plant may come from the grower in one of several ways. Young plants, whether produced from grafts or seeds, will probably be in containers. Medium-sized to very old plants can also be purchased in containers. This allows for successful transplanting into the permanent landscape with very little transplant shock. In today's modern nursery production, maples of any age are successfully produced as "containerized stock". The planting season is extended to any month of the year.

Young plants up to 3 or 4 years of age, when purchased in the dormant season may be "bare-rooted." These are dug, or taken out of containers, and shipped without soil on the roots. This saves transporting heavy growing medium. This is done safely only during the very dormant growth months and usually with young plants.

Field-grown material several years of age is usually dug with an earthen ball intact around the roots. This comes from the nursery with the root ball often wrapped in burlap, or similar material, to prevent the root zone from drying. "Ball and burlap" plants are usually safe to transport during the dormant season only.

When moving to a different location within a landscape, the plant must be dug with an earth ball intact around the roots. If the plant is of any size or age at all, this root protection is important.

It is imperative, whatever the method, material, or timing, that the roots not be exposed to air or direct sunlight for any length of time. Such care will prevent them from becoming dessicated thus producing too much transplant shock and possible loss of the tree.

The planting hole should be dug slightly larger than the root mass of the plant. If planting into very tight soils such as heavy clay, success will be greater if the hole is rather shallow and the plant left slightly above the ground level. The root zones should then be mounded up to a satisfactory depth to assure root coverage. If deep holes are dug in tight soil, it is like planting the tree in a large iron kettle with no drainage. Surely the plant will soon drown and die.

The reverse is true, of course, with light, sandy situations. Before planting, a large amount of organic material should be incorporated to assist in water retention. Ground bark is excellent for this purpose and better than the "sawdust" now widely used. Sawdust rots down at a rapid rate, not only eliminating its conditioning effect but also it rapidly uses up available nitrogen during the rotting process thereby robbing the tree. Ground conifer bark, which decays at a much slower rate, is more useful for this purpose. If bark dust is not available, other stable organic matter which is readily available should be used to condition extremely sandy sites.

In any case, the tree should not be set in deeper than the ground line at which the young plant was grown. The roots will find their own level during the first year or two. Deep planting and overwatering will surely kill the plant.

Conversely, planting in too shallow a space will allow the roots to dry excessively. As mentioned, it is possible to plant quite shallowly if covering for the root zone with a mound of soil and protective material is provided. After the first few seasons, the plant will have found the level of root activity at which it can exist. We have seen maples growing in some surprisingly dry, shallow and exposed conditions.

Mulching over the roots will prevent high temperatures from drying out the root zone in times of short water. Mulching is also important for winter protection of the roots. Practically all of the cultivars will stand Winter freezing and temperatures down to —18°C (0°F) and below. The critical point, which can only tolerate temperatures to —10°C (14°F) is the root zone. When planted normally in the soil, these plants will withstand extreme temperatures as the roots are protected in the deeper soils.

To put the matter in another light, we find that a surprisingly large number of maple enthusiasts also have fine plantings of rhododendrons and azaleas. We mention it here because the culture of Japanese Maples is very similar to rhododendrons.

MICROCLIMATES

By microclimates we mean those small areas which differ slightly from the conditions in the major portion of the garden and landscape. These spots may be warmer, colder, windier, drier, or wetter. Japanese Maples do not differ from other landscape plants in adverse response to such conditions. A spot with a constant strong wind will misshape the plant and may burn the leaves. In winter, the chill factor may cause bark and cambium damage.

If planted quite close to a pure white wall, the intense reflected light can cause foliage burn. In foundation plantings around a building, people tend to plant too closely to walls. Plant location should provide for at least ten years of growth and this should be envisioned when planting. The more dwarf cultivars work well for the lower foundation sites.

Drought and waterlogged sites are discussed in the section on soils. If the problem is recognized, corrective measures can be taken at planting time. In areas of strong marine breezes leaf damage may occasionally occur from the salt deposit. Those growing plants under such conditions are familiar with the necessary protection and the need for periodic washing of the foliage with fresh water. Many successful maples are grown on seashore sites.

If some additional care is given the first year or two of establishment, the Japanese Maples will adapt to most situations even though somewhat adverse.

SOILS

The ideal soil for Japanese Maples is a sandy loam with a low to medium amount of organic matter. This ideal soil is hard to find in many parts of the country. However, the plants will do well on less-than perfect soils of most types. In tight soils or very sandy soils the growth rate will be reduced somewhat. Sometimes simple procedures of planting or moisture management will make up for poorer soils.

The richer the soils, the more rapid the growth. However, this can also be a drawback. Some of the upright type cultivars can get too "leggy" when forced by rich soils or high fertility.

The site must be well-drained. This species will not do well in a wet or swampy location, but they may be grown along pools and little streams provided the root zones still have sufficient drainage and aeration.

We have seen these plants growing on dry hillside locations in a clay soil and in hot sun. However, the annual rate of growth on these latter plants was limited and certainly could not be called lush, but at least they were fine small trees filling a particular need.

The roots of Japanese Maples are not deep and mulching is quite important in a tight, hard soil type. Since the shallow roots cannot penetrate readily, mulching helps retain moisture and keeps the roots cool in the heat of Summer.

Extremes in alkaline conditions prevent the maples from performing well. Those with gardens of high pH soils need to adjust with acid fertilizers or neutralizing soil amendments. Container growing offers an alternate choice where "impossible" soil conditions exist.

The acid type or neutral soils in which rhododendrons do well seem to be suited equally well to the maples. Soils of extremely sandy nature will need considerable organic matter incorporated to help in water retention.

MOISTURE

Japanese Maples do not have any unusual moisture requirement. The "average" amount of water supplied to the normal range of landscape shrubs is usually adequate. Grown as companions with most other shrubs and perennials normal irrigation will carry them along nicely.

The principal water requirement, in our opinion, is a uniform supply of moisture. By this we mean: (1) if the plant is in a fairly dry situation, it should not be flooded with water at irregular intervals; (2) if grown where moisture is plentiful, it should not experience a sudden drying occasion. The moisture supply whether little or much should be constant.

Maples will grow with limited water but produce a shrubbier type of plant. This can be an advantage with the taller-growing types if larger trees are not desired, but remember even though the supply of moisture is limited, it should remain constant.

The main point to guard against is very wet periods followed by very dry periods or vice versa. This will surely cause mid-Summer leaf drop or leaf scorch. One of the most common causes of leaf scorch is an excessively dry period of a few days in a normally-watered landscaping. In fact, the leaves may all fall off as though it were the beginning of Winter—completely defoliating. We have seen this occur in mid-Summer. A thorough soaking into the deepest part of the root zone will probably save the tree and perhaps even cause a new crop of leaves to grow in late Summer and early Fall if the tree has not been damaged too badly.

Another leaf-scorch problem, especially in container-grown specimens, is caused by watering the leaves in full sun during the hot Summer months. Watering in very early morning or early evening during the hottest weather will prevent this type of scorch.

Containers must not be allowed to waterlog. The grower must determine the requirement of water for his particular type of soil mix and container quickly as overwatering is almost worse than underwatering.

Proper water management is far more important than fertilizer or soil types!

FERTILITY

Japanese Maples do not demand large amounts of fertilizer. One can hardly generalize in this book about the needs in all the locations in which they grow around the world. If the soils are generally fertile for most landscape plants, the maples will do well with little or no additional attention. In the Northwest soils palmatums seem to resent the ammonium sources of nitrogen. We have found calcium nitrate the best. Other non-ammonium sources also work well. A balanced "garden" fertilizer applied lightly not more than once a year will provide for these non-greedy plants. If very rapid growth is required for some purpose, calcium nitrate applied to the landscape plant in early Spring and again in July will give rapid results. It must be watered in well.

On very poor soils and problem areas, a "complete" fertilizer for shrubs and trees may be used. Early Spring feeding is generally best, applied prior to emergence of leaves. Aged barnyard manure is an excellent fertilizer and mulch where one is fortunate enough to have it available. The low nitrogen content may have to be supplemented with commercial fertilizer. Newer "slow release" fertilizer mixes now on the market work well. The risk of chemical burn is reduced, but the cost is higher.

PRUNING

We are convinced that a major sin in landscaping and gardening is the constant neglect of pruning and shaping of our plants. So many enthusiasts get busy and let their plants (rhododendrons for one example) get too high, too wide, or too floppy. This is true of flowering shrubs, dwarf conifers, and even perennials in most gardens. We, too, are guilty of this misdemeanor. In far too many cases we let a fine plant go unchecked for a few years and then suddenly realize that it just can't be that big anymore and live in its allotted space. So we either have to tear it out or prune it back drastically and start over. There is nothing wrong with this except it leads to several years of unsightliness. Thoughtful pruning and shaping should be done each year. Better still, limited but constant pruning-shaping every season of the year is desirable. These detailed remarks are given to emphasize the need of pruning on all Japanese Maples.

Where large plants and great expanses allow, it is magnificent to allow these trees to grow unhindered. However, unless one wants to have a very tall Japanese Maple of the upright cultivars, top shaping and pruning should be started rather early in the life of the tree.

Major pruning should be done during the dormant season and just prior to leaf production in the Spring. Corrective pruning and training can be done at any time of the year, however. Cuts should be made just beyond a pair of buds on the twig or branch. Usually this will then produce two side shoots. When removing a larger limb, like any other pruning, the cut should be made as close to the base as possible so a dead "stub" is not left for disease and insect entry. Should we emphasize the need for SHARP pruning tools? Quick callusing over the cut, whether large or small, is nature's protection against disorders. Tree wound paint should be used on larger cuts.

All the fine "twiggy" growth in some of the larger types of Japanese Maples must be removed. This is especially true with the lace-leaf, dissectum, types of cultivars. One that is too brushy inside invites insect and disease problems. But, perhaps more important is proper display of the plant. The cascading and undulating branches of the dissectum types are as beautiful and interesting as the foliage. Part of the beauty of these maples is the trunk and limb structure and texture. In dissectums the bulk of the inside growth should be removed periodically so that the graceful trunk and branch structure are enhanced and displayed. In the case of 'Sango kaku' (coral) and 'Aoyagi' (green) the bark and twig color is the outstanding feature and should be exposed.

The planting at the nursery is quite limited in area. It was necessary to plant hundreds of stock plants of numerous cultivars in a small area. Therefore, they are much too close to let them mature to the size which they would reach if unchecked. With judicious pruning and shaping, these plants still fulfill their purpose and make specimen plants. It would be nice to own unlimited areas, but all of us are not that fortunate. Pruning and shaping is the answer.

CONTAINER GROWING

Japanese Maples lend themselves admirably to container growing. Care is minimal, although it has to be constant since plants in containers will naturally dry out more rapidly than the same plants in the ground.

The dwarf forms, such as 'Kamagata,' 'Tsuchigumo,' 'Kyohime,' the various "Yatsubusa" group, and especially 'Goshiki kotohime' are excellent in containers. The various color forms of the dissectums as a total group will adapt quite well to container growing. Even old specimens can be kept in containers indefinitely with the proper attention to fertilization, watering, and occasional pruning for shaping.

Not everyone is aware of the excellence of Japanese Maples for bonsai work. Here is the extreme example of growing even the more vigorous forms of the species as very small specimens. The occasional root and top pruning and proper attention to watering and fertilizing create this art form.

Those who wish specimen plants for medium to large-size planters for patio type culture will find most of the more colorful and interesting leaf-shape cultivars make outstanding and unusual container plants. Collectors with limited space may utilize the adaptability of containering to maintain a large collection of cultivars in a small area.

The planting mix requires only adequate drainage and an even level of fertility and moisture. There are as many planting mixes as there are growers. The soil mix must not be "tight" but should have good water retention capabilities and good drainage. We have grown red and green dissectums, as well as other cultivars, for several years in wooden cedar tubs with a basic container mix of about 90% Douglas Fir bark and the balance of sand for weight and a little perlite. The plants maintain a healthy and vigorous condition even located on a cement patio slab in full sun. Most of the commercial soil mixes for containers are adequate. A mixture of good loam with a high percentage of peat moss, or better yet ground conifer bark, will maintain a good specimen indefinitely. Slow-release fertilizers now on the market lend themselves quite well to a constant flow of fertility in containers.

In extremely cold climates protection must be given the root zones of container-grown plants. Recent research has indicated that the destruction point of the roots of *Acer palmatum* is —10°C (14°F). Below this point complete root destruction occurs. We have had containers freeze solid at about —7°C (20°F) with no apparent damage to the root zone the following year. Some type of protection that will adequately guard the entire container from extremes of low temperatures is necessary. Wrapping in thin poly-foam sheets, in turn covered by several thicknesses of burlap, is effective for large ceramic planters which cannot be moved easily. Smaller containers can be set in beds of sawdust or other winter protection mulch. The mulching should cover the containers for 2 to 5 inches with the top of the plant exposed. The tops of the plants, both in containers and in the ground, will survive below —18°C (0°F) when the plants have gone into proper dormancy. In mild winters an occasional cold snap may cause some twig tip loss if the plants have experienced a mild Fall and not hardened off properly. This natural pruning is of no great consequence. In areas of extreme winters the tops of the plants should be protected from strong freezing winds which rapidly dessicate the bark and cambium.

Pests and Problems

At the beginning of this chapter on pests, diseases and problems I would like to emphasize that I make no attempt to present specific chemical controls. With the wide range of chemicals in use today, the constant change in control measures growing out of research, and the fluctuating status of chemical residues and safety, it would be unwise to include specific recommendations for specific controls.

If problems arise, I suggest immediate contact with local authorities in plant disease and insect control or the nearest agricultural and horticultural research station. For the individual gardener, the experienced commercial nurseryman is a dependable source of advice.

INSECT PROBLEMS

Japanese Maples are not often subject to serious insect infestations. Other than the range of insects normally found in any concentrated landscaping, no specific insects are major predators on these plants.

APHIDS

As with most broadleafed plants, various species of aphids (plant lice) may increase seasonally to a problem level. There are several types of aphids which may be involved. Uusually the most serious build-up occurs in the Spring when the new foliage is most succulent. Overwintering forms emerge and increase rapidly. Occasionally they are found in great numbers on the new tips of shoots and young leaves. If left uncontrolled, they can stunt the terminals and cause misshapened leaves. Rarely, sporadic infestations will be serious again in early Summer or early Fall. In these cases the production of "honeydew" exudates can cause unsightly stickiness on the foliage. Normal aphid sprays for the garden will control most of the above problems.

MITES

Even more unusual are the occasional infestations of "Spider mites" (usually a species of the *Tetranychidae*). These infestations occur under unfavorable growing conditions and usually in times of moisture stress. Leaves on portions of the plant, or even the entire plant, can dry quickly, shrivel, and turn brown. An experienced eye will detect the difference between mite damage and lack of water. Sometimes spraying with strong streams of water, repeated each day for several days, plus increased irrigation, will offer some relief although not a control. Several mite control chemicals are on the market for garden use.

WORMS (*Lepidoptera*)

There are numerous types of moth larvae which will feed on maple leaves as well as other garden plants. Normally worms are not enough of a problem to cause much concern. Occasionally adult moths will deposit eggs, the larvae of which feed on the foliage. We find that this causes only scattered damage. In areas where mass-feeding larvae occur in outbreaks of serious proportions these masses will sweep across a landscape planting consuming maples along with other landscape material.

Some of the larvae belong to the "leaf-roller" type. As the larva feeds, it spins a web, rolls the edges of the leaf together, and feeds in the enclosure. These are the most difficult to control with sprays for they are protected inside the leaf-roll. For small areas, hand picking is effective. For a large planting, a good "wetting agent" (surfactant) must be added to the insecticide to allow the spray to enter the enclosed leaf area.

Other larvae, usually minute, feed on an unopened leaf bud, perhaps taking one or two bites. When this leaf unfolds, the holes appear in several areas. Small weevils also cause similar damage. There is no control for this problem as the insect has already eaten and gone.

Gardeners experiencing serious or repeated problems with these leaf-eating larvae may have to resort to control chemicals. These should be the types which either contact the insect or leave a short-term residue on the foliage which the insect will consume as it feeds. We find that in most cases widespread controls are unnecessary.

BEETLES

Occasionally leaf-eating beetles travel through the garden with much the same results as described for worms. Except for localized epidemics, chemical control is rarely necessary.

Bark beetles occasionally attack the stems and small limbs of Japanese maples, particularly in large concentrations of young trees. Except in very unusual circumstances the damage on mature plants is confined to a small limb or two. These tiny beetles (usually of the Genus *Scolytus*) attack a wide range of woody plants. In almost every instance the plant is in poor condition prior to the attack. They are attracted to "sick" trees. The eggs are laid on the bark and result in minute larvae entering and tunneling in the cambium area, thereby cutting off the nutrient flow. The damage occurs during the Summer, but the results may not be noticed until the following Spring when the affected portion is dead. In the very early Spring the small beetles emerge from the bark to disperse and lay more eggs. The result is many small holes in the bark, giving rise to the common name "shot-hole" borers. Cutting and burning infected portions of the tree before the beetles emerge will help prevent further spread. The exacting methods for spray control usually preclude this type of control for the average gardener. Maintaining plants in good vigor is the best protection against this type of injury.

ROOT WEEVILS

These insects can be an occasional but specialized pest. There are several species which do similar damage, usually of the Genus *Brachyrhinus* and closely related genera. They are the same insects which cause much leaf and root damage in rhododendrons and feed heavily on the roots of both plants. Weevils enjoy a very long list of host plants, including strawberries, which gives rise to the common name "Strawberry root weevil." Fortunately, they do not attack maple foliage. Larval damage to the roots can cause a great loss. The adult weevils lay eggs during the late Summer and early Fall. Upon hatching, the larvae enter the soil and start feeding on roots. In mild climates, they will feed throughout the Winter months. By Spring only the woody portions of the roots remain, totally stripped of the cambium layers.

In our experience the greatest damage is found in overwintering seedling flats prior to transplanting in the Spring. Fall transplanting eliminates this problem. Serious loss can also occur in grafting pots. Growing the one-year understock in small containers for the second season gives the larvae the opportunity to go on feeding in the pots, thereby causing serious loss to the two-year old understock. Soil drenches, or potting up two-year stock the Fall prior to grafting, prevent this loss.

Young transplanted grafts and seedling selections are also subject to this threat in nursery beds. Rarely are more mature trees endangered by root weevil. If root damage does occur, it is often limited and the tree overcomes the loss.

Container-grown nursery stock, and in some instances, bonsai plants are subject to the same threat of root damage. Close observation for this potential problem should be carried out constantly. Root inspection in late Fall or early Winter will reveal the presence of larvae or damaged roots.

At present we know of no control which is infallible. Research continues for root weevil control methods in nursery stock. There are several insecticides which when used properly will give a satisfactory degree of protection but not total prevention.

MISCELLANEOUS PLANT PESTS

I mention such insects as thrips, plant-sucking bugs (*Hemiptera*), various scale insects, and leaf-miner flies (*Diptera*) as rare or occasional pests. Perhaps localized problems will occur with these, but they are not general threats of any magnitude.

PLANT DISEASES

One of the most talked about and least understood problems of maples is "twig die-back." This can be caused by one or more of several organisms, individually or in combination. Also, cultural practices, climatic conditions, and soil chemistry can produce this symptom. But, disease should not be confused with a certain amount of "natural pruning" which takes place as the plants mature.

VERTICILLIUM

One of the main causes of "die-back" is *Verticillium* wilt. This fungus, and its various strains, affects an extremely large range of host plants. The effects of this disease are apparent in the native forests of *Acers* across the United States. It is a threat in arboreta and large landscapes in all parts of this continent, if not the whole Northern Hemisphere.

Verticillium wilt enters the cambium layers of plants, blocking the transmission of nutrients within the tissues. In most cases, this will cause a brown "streaking" within the layers under the bark. New shoots, twigs, limbs, branches, and in some cases the entire tree will die quickly.

This same effect, however, may also be caused by other diseases and conditions. It is unfortunate that this disease is so widespread but so little understood. In general practice, non-pathologists will note dying branches and immediately cry, "Verticillium wilt," which may or may not be the causative agent.

This fungus is widespread and can be of serious consequence, but research has not yet provided definitive answers. Still not fully understood are the possible methods of contamination, exact stage of infection, complete means of plant protection, or any dependable method of cure. Such things as meticulous sanitation during propagation, maintenance of plant vigor, removal and burning of infected parts will assist in limiting further spread. One common method of transmitting *Verticillium* wilt is carrying it from plant to plant on contaminated pruning or grafting tools. It is possible to spread the disease by cutting into healthy wood after cutting an infected plant while pruning. It also is possible to spread it in the propagating house while cutting scions if knives are not frequently sterilized. In landscapes where presence of the disease is suspected, pruning equipment should be cleaned often with proper sterilants. But this is a wise practice in any pruning operation. There is no specific chemical control recommended at this time.

FUSARIUM

This is another fungus involved in "die-back" or loss of young plants. This disease affects young seedlings as well as older plants. Damage may occur at ground level, destroying the cambium at the base, or on twigs and limbs, destroying new buds and shoots.

BOTRYTIS SPS.

The fungus, *Botrytis* sps., is also a serious threat. It is manifest as twig die-back, destruction of buds as they unfold, or a breakdown of tissue at the base of young plants. During propagation in the warm humid greenhouse total destruction of new shoots and leaves can occur.

Field losses may be increased by overfeeding of the young plants, particularly with nitrogen. The danger increases in warm humid conditions without sufficient air circulation.

We experienced losses in one instance following frost damage. With a long, humid, warm Fall, the growth continued to be very soft and sensitive into November. A sharp frost occurred, "burning" back these unseasonably soft shoots. After they were killed back, remaining tissue was left susceptible to the entrance of *Botrytis* organisms. The normal hardening off process eliminates some of this vulnerability. Too much shade, protection, and humidity on young plants in the nursery can increase the risk of this and other destructive organisms.

ANTHRACNOSE

This leaf blight may occur in all *Acers*, usually in wet, warm Spring conditions. The symptoms are various sized reddish-brown to purplish-brown spots on the leaves. Often the entire leaf will subsequently die. Leaves may appear as scorched by heat or frost. Chemical sprays and pruning aid in control.

LEAF SCORCH AND TWIG BURN

This condition is caused by a wide range of untoward conditions, usually not pathogenetic. Examples include wind burn, exposure to extremely hot sun, salt-laden breezes, late Spring frosts, salt runoff from Winter-treated roadways, or excessive alkalinity in soils. Container plants and certain cultivars, such as the red dissectums, when grown in full hot sun exposure will have serious leaf burn if the foliage is wetted during the extreme heat of the day. Leaf burn, or twig die-back, including the sudden loss of all foliage may result from irregular irrigation. The flow of available moisture should be consistent. Short intense drought periods may cause leaf burn or defoliation. Normally the plant is not lost, but appearance and vigor for at least that season are damaged. I should also mention that excessive use of nitrogen will cause quick foliage burn as it does with other plants.

CHLOROSIS

Defined as a general or partial yellowing of the leaves, this disorder is usually associated with the chemistry of the soil. A lack of one or a combination of minor elements is usually the cause. Lime-induced chlorosis, usually caused in soils of high pH, is indicated by the yellow tones in between the greener veins. This is usually caused by the lack of iron avilable to the plant because of the presence of excessive alkaline materials.

MISCELLANEOUS PATHOGENS

Nectria cankers and *Phytophthora* cankers are problems in some areas. Normally these are not major threats. Sooty mold, black mildew, and powdery mildews also are known to occur. These problems are only sporadic and not a general threat. Virus diseases are also known to infect *Acers.* Leading texts on plant disease will aid the reader to determine the cause and control of some of these lesser diseases.

In general, we have had fewer pathological problems with Japanese Maples than with many other genera of ornamentals. When grown under normal conditions and with good culture, they are remarkably free of disease and insect problems.

A. palmatum 'Koto ito komachi'. An example of the unusual leaf forms found among the cultivars of this species.

IV

PROPAGATION

Methods of Propagation

Japanese Maples are produced primarily from seed and by grafting. Other methods used in a limited way include production from rooted cuttings, budding, and layering. Seedlings are grown widely in the United States both by nurserymen and amateur gardeners. Presently most commercial production is done by grafting named cultivars onto *A. palmatum* understock.

SEEDLING PRODUCTION

The primary purpose of seedling production is to obtain large quantities of understock for propagation by grafting. Also of importance in the United States is the production of strong seedling-grown planting stock of *A. palmatum* to be grown out for landscape material. They are less expensive than grafted plants of named cultivars. Many of these seedling-produced plants are excellent trees, some even better than certain named cultivars. In a few cases a particular parent seed tree will yield a very uniform strain of red-leafed seedlings which lend themselves to growing-on for landscape material. These are usually sold as the "palmatum atropurpureum" of the nursery trade. Good red-leafed strains of the upright forms of palmatum are often grown to larger sizes, making an excellent nursery item for larger scale plantings. Also, for large-scale plants the green-leafed trees of the species are most impressive.

Most propagators prefer the green-leafed strain of the species for grafting understock. Some grafters even claim that grafting cannot be done on the red-leaf varieties. I find this completely untrue. Under like conditions I find grafting as successful and the plants grown out to five-year tests perform equally well whether on red- or green-leafed understock. However, since green-leafed understock is so easy to obtain, it is only logical to save the red selections for growing-on purposes.

Germination of palmatum seed can be a most frustrating problem (and here we include most other Asiatic *Acer* seed). An example will illustrate the manifold problems associated with seed.

Many years ago, when I first started, I could not find local sources of seed. I ordered "Japanese Maple" seed through a seed house from a Japanese source. By the time the order was processed, the seed was received from Japan and was forwarded to me, it was early June—too late to plant. The seed was held under refrigeration and planted the following Spring. I had not learned of the stratification needed for *A. palmatum*. About 5% of the seed germinated that Spring (19 months after I had placed the seed order). I left the seed beds undisturbed. The following Spring another 25% germinated. That seed bed produced new germinants for a five-year period. I detail this because many readers have experienced delayed dormancy, and I constantly receive questions on how to germinate *A. palmatum* seed. Many people, unfortunately, discard the seed flats or destroy the seed beds the first year, thereby losing all their seed. I stress the importance of stratification and the desirability of fresh seed.

Since early times plant propagators have known that seeds of certain trees and shrubs must be chilled prior to germination. This is especially true with the species of the Temperate Zone. In a natural setting the seeds fall on moist ground in the Fall and may even freeze prior to Spring emergence. Sometimes it takes two years or more for this to occur in the wild. This knowledge led to the nursery practice of "stratification." The term originally meant that seeds were layered in moist sand or soil and kept near the freezing temperature until time to plant in the Spring. A more accurate term might be "moist chilling." In the *Acers* generally and with Japanese Maples in particular, the seeds are mixed with moist peat or sand, enclosed in plastic bags or tight containers, and refrigerated at 1° to 8° C.

I have had excellent results with both imported and domestic seed which has been allowed to dry thoroughly, by pre-soaking before stratification. This is imperative. Whether the seed is de-winged or comes with the wings attached, we immediately soak it in 40° to 50° C water (120° F). The seed is then covered completely and held for 24 to 48 hours while the water is allowed to cool gradually. After cooling, the seed is drained and mixed with peat moss for stratification and immediately treated with a fungicide (Captan or similar product). I use peat moss for stratification, although damp sand and other similar materials can be used successfully. The seed is mixed about 50% by volume with peat and enclosed tightly in a polyethelene bag (WELL LABELED!). The bags are stored at 1° to 8° C (34° to 40°F) for a period of not less than 60 days and up to 120 days. The cooler temperature is desirable to prevent germination in the bag prior to preparation for planting out.

Production from fresh-picked seed is almost identical to the procedure described above. However, pre-soaking should NOT be done if the seed has been collected properly. I have 75% to 90% germination when the seed is picked fairly early in the Fall. Stock seed is gathered when the wings have become brown and dried but while the seed itself retains its green color. In Oregon I usually find that the best collecting period is September. This seed is immediately stratified. I do not de-wing the seed because this is not only extra labor but the process can allow the seed to dry out to an unacceptable degree. Maple seed is usually produced in pairs of seed attached at the base with the wings extended. These pairs are called "samaras." As soon as the seed is picked, the samaras are separated, cleaned and refrigerated in polyethelene bags until the harvest is completed. Then I immediately go through the stock, dust with fungicide, mix with the damp peat (not soggy wet), label, and stratify as described. In direct planting, I plant upon harvest into outside seed beds and depend upon natural processes to stratify the seed. (Unfortunately all the enemies of the seeds are at work as well.)

At our nursery we plant the stratified seed out in flats during late February and through March. Light frosts have not hurt our germinating palmatums. I plant no deeper than about twice the diameter of the seed and then cover the seeds with the same medium in which I grow the seed, whether in flats or in ground beds. I plant both in seed flats in a lathhouse and in ground beds. I prefer seed flats off the ground to help prevent infection from soil bacteria, fungus, and other pathogens as well as attacks by soil-inhabiting insects and other soil pests. Planting directly into well-prepared soil beds with the proper protection from soil pests and external problems such as squirrels, cats, and other digging animals is equally effective.

Seed flats are prepared with a mixture of 60% medium coarse peat and 40% perlite. Light amounts of the proper fertilizers are calculated and added to the mix. Every propagator has his favorite fertilizer mix. *A. palmatum* do best with a slow-release nitrogen source plus a low level of phosphate and potash and minor elements. I have excellent response to both organic and synthetic nitrogen. In our acid soils I find that ammonium sulphate is not the best choice for Japanese Maples, either seedlings or older stock. Seed beds prepared with good loam soil should have coarse sand, perlite, organic matter, or any material suitable to the particular location added to assure a slightly fluffy and well-drained seed bed. The bed must not be allowed to become waterlogged at any time during the growing or dormant period.

Every effort should be made to maintain a high level of fertility in the ground seed beds during the growing season. Small feedings at frequent intervals are best. In our particular soils, we have good results with the calcium nitrates. In seed beds I get excellent response from the use of bloodmeal as a slower-release form of nitrogen. Of course, the phosphate, potash, and the minor element factors should be supplemented when needed. These needs should be established before planting by having the soil tested. The seedlings should make a good growth from germination and go through a brief Summer rest period. In late Summer a second growth will occur. If prepared for this second growth period, the producer can obtain surprisingly large one-year-old seedlings with proper fertilization and moisture.

Constant attention to pests is necessary. Small leaf-eating caterpillars, aphids, spider mites, slugs, root weevils, birds, and squirrels all present a threat to valuable seed beds. Diseases can quickly damage a concentrated planting of seedling maples. Damping-off fungi and grey-mold *Botrytis* are particular threats at this time.

It is best that young seedlings have partial shade at least the first growing season. Watering should be done carefully to assure a constant supply of moisture, but the seedlings should never become waterlogged.

Usually the *A. palmatum* will make an original early growth upon germination. Following a short Summer resting period they will then make considerable growth in late Summer and early Fall. I have had one-year seedlings up to 1 m (3 ft.) tall in seed flats. In early Fall it is important to withdraw water gradually and begin to harden off the seedlings so they will be prepared for the first freezes. They should not be in "soft-tip" condition at that time.

Usually the one-year seedlings are separated during dormancy and either potted up in grafting pots for the following year or lined out in ground beds for the second year growth. Handling of understock is discussed in the section on grafting.

Much variation will be noted in the crop of seedlings of *A. palmatum*, depending upon the source of seed. Seed from some trees and some imported seed will be quite uniform in either the green-leaf or occasionally the red-leafed varieties, depending upon the parent tree. However, seedlings from some trees will show variations in almost every seedling. This is especially true with seed gathered from some form or cultivar of the *matsumurae* variety of *A. palmatum*. Some of the most beautiful individual plants will be found among these seedlings.

I caution producers and hobbyists about naming "new" seedlings, especially in the red-leafed forms. There are probably 20 or more named cultivars of the "atropurpureum" type. Only a particularly outstanding clone will warrant naming to compete with the already-plentiful supply of "red palmatums." Many excellent seedlings are raised each year and sold as "Red Leafed Maples" and make wonderful landscape plants.

The same is true in the dissectum group. Usually the seed from the dissectums do not come true to color and most do not come true to "dissectum" form. In most instances, the regular palmatum leaf and upright habit of the species will result. However, a certain percentage of dissectum seedlings will result from some seed trees. Quite often these are small, weak-rooted, and slow-growing. With patience many good dissectums can be produced by this method. However, confusion with the named cultivars should be avoided for much of the present disarray in nomenclature has arisen for lack of care in the past, especially among the red dissectum cultivars.

HYBRIDIZATION

At our nursery I have been doing a limited amount of controlled hybridization. Hand pollination of selected male and female blossoms has been completed between various named cultivars of interest. Also, open pollinated seed between interesting named cultivars has been grown-on. This results in a tremendous variation in the seed beds. Very rigorous selection is made after the second year. Many outstanding red forms and other worthwhile seedlings have resulted. However, as stated before, only truly outstanding clones should be retained. There is no need to add to the already confusing abundance of red upright forms of named palmatum cultivars.

I normally wait until the second year to judge the leaf form and color of the seedling. Usually the true character of the seedling does not show until leaves develop from 2-year old wood. The same practice should be followed when evaluating named cultivars as new growth often does not show fully the true character of the cultivar. This characteristic is described more fully in the chapter dealing with cultivars of species.

An example of extreme variance which may occur in hybridizing *Acer palmatum*. The large leaf form (*A. palmatum* 'Ōsakazuki') was the female parent of the cross from which the filament-leaf form (*A. palmatum* 'Koto ito komachi') was selected.

Of the tens of thousands of seedlings produced here over the years, I have found only two or three so outstandingly different that I felt that they warranted the status of named cultivars. One, a dwarf with divided and re-curved leaves, was named 'Kamagata.' A second with extremely fine and delicate linear separations of the leaf—almost hair-like—is a very dwarf form named 'Koto ito komachi.' These are well adapted for container, patio, or alpine gardens but not large landscapes. We also are observing at this writing an entirely different deep crimson-maroon variegate together with an entirely different form of green-white variegant, both of which show considerable promise.

Cross hybridization within *A. japonicum* clones produced some extreme forms. These range from very finely dissected leaves (approaching the delicacy of the *A. palmatum dissectums*) to the other extreme of very large leaves, exceeding the cultivar *A. japonicum* 'Vitifolium.' After a few more years of observation and evaluation, merit judgments will be made on them.

Distinct opportunites to develop worthwhile plants by crossing the cultivars of *A. palmatum* and other species in the Series *Palmata* remain available to the interested. Hybrids between *A. palmatum* and such species as *A. pseudo-*

sieboldianum, A. shirasawanum, and *A. circinatum* offer possiblities for the serious propagator or hobbyist willing to expend the time and informed effort.

GRAFTING

Grafting is the principal method of propagating the Japanese Maples both in commercial production and for the hobbyist.

In collecting data from commercial operations in the United States as well as in Japan and Europe I find that the timing and methods of grafting vary considerably among producers. However, I have also found that each propagator adapts his own variant of the same basic operation. Though there are many variations on the same basic principles, I stress the fact that each variation is proper for that particular propagator. I want to emphasize that because there are wide differences in methods it does not follow that some are right and some are wrong. Each adapts to his own conditions and purposes.

Timing varies widely. In the United States most of the grafting is done during the Winter months, January to March. Some, however, do successful grafting in October and November. In Holland and to a limited extent in the United States grafting is done in July. In Japan grafting is done with both the understock and scions dormant. This is usually done in January or February.

Understock used varies from 1-year old plants to 3-year old stock. Grafting pots vary from 2-inch "rose pots" to one-gallon containers. All these variations plus many more only point out that no one way is absolute. Propagators soon adapt to the variation of the basic method which suits them best.

Most grafting is done with a 2-year old *A. palmatum* seedling in a 7 to 10 cm (3 to 4 in.) grafting pot. Some producers pot up 1-year old seedlings and grow them the second year in the grafting pot. Others field-grow the stock until the second Fall and then pot up and prepare for the grafting house in the Winter. Summer grafting requires potting the understock in the Fall prior to grafting.

Carrying the potted understock during the second growing season demands extra care. Water stress must be avoided to produce good growth and full root systems. As in ground beds, the potted understock must be protected against soil insects and disease. It is most disappointing to fill the greenhouse with potted understock which has had unknown insect or disease damage, for the grafting effort will be wasted.

The variation of foliage in *Acer japonicum* hybrids which resulted from the crossing of two outstanding clones of the species.

The understock is placed in the cold greenhouse in late Fall, having been trimmed back to about 15 cm. (6 in.) in height. About two weeks prior to grafting, the temperature in the greenhouse is raised to 15° C (60° F) to bring the understock into active growth. As the grafting is done, I increase the night temperatures to 18° C (65°F). I try, although not always possible, to keep daytime temperatures below 27-30°C (80-85°F) when the grafts are producing leaves. I use shading and ventilation to protect the young growth from excessive heat and light which could burn the new tips.

The stock is ready to graft about the time the buds begin to swell actively but are not producing leaves. One good method of determining if the stock is ready, is to turn out several pots gently and observe if white roots are starting in the root ball. If there is good root activity, grafting should begin. One problem of having the understock too advanced is that maples (and a few other species, such as Beech, *Fagus*) will "bleed" or produce excessive sap flow. This can quite often drown the graft and prevent healing of the cut surfaces.

Scions are collected from the named cultivar stock plants while they are in full dormancy. The scion is a short piece of wood which is to be inserted to form the graft. If large amounts of scions are to be collected, they should be trimmed to proper length and stored, slightly moist (not saturated) in a plastic wrap or polyethelene bag in a refrigerator very close to freezing—1°C (33°F). They should retain dormancy until actually grafted and be protected from drying during the handling for grafting.

I prefer a scion of the current-year wood, or when necessary not older than 2-year old wood. Young wood heals more quickly. In the extremely dwarf cultivars, with only ¼ to ½ inch of current-year wood, I have grafted up to 4-year old wood but prefer not to do this for commercial types. The scion should have at least three pairs of buds. The length will vary with the cultivar from 3 cm (1 in.) to perhaps as long as 20 cm (8 in.).

Very special care should be taken when selecting the scion wood. Terminal shoots are often selected and are usually excellent wood for grafting. However, winter damage, hidden disease, and other weaknesses might be present in the terminal wood. Each scion should be closely inspected prior to use. Wood damaged by winter temperatures may not show the weakness at time of collection in January.

I cannot emphasize too strongly the necessity of having an extremely sharp knife for cutting the wood at grafting. It is not possible to have a knife too sharp. The cambium layer on *A. palmatum* and similar maples is so thin that it is easily bruised. The smaller cultivars with tiny scions have an unbelievably thin cambium—only a very few layers of tiny cells in thickness. A knife which may be thought "sharp" may be comparatively dull. All cuts must be very clean. Bruised cambium cells do not heal or at best heal weakly. Bruised cambium can cause up to 50% loss in grafting. I have found that a single-edged razor blade does an excellent job and is easily replaced when dull.

The most important single aspect of grafting is the successful union of the cambium layers. It is important to understand exactly what this layer is and how to unite it so the new graft will heal.

The structure of roots, stems, and twigs of all woody plants is divided into three basic parts. The bark is an outer covering mainly for protection. The innermost area is the wood which provides structural strength and serves to support the plant. This is the major portion of the plant. Between these two portions is the circle of tissue called the cambium layer. In this layer most of the life functions take place. It contains growth production cells; tubes conducting the moisture and plant nutrients up and down the plant system; and regenerative tissue.

For the non-professional I present an over-simplified explanation to help visualize the important plant structures involved. First, picture a broomstick: this represents the woody scaffold of the plant structure, including the roots. Next, imagine a pipe slipped tightly over the broomstick. This represents the cambium layer. The outside layer is strong burlap wrapped uniformly around the pipe. This represents the bark. It is the "pipe" with which we are most concerned in grafting. The "pipe" is composed of the tissue which carries the moisture and plant food up and down the plant system. Also, it is the location of the cells responsible for growth of the plant and for regeneration of cells when damage occurs. Grafting is a form of temporary damage. The plant attempts to heal this damage quickly. If the cambium layers of the scion and understock fit closely, the cells will unite and repair the "damage" and a graft union will result.

All other aspects of grafting are essentially either "culture" or "mechanics," such as : the handling of understock and scions, growth and care of understock, choice of grafting methods, and post-grafting care. Each is variable. The one non-variable item is that cambium layers *MUST* match, or join, at some point in the graft to start regeneration of cells and result in the union of scions and understock.

It is true that a graft can succeed to a limited degree if only a few cells unite. Naturally, the more that do, the better the graft. The ideal graft would be one with the diameter of the scion exactly matching the diameter of the understock. This is normally not possible. Therefore, specific attention must be given to the matching of at least one side of the scion cambium to one side of the understock cambium. It should be kept in mind that in older understock the cambium is deeper under the thicker bark layer. Conversely, in small scions the cambium is a very thin layer under very thin bark. Matching these can be extremely difficult. When we graft certain tiny dwarf cultivars or types with very small diameter twigs, the matching of cambiums becomes exceedingly trying. It is often impossible to place these on understock of equal diameter as this size base would be too weak.

With a very sharp knife a long, slanting slice is removed from the base of the scion. The cut will be from 1½-3 cm (½-1 in.) long. The thickness of the cut on different cultivars will vary according to the diameter of the scion. On the opposite side a very short cut is removed in order to point the scion.

A corresponding slice is made on the side of the understock. The cut should be slightly longer than on the scion. This will assure a closely-matched placement of the graft. This cut should be very low on the plant when grafting most cultivars. The understock cut should not go into the center of the stem but remain on the outer one-third of the diameter. The resulting "flap" should have the upper ⅔ of the end removed.

The scion is then slipped gently into the matching cut in the understock. The point should be pressed firmly into the matching notch in the stock and the end of the "flap" brought up over the short cut on the outside of the scion. The graft should be tied firmly. I use the strips of "budding rubbers" pulled firmly tight but not tight enough to choke the cambium layers. Holding the scion firmly in place, the tie is wrapped around the graft in a spiral manner to immobilize the scion until the cuts are healed and a good union is completed. We usually start wrapping from the lower end. Some propagators tie with plastic strips, cotton thread, grafting tape, etc. The important point is to keep the scion firm in the understock until healing is completed. The ties are usually cut later in the season when the grafts are planted out of the greenhouse.

After tying, it is usually necessary to do some waxing. Any of the good grafting waxes and compounds will work. Some grafters paint with the beeswax mixtures or paraffin. Others dip the entire graft, understock and scion, into melted wax. I prefer the grafting wax emulsions, only coating the cut and joined surfaces on both sides of the understock. Some of the new "plastic base" pruning paints are too constrictive on the very small grafts of some cultivars. As growth starts, these preparations will constrict and choke the growth.

There are about as many variations to this method as there are propagators! Each is correct in his own adaptation. I observed that in Europe many grafters will make a shorter tapered cut in the scion, rarely over 1 cm in length and a rather stubby point on the scion. In Japan some grafting is done on understock with the top completely removed, grafting directly on the stub. The entire stub and base of scion are then wrapped to keep out the air. I have also seen direct cleft grafting and the reverse, which is saddle grafting. My feeling is that this does not result is as smooth a union as side or veneer grafting. I also know of commercial grafting done with these plants when the understock is not potted. This "bench-graft" attaches a dormant scion on a bare-root dormant understock with a short side graft into the top of the stub. The entire graft is then plunged into moist peat, covering the graft union. As growth develops, these grafts are then potted up and kept in a protected house for the growth season.

As stated, most grafting is done very low on the understock, especially for the upright cultivar forms. This makes a nice trunk when planted out and the plant matures. In the cultivars of dissectums, low grafting is also done and then the cascading new growth is staked and trained for a few years. Some propagators also graft dissectums on "standards." Scions are grafted 30, 50, or even 90 cm tall understock (12, 20, or 36 in.). This gives a good, strong, straight understock from which the cascading varieties can arch down. I have seen and have made a few grafts on good, straight 3-year old understock which were 1½ to 2 m tall. With a few years of training these special grafts form spectacular specimens of dissectum cultivars.

Summer grafting follows the same process with the following variations in handling. The understock is potted the previous Fall during dormancy. Following the Spring growth period, the understock is dried out in the pots until the leaves approach the wilting point. The understock is then cut back to the short height desired. Leaves are stripped from the understock at this time. Meanwhile the new growth on stock plants has gone into a Summer rest period. This new growth is collected and protected from drying. The scions are cut and inserted by the same side-graft method. The leaves are removed from the scions, leaving usually only the terminal pair. After wrapping, the grafts are placed immediately under an automatic mist system. Waxing is not necessary when they are placed under the mist system. No delay in getting the graft under the mist can be allowed. The timing of the mist frequency should be controlled to keep the new grafts from dessicating but not to the point of overwatering the understock. The graft will heal within a very few days (temperature also determining the length of time), and the union will be complete. The new grafts will not always put out a new shoot of growth. In fact, it is just as well if they do not. Misting should be reduced as soon as the graft union has healed. As Fall approaches, these plants should be well hardened off and prepared for overwintering. This can be done either in larger containers or held in the small pots with protection until lined out in the regular manner.

I have also been successful with "T-budding," chip-budding, budsticks, and patch budding. I have even seen good grafts made with short bud sticks inserted at right angles to the understock. This method of using limited material assures that more cambium cells are in contact with the understock. The final graft may not be as smooth, but it is a method which will allow more successful grafts to increase the stock plants of a very rare and limited cultivar. "T" and patch budding work well in cultivars with larger buds, but the dwarf forms such as the many "yatsubusa" types are difficult. The extremely small buds are difficult to place properly. Any good propagating reference will show these basic procedures. Budding, patch buds, and bud sticks may be done in the Summer grafting method as described above. It is also possible to field-bud on understock lined out in the field if necessary. Budding of various types is also successful when done in the Winter in the greenhouse. None of these methods is widely used because the size of the material is quite small and so hard to handle properly. It is an excellent way, however, of getting more material out of an extremely limited supply of a rare or unusual cultivar by using one or perhaps two buds instead of a long scion.

Post-graft handling must be given close attention. After the scion produces new growth in the greenhouse, the understock should be clipped off immediately above the graft. Care should be taken that the new graft is not pressed, breaking the union of the newly-healed scar tissue. The newly-trimmed grafts should have shading in hot areas, adequate water, fertilizer, and temperatures controlled to prevent excessive chilling or overheating. The scions will go through a new period of growth, and within about two months the new growth will form a terminal bud and harden. At this time, the plants can be given increased amounts of "outside" air and temperature, preparatory to hardening off for transplanting outside. Transplanting should be done by early Summer, either directly into prepared ground beds or into larger growing-on containers. They can be transplanted safely at this end of growth period with protection. It is essential that they be given at least 50% shading for the balance of the first growing season. Proper care, fertility, and moisture for the new grafts will assure a second growth production in the late Summer period. This is often the most important period for the new graft, making up its size and strength at this time. As Fall approaches, moisture should be withheld gradually to harden the young plants off for Winter protection.

CUTTINGS

Several large-production operations have used the rooted cutting method of propagation. We were told in Holland that this is usually confined to one cultivar of upright red palmatums. All other production is by grafting. It is felt that the plants were better grafted than on their own roots from cuttings. There has been some discussion and disagreement in the United States over this point. Some feel that many of the cultivars are not as strong on their own roots as when grafted onto good seedling understock. Some plant failure in rooted cultivars, as they get older, is attributed to their being on their own roots. However, I have observed that plants from two nurseries show very satisfactory plants resulting from rooted cuttings of several cultivars.

I have made cuttings of many of the cultivars of *A. palmatum* and *A. japonicum* and demonstrated to my satisfaction that some root very poorly, if at all. Other cultivars, such as 'Bloodgood' root very well and seem to make very strong older plants. Dissectums in general are not readily rooted, although certain cultivars do fairly well. Young dissectums must be staked for several years to attain any height.

Propagation by the cutting method can be done several ways. Various procedural methods have been reported in research papers for several decades. Satisfactory results are possible with both Summer cuttings and the dormant hardwood method.

Summer cuttings of semi-hard wood is one method used. The Spring growth, after the terminal bud is hardened, is cut into 8 to 15 cm (3 to 6 in.) lengths and protected from any wilting. All but the last pair of leaves are removed. A 2 cm long, slanting cut, with a very sharp blade, is made in the base of the cutting. This cut should not extend into the center of the cutting. Hormone treatment, dust or soak, is usually necessary. I have tried several strengths, combinations and types, and do not find much difference. Cuttings are inserted into mixes of peat-sand, perlite-sand or other mixes which allow for good drainage. The cuttings must not become waterlogged, so good drainage is essential. The cuttings are put under an automatic mist system set to prevent any drying of the new foliage. Bottom heat is supplied with electric cables set at about 22° to 24° C (72° to 75°F.). Some shading is essential for new growth on palmatums. In some operations a "double case" of plastic tents or glass frames is used instead of mist system with great success.

Some propagators have equal success with dormant cuttings. Material gathered in January and stuck in well-drained rooting medium is treated with a hormone rooting compound. Bottom heat is held fairly low at 18°C (65°F) for the first week or ten days until some callusing occurs. Heat is then increased to 21° or 22° C (72°F). As new growth develops, close attention must be given to moisture supply and shade.

LAYERING

Layering and air-layering are methods of obtaining a few larger plants in a short time or of expanding the supply of a choice plant. This is sometimes easier to perform for a hobbyist who does not have grafting or other propagating facilities.

Air layering procedures described in any good propagating text are about the same for palmatums as other horticultural plants. In our area, April and very early May is the most desirable time, for active cambium cells and some leaf production will speed up the callusing. With a sharp, clean knife, a slanting cut is made at the point chosen for the new base of the plant. The cut is dusted with a hormone powder just before wrapping. The cut area is packed with damp sphagnum moss and then enclosed with polyethelene sheeting. The covering must be tightly tied at both ends to prevent drying and also to prevent rain from entering and wetting the rooting area excessively. The plastic enclosure must then be covered with black paper, aluminum foil, or some other material to divert the direct rays of the the sun to prevent excessive temperature within the root material. New roots can be observed the following Fall or the next Spring. The limb is then cut off just below the rooted area. The new roots are quite brittle and should be planted with care. Also, shade should be given the new plant the first season.

Layering or "stooling" works well for special conditions. A stock plant can be cut back, thereby inducing bottom sprouting the following season. Or, if a low branch of young wood can be bent to the ground, this will root well. A mix of peat moss, bark, open loam, or any good friable material with good drainage can be mounded up around the base of the young sprouts or over the low twig held to the ground firmly. It is best to make a small slice or wound in the bark of the young growth prior to covering with the rooting material. This arrangement should usually be left for two seasons to assure a new root system before removal from the parent plant. After rooting, the new shoots can be removed during the following dormant season and transplanted for growing-on.

The "mound" method or "stooling" may give several good plants from a stock plant at one time. However, this method is very hard on the stock plant. The stock plant should be rested for a year or two before cutting back for re-stooling and additional plant production.

I would like to re-emphasize one point relating to propagation before closing. There is a very large variation in the methods used in various parts of the world. I emphasize that each propagator has developed his own technique. Each adapted his own procedure depending upon locality, facilities, climate, and personal abilities. I am convinced that Japanese Maples can be propagated by almost any method used for other plants. One must choose the method which gives him the best plants consistently and economically under his own conditions.

Acer Sieboldianum in Fall coloration. Many of the other species of *Acer* from Japan are as desirable as the "Japanese Maple" of the horticultural trade but are not as well known.

V

THE CULTIVARS DISPLAYED

How to "Read" Cultivars

This part of the book is devoted to the description of the cultivars of Japanese Maples. It is important to consider several factors if one is seeing a cultivar for the first time, especially a young plant or a new graft. Different cultural conditions can alter the immediate appearance of many of the cultivars, and this should be taken into consideration when comparing written descriptions with the plant growing in a garden location.

SUN

Red cultivars, particularly the dissectums, will "bronze" more severely under situations of extremely hot, direct sun rays. Some of the variegated forms also need afternoon relief in areas with very hot exposures.

SHADE

The red-leaf forms, both diesectum and palmate types, alter color considerably when grown under deep shade. 'Garnet' for example, will be a shade of green rather than the garnet color for which it was named. Other red dissectums will be predominately green with subdued red. New propagates grown under shade-cloth (55%) will not develop red colors or the variegations in true color tones.

Light colored leaves (such as the 'Aureum' of *A. japonicum* and *A. palmatum*) will not show the gold undertone which is so desirable. Variegated leaves may be more predominately green under deep-shade conditions.

FERTILITY

Plants grown under high fertility may mask the characteristics for which they were originally selected. This is particularly true of the variegated forms. Odd-leafed forms may produce non-cultivar shapes. Dwarf plants may grow to a-typical shapes and size. Good health is important, but over-fertilizing can cause several types of difficulties.

AGE

A cultivar should be judged only by the foliage produced on older wood. Leaves which appear on new growth (current season shoots) are quite often non-typical for the cultivar. They will usually appear more "typical" for the species. This is especially true in the linearilobum and variegated groups as well as the odd-leaf types, such as 'Higasayama,' 'Tsuchigumo' and similar forms. Especially in the linearilobums, the new foliage may have rather coarse lobes, even on two-year wood.

This is also a very important consideration when judging the future quality of a seedling. Any important feature, which may make it a possible candidate for naming, may not appear until the third or fourth year. I have found several unusual forms in the two- or three-year old seedling beds which were not apparent the first year. It is best to make final judgment of a new seedling selection about the fifth year.

"Juvenile" foliage compared with leaves on older wood of cultivars. The new, vigorous foliage will show "non-typical" form. Top row: foliage from older wood, left: *A. palmatum* 'Scolopendrifolium', left center: *A. palmatum* 'Trompenburg', center: *A. palmatum* 'Okushimo', right center: *A. palmatum* 'Higasayama', right: *A. palmatum* 'Red Pygmy'. Bottom row: new foliage.

"REVERTING"

Variegated cultivars are most often suspected of "reverting," i.e., losing the color form for which they were named. I am convinced some of this is directly linked with over-fertility on certain soil types. Plants which have gone "plain" have been observed in later seasons to return to the variegated form as they matured and had less nitrogen available. This may not be applicable in all areas due to varying soil types.

I have repeatedly made grafts of "non-cultivar" tips of 'Higasayama' and 'Hagoromo' (as well as some of the variegates). In every case, the second season from graft produced the type-foliage of the cultivar.

If strong, non-typical shoots which occasionally appear become disturbing to the plant owner, they can be removed easily at any season of the year.

I do not mean to imply by the above paragraphs that the Japanese Maples are overly delicate in culture. The reverse is true. However, the dissectum, variegated, and red-leaf cultivars are rather sensitive to excessive shade and fertility and may not show each individual character to the fullest extent.

Cultivars and Selections of *Acer Palmatum*

The cultivars of *A. palmatum* are described in the following section. I include most of those which still exist in cultivation. The descriptions are primarily derived from specimens growing in our collection, augmented by written material from early literature. (See bibliography.) It has been difficult for me to describe adequately all the subtle differences which occur in some of the cultivars. The color illustrations of the foliage were planned to assist in identification and not to present landscape situations.

The cultivars of *A. palmatum* are separated here into seven groups. I have based this division mainly on basic leaf shape, except for the dwarf type plants. The sections are: (1) palmate leaves (2) dissected leaves (3) deeply-divided leaves (4) linearilobed leaves (5) dwarf forms (6) variegated leaves (7) unusual features.

It is difficult to describe the slight differences in leaf form among some of the dissectums. However, when seen on the plant, the total effect of the foliage is quite apparent. Individually, a leaf of 'Sekimori' placed beside one of 'Ao shidare', or even 'Seiryu' may look almost identical. When viewed on the plant, especially through the various seasons of the year, it becomes apparent that there are great differences. This is true of all the "groups" of cultivars that may seem to have identical written individual leaf descriptions.

Some plants in our collection are only a few years old, and so details such as ultimate height have been omitted. For some cultivars descriptions from early literature were not available. Cultural conditions in widely-varying localities may account for differences in leaf and plant sizes. Whenever possible, composite data has been used to describe the true nature of the cultivar habit.

Acer palmatum Thunberg. This excellent example of the species is growing on the Dixson estate at The Ford, Wiveliscombe, Somerset, England, and was planted about 1850. It typifies the open-crown growth habit of the species.

PALMATE GROUP

The cultivars and varieties grouped in this section all have the palmate type leaf. They include those with five, seven, and rarely nine-lobed foliage. They are similar to the foliage of the species *Acer palmatum* and include those similar to the subspecies and varieties.

They are mostly upright plants, forming either tall shrubs up to 3 meters or tree forms reaching a mature height of 4 to 8 meters. Both green and red cultivars and varieties of this leaf type are included in this section.

Acer palmatum Thunberg 1783
  Series *Palmata*
  "Japanese Maple"
  Japanese names: Momiji, Kaede noki, Iroha momiji, Tako kaede, Iwato beni

Acer palmatum is the species from which most of the cultivars of "Japanese Maples" have arisen. This is a complex species, quite variable, which consists of several subspecies, varieties, and forms. *Acer amoenum* is given full species status by some authors, while other authorities place it as a sub-species. Variety *Matsumurae* has also been given various placements. For the purposes of this book, I have preferred to use the inclusive name "Palmatum" as the reference point without delving into the complexities of the sub-divisions. For exacting taxonomic separations, I would suggest the writings of Ogata, Ohwi, Koidzumi, and de Jong.

The type foliage is a bright green, 4 to 7 cm in diameter, with 2 to 4 cm petioles. The 5 to 7 (9) lobes are palmately arranged, separating half way or even entirely to the center of the leaf. The lobes are lanceolate, sometimes broadly so, and acuminate, terminating in a sharp tip. The margins are serrate or double-serrate.

These are upright-growing trees, usually with rounded-tops or broad canopy. In their natural habitat, they reach a height of 10 to 12 meters, although trees this tall are rarely seen in cultivation. They are thrifty, hardy, and in cultivation seem to adapt to a wide variety of culture and locale.

The species is almost entirely confined to Central and Southern Japan. However, it does extend west through the Island of Tsushima, the Southern part of Korea, to the coastal regions of the Yellow Sea and the East China Sea in continental China. There are very few specimens in the last-named regions. (Ogata)

These maples grow in a wide range of soil types and occur at elevations from 200 to 1300 meters. They grow in areas with variations of moisture, but never in wet, soggy soils.

Some of the major taxonomic divisions are:

amoenum "Ō momiji" (either a species, variety, or subspecies by differenct authors) Differs mainly in leaf size, which can measure up to 2 cm greater in diameter. Also the lobes are usually 7 to 9 in number, are more deeply separated in the leaf, and the margins are regularly-serrulate.

Var. *Matsumurae* "Yama momiji" These are also larger leaves than *palmatum* but have prominently duplicate or incised-serrate margins. Also, the lobes are more broadly lanceolate or narrowly ovate than *amoenum*. They separate to the center of the leaf.

Form *latilobatum (septemlobum)* "Hiroha momiji" Has seven lobes which are broader, deltoid or deltoid-ovate, not so deeply separated into the leaf.

Form *horonaiense* (Ogata) "Horonai kaede" Has large leaves, up to 10 to 12 cm, broad lobes, and roughly serrated margins.

Var. *nambuanum* (Ogata) "Nanbu koha momiji" Is separated from f. *latilobatum* by the consistently smaller size leaves.

It is important to recognize, also, that there is a general inter-gradation of leaf size and shape among these various forms and varieties.

The Var. *Matsumurae* probably gives rise to more cultivars than any of the other subspecies or varieties.

A. palmatum 'Akegarasu'
  (The crows at dawn)

One of the large, upright red forms of palmatum, this is probably a cultivar of the *Matsumurae* group.

The large leaves are divided only ½ or ⅔ into the center. The lobes are ovate-elliptic, coming to a very sharp point, with the edges slightly toothed. Leaves are from 8 cm to 12 cm wide as well as long. The early season color is a very deep purple-red, or black red, depending on the light. In later Summer the leaves will bronze somewhat, showing more green. Like other reds, when grown in shady conditions, the red is not as intense in early Summer. Petioles are up to 4 cm or 5 cm and are a deep red. The branches are green.

This is a strong, upright-growing type and will reach 3 or 4 meters at maturity. It tends to widen into a broad-topped, short tree. It is a hardy cultivar for landscape use, the color contrasting slightly with other "red" forms, and is a good choice among the larger-leafed cultivars.

A. palmatum 'Aoba fuke'
See: A. palmatum f. volubile

A. palmatum 'Aoyagi'
(Beautiful green, or green willow)

The bright pea-green color of the bark on twigs, small branches and limbs is the outstanding feature of this cultivar. It is sometimes referred to as the green counterpart of 'Sango kaku.'

The foliage is typical palmatum type with leaves about 5 cm long and wide. The lobes radiate outward, separate ⅔ the distance to the center, and taper gradually to a long sharp point. The margins are serrated. The bright green is of a light tone and becomes a pleasing yellow in the Fall. The leaf texture is rather thin. Petioles are normally about 2 cm long, making the leaves rather compact along the twigs.

While this is an upright-growing small tree, it is not quite as vigorous as 'Sango kaku.' It will become a spreading-topped tree of 3 meters as it matures.

The brilliance of the bark is surprising for a green tone. When planted near the contrasting 'Sango kaku,' the effect is pleasing. The colors are most intense during the Winter season. A snowfall enhances the beauty of this cultivar by emphasizing the bark color.

"Yagi" is the Japanese name for a species of coral, Ao-green. Therefore, this could infer "the green type of coral-bark."

A. palmatum 'Ariake nomura'

This is one of the upright red forms of palmatum.

It is reported to be a seedling of 'Nomura kaede.' From the palmatum shape of the leaf and the plant habit it is difficult to distinguish from 'Nomura' which has been known for a long time. The distinguishing feature is a slightly different tone of red. 'Ariake' is a little more brown-red in color in Spring, a lighter purplish-red bronze in late Summer, and a bright crimson when Fall colors occur.

Not widely found in collections or nurseries.

A. palmatum 'Aoyagi'

A. palmatum 'Atropurpureum Superbum'

I imported this cultivar several years ago from Holland. It grows vigorously and is hardy. It is a selection from A. palmatum atropurpureum. Its color is deeper and holds better in the Summer than the usual seedlings of atropurpureum.

Leaves have 7(5) lobes which are long ovate and separate to within 1 cm of the petiole attachment. The outer end gradually tapers to a sharp point. The inner ⅓ of the margin is rather smooth, while the outer portion is sharply and regularly toothed or double-serrated. Leaf size ranges from 6 to 9 cm long and up to 11 cm wide. The stiff, red petiole is 4 to 5 cm long.

The color is a deep purple-red or maroon. Tones are brightest on new leaves and then change to the good, deep tone in Summer. The color holds almost as well as 'Bloodgood' but will burn in hot locations.

As a young plant, this is a vigorous and sturdy grower. It will reach the height and size of the atropurpureum palmatums—small trees up to 7 or more meters at maturity. A good landscape plant.

A. *palmatum* 'Aureum'
Gold Leaf Palmatum
(Not to be confused with the Golden Full
Moon Maple, A. *japonicum* 'Aureum')

The distinctive yellow of this cultivar is quite dominant. However, there is an undertone of light green. When the new foliage appears, the margins of the lobes have a slight tinge of rust color which soon disappears. As the season progresses, the leaves age into a more pure light green, the "golden" tone softening. In our plants, the yellow tones are even more pronounced as the second growth occurs in early August. This seasonal flush of growth is also more vigorous and quite often more branched.

Foliage is composed of 5 (7) lobed, typically palmate leaves of medium size. The lobes extend outward forming a 5 to 6 cm diameter leaf with slightly toothed margins. Petioles are about 3 cm long. The twigs and petioles are bright red.

A. *palmatum* 'Aureum'

The form of the plant is upright, bushy, and does not reach great heights. I would rarely expect to find a tree over 6 or 7 meters tall at maturity. They tend toward a twiggy type of growth on older wood.

This cultivar does not have the same type of golden cast as the more familiar A. *japonicum* cultivar, 'Aureum.' In shade the yellow will be rather masked and assume a light green tone. In full sun the color develops into the golden shades. Fall coloration produces a display of bright yellow.

A. *palmatum* 'Autumn Glory'

This is not a cultivar in the true sense of the word. The name applies to a few selected seedlings which are most notable for their beautiful Fall coloration patterns—mostly crimson. This is an excellent selection of plants commercially distributed out of The Netherlands. The selection and introduction were done by R. de Belder of the Arboretum Kalmthout, Belgium, about 1958.

These are upright small trees of 4 to 6 meters which form a broad canopy. The leaves are broad and of good texture as found in the *heptalobum* type. I believe they are rightfully classed as seedlings of *amoenum*.

A. *palmatum* atropurpureum
Red Leaf
Japanese Maple

The red tones of the leaves distinguish this as a variant of the palmatum species. It is usually produced from seed and not a grafted variety. Leaves are 5 to 7 lobed, typically palmate, but variable. They will vary in size from 4 to 10 cm in diameter, generally sub-orbicular, but with the lobes separated from ⅓ to ⅔ the distance into the center. The lobes are ovate to ovate-lanceolate and acuminate with margins indistinctly to prominently serrate. Being seedling produced, each tree will have minute individual differences.

Classed in the upright group of palmatums, this is a strong-growing landscape tree. It will ultimately form a round-topped canopy up to 10 meters high.

Early literature indicates that at one time there was a cultivar of this name. However, through general practice in various countries, the red-leaf selections have become a general classification in the nursery trade. If it ever had true cultivar status, it became so diluted as to be no longer valid.

A. *palmatum* atropurpureum

At present in the United States this type of Japanese Maple is heavily propagated. They are produced from seed sources of choice parent trees. Some of these trees produce surprisingly uniform seedlings of a uniform color tone throughout. Other parent trees produce some very interesting deviations in leaf size, shape, and color in the individual plants. Some of these seedling types may even exceed the beauty of some of the named cultivars.

It is from these seedling-produced atropurpureum types that selected cultivars have arisen over the centuries. Older types such as 'Shōjō', 'Nomura', 'Nuresagi', and the more recent 'Bloodgood' and 'Moonfire' have all come from the selection of outstanding types.

The main failing of this general group is that the red colors are not as stable as those of the named cultivars. Usually Spring and early Summer color will be red followed by a general fading into bronze tones which are often rather dull. Many will change to green, and the red landscape effect is lost. Fall colors, however, will usually return to bright tones in most seedling trees.

Many propagators continue to select red seedlings with the aim of naming new cultivars. We have raised thousands of these red seedlings, some of exceptional character and quality. However, I feel that there are so many 'Red-leafed' cultivars named and on the market that there is a risk of further confusing and loading the market with more "names." Unless the new selection has outstanding and unusually desirable characteristics, I am loathe to see more named clones appear.

A. palmatum atropurpureum 'The Bishop'

This is one of the late Henry Hohman's selections out of atropurpureum. Mr. Hohman's ability to select outstanding plants for propagation was one of his well-known attributes.

It has seven-lobed leaves. Each lobe is oblong-ovate, gradually tapering to a long, slender tip. The lobes extend outward and are separated to within 1 or 1½ cm of the leaf center. The margins are serrated uniformly. Leaves measure 6 to 7 cm long and 7 to 8 cm wide with slender petioles about 4 to 5 cm long.

The purple-red is bright in the Spring, and the color does not "bronze" until late Summer.

This is an upright-growing specimen, vigorous and hardy, with excellent crimson Fall colors. It reaches 3 to 4 meters at maturity.

A. palmatum 'Bloodgood'

'Bloodgood' has become one of the very popular large-leafed, upright-growing tree forms of palmatum in the United States and Europe. It is a very good deep red or black-red and holds its color into late Summer better than most red-leafed forms. It will not "bronze out" as most of the broad-leafed forms. In extreme hot sun it will sunburn slightly as will most palmatums. Some afternoon protection is beneficial.

The leaf shape is typical palmatum with lobes divided approximately one-half distance to the center. Length is up to 10 cm, with width up to 12 cm. The dark red petioles are up to 5 cm long. The underside is usually a shiny, dark green. Light transmitted through the leaves on a bright day gives a beautiful red effect. Fall colors are usually bright crimson. The prominent seeds are a beautiful red and add to the overall beauty of the plant.

This strong-growing variety makes an upright tree maturing at 5 or 6 meters. Strong branches form a broad-topped tree with a spread about equal to the height.

I noted that this was about the only cultivar being grown from cuttings in Holland nurseries. It is also grafted there. In the United States there are thousands being grafted onto strong understock. These make vigorous trees in a short time.

I hope this cultivar is kept "pure", for it has very good qualities not found in some other red-leafed cultivars.

It is suggested (Carville) that this was a selection from A. palmatum atropurpureum seedlings by the Bloodgood Nursery, Long Island, New York. Vrugtman suggests the possibility that this cultivar had its origin in Boskoop, Holland, and was propagated by Ebbinge & van Groos (nursery discontinued). It was subsequently exported to the United States where it was named and the propagation expanded.

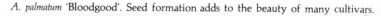

A. *palmatum* 'Bloodgood'. Seed formation adds to the beauty of many cultivars.

A. palmatum 'Hōgyoku'

A. palmatum 'Hōgyoku'. Compact growth and distinctive Fall coloration typify this cultivar.

A. palmatum 'Chikushigata'
   Alternate spelling: 'Shikishigata'
   See: *A. palmatum* 'Tsukushigata'

A. palmatum 'Daimyo'
   See: *A. palmatum* 'Taimin'

This is an old cultivar of the red palmatum type.

A. palmatum var. *heptalobum*
   Syn.: septemlobum, Thunbergi, meikots, septenlobum

While this is sometimes sold as a cultivar, it is a variety or a subspecies, depending upon which authority is used as reference. There are several choice cultivars in the heptalobum group. An outstanding character of heptalobums and selections therefrom is their bright Fall coloration.

Leaves are of good green substance and tend to be the largest foliage in the palmatum group. The seven (9) lobed leaves range up to as large as 10 to 12 cm long and wide. Lobes spread widely and normally do not divide over half way to the center. Each lobe is broad but comes to a sharp point. There is much variation between leaves on the same plant.

The crowning glory comes in the Fall with almost fluorescent tones ranging from strong orange to blends of scarlet.

This is a sturdy, upright tree which tends to spread, thus becoming wider and shorter than the typical palmatum. It will mature at 5 or perhaps 6 meters. The branches and twigs are stocky.

A. palmatum 'Hichihenge'
   See: *A. palmatum* 'Shichihenge'

The most common spelling of this cultivar when translated into English is 'Shichihenge.' In some areas the Japanese do not pronounce the syllable "hi", so more often this cultivar is spelled with "shi."

A. palmatum 'Hiugayama'

This is not a widely-grown cultivar of palmatum probably because it is not outstandingly different from many other named red cultivars. It is reportedly a seedling selection of 'Nomura', one of the older cultivars. The leaf lobes are longer and more slender than 'Nomura.'

The color in the early season is a deep purple red. It will become less intense as the season progresses. The leaves are palmatum type, regularly 5 lobed. The lobes radiate outward and are widely open. Each lobe is long ovate-elliptical, and the margins are sharply toothed. Leaves are about 6 cm long and 7 cm wide. Petioles are usually about 2 cm long. The branches are green and slender, and the growth habit is rather erect.

A. palmatum 'Hōgyoku'

Surely this cultivar was selected for its rich, deep orange Fall color. Usually our stock plant turns a bright pumpkin orange. The Spring and Summer foliage is a deep, rich green.

Leaves range up to 6 cm long and to 9 cm wide. They are seven-lobed and broadly palmate. The lobes radiate out and are divided only about ⅓ the distance to the center. Lobes are ovate-triangular, with edges very finely serrate. Petioles are up to 4 cm long. The leaves have heavy texture and good substance. The surface is glabrous.

This is a sturdy and hardy cultivar. New growth is thick and sometimes stubby. The tree will reach probably 4 to 5 meters with age. It responds to pruning and shaping very well.

Although not widely distributed, this is a very worthwhile plant since most of the year it is an attractive rich green, followed by the unique orange of Fall.

A. palmatum heptalobum. Noted for Fall colors.

A. palmatum 'Ichigyōji'
  Alternate spelling: 'Ichijōji'

This plant is almost identical to 'Ōsakazuki' except for Fall color. 'Ichigyōji' has intense, brilliant yellow or yellow-orange color while 'Ōsakazuki' has crimson. The plant stands out among all others for its brilliance. Because of its large leaves, the colors are flamboyant. During the growing season when the leaves are a pleasant green, the tree looks identical to 'Ōsakazuki.' (Some authors class these two as synonyms.) It is reported that they may have been sister seedlings when selected over 100 years ago.

These trees have very large leaves of the heptalobum group. Leaves measure up to 12 cm long on the center lobe with a spread of 15 cm from tip to tip on the side lobes. The seven lobes are broadly ovate, shaping to a sharp point with edges slightly toothed. The lobes are joined about half way to the base, forming a broad and substantial leaf. Petioles are up to 7 cm long.

The tree is upright and broad and in maturity forms a round-headed tree. It will perhaps attain a height of 6 to 7 meters, although it is not usually seen this tall in the landscape. With pruning the tree shapes well, and there need be no fear of keeping this type in bounds in the smaller plantings. It is of sturdy branch structure and not willowy.

Japanese writers wisely suggest planting 'Ichigyōji' and 'Ōsakazuki' near each other and on a rise or hillside, or near a pond, to allow the full glory of the Fall brilliance to be appreciated.

A. palmatum 'Ki hachijō'
  (tree from Island of Hachijō)

The sturdy leaves of this cultivar are a bright green. The lobes are usually 9 in number but occasionally 7. Lobes are long, ovate-acuminate with deep double serrations on the margins. The very narrow point of each lobe gives a distinctive effect. Leaves are 6 to 7 cm long and 8 to 9 cm at spread of tips. Leaves lie flat and are attached with short petioles about 1 to 2 cm long.

Fall coloration develops into a distinct yellow-gold with rosy tones. It becomes blended with light orange and reds. It is quite a unique Fall color.

The sturdy branches angle out, thus developing a well-rounded, short tree or tall bush about 4 m high. The bark is a strong green with an overtone of bluish grey. White streaking is prominent, especially as the bark ages.

This is a good, hardy, sturdy cultivar for landscaping which adds a "different" appearance.

A. palmatum 'Kingsville Red'

This is one of the selections of Henry Hohman of Kingsville Nurseries, Maryland. He was a very observant plantsman and selected outstanding clones of several genera of plants.

'Kingsville Red' is an atropurpureum selection which is vigorous, hardy, upright, and grows to about 7 meters. The bright red-purple tone holds well in our climate into the late Summer. It does not seem to sunburn as do some other "reds."

The large leaves are seven-lobed, separated to within 1 cm of the leaf center. Lobes are oblong, tapering to a slender tip. Margins are finely double serrated most prominently on the outer half of the lobe. The leaves are 6 to 7 cm long and up to 10 cm wide. Petioles are 3 to 4 cm long and are stiff. The smaller base lobes of the palmate leaves tend to cup slightly upward.

A. palmatum var. *koreanum*
  Alternate spelling: var. *coreanum*

This is a green leafed variety of the species palmatum which is indigenous to South Korea. It is a fairly vigorous, upright-growing, small tree and will form a round-headed specimen much like the type species.

A. palmatum 'Ichigyōji'

A. palmatum var. *koreanum*. A geographical variety of the species.

The leaves are a bright green and of light tone. The margins have a very narrow and faint red marking in Spring. Lobes are usually 7 in number, but 5 is not uncommon. They are long ovate, separated about ⅔ the distance to the center and radiating outward. The lobes taper to a fairly sharp point with the margins very delicately double-serrate. Petioles are red and up to 4 cm long.

Fall colors are fairly brilliant and typical of the species they range from yellows to oranges occasionally blended with red. The twig coloration is very dark, especially in the Fall and Winter.

This tree is strong-growing and hardy and will attain a height of several meters. However, with proper pruning it can also be made to form a round-headed, short tree.

A. palmatum heptalobum 'Lutescens'

The leaves of this cultivar are of the larger type of palmatum leaf and are 7-lobed. Leaves range up to 6 to 9 cm long and 1 cm wider. They are divided over half way to the center. Lobes are ovate but taper to a sharp point and have a toothed margin. Petioles range from 4 to 5 cm in length.

The new Spring growth is yellowish-green which soon changes to a rich green. Leaves have good substance and are durable. The real glory is the Fall coloration which becomes a very rich yellow or gold.

This will become a large tree, probably maturing at 7 meters or more. It is a good tree to blend with other crimson and orange forms in a larger planting.

A. palmatum 'Monzukushi'

Another of the green-leaf form of palmatum. The leaf color is a bright, pleasant green of lighter value. Early in the season there is a hint of reddish overtone, and sometimes the veins show a faint red. This soon changes to a solid green. The texture of the leaf is firm but not thick. Fall colors are brilliant orange-reds.

The leaf is an open palmate shape with five radiating lobes. Occasionally the base lobe produces a small "spur" lobe. Each lobe is a smooth ovate form, tapering to an elongated

tip. The margins are very finely serrate. Lobes unite ⅔ the distance to the center. Leaves are 7 cm long and spread about 8 cm. The stiff petioles are 2 to 3 cm long.

This is a rather vigorous, hardy plant which will reach a height of 3 to 4 meters.

A. palmatum atropurpureum 'Moonfire'

The excellent purple-red, almost black-red, color of this cultivar has a quality of being almost "opalescent." Diffused sun gives it a faint blue overtone similar to 'Nuresagi.' The good, deep colors last very well throughout the Summer and do not "bronze-out" as do so many of the red cultivars. Later the leaves turn crimson for a delightful Fall display.

The large leaves are 7- (5) lobed, separated almost to the center. Each lobe is elongate-ovate with finely double-serrated margins. It gradually tapers to a fine point. Leaf size ranges from 7 or 8 cm long on older wood to 10 to 11 cm or even more on new shoots. Lobes radiate outward to a width of 11 cm. Petioles are rather short for the leaf size—1 to 2 cm long. Center veins of the leaf are also a deep purple-red, and the underside of the leaf is a very rich, deep reddish-green.

This is a strong, upright-growing form of palmatum atropurpureum. New shoots on vigorous young plants will grow at least 1 meter in a season. It is a fast-growing tree when young but broadens and slows down as it matures. Older trees will assume the upright, round canopy of the species type, and reach 4 or 5 meters.

A recent introduction selected from seedlings by Richard P. Wolff of the Red Maple Nursery at Media, Pennsylvania, it is a very worthwhile cultivar. It is durable and its long-lasting season color rivals the well-known cultivar, 'Bloodgood.'

A. palmatum atropurpureum 'Muragumo'
Alternate spelling: 'Murakumo'

This is an outstanding red-leaf form of palmatum.

The palmate leaves are usually 7-lobed and divided almost to the center. The ovate-elongate lobes are wide in the center and come to a strong point. Basal lobes are quite small. Edges are finely double-serrate. Petiole is reddish and 2 to 3 cm long. The leaf has good texture and measures about 7 cm long and 8 cm wide.

Early Spring color as the leaves unfold is almost crimson and soon becomes a very good, deep purple-red. Leaf veins are also red and are noticeable. Fall colors range into the good crimson shades.

A. palmatum 'Moonfire'

This is an upright cultivar which is quite hardy. It will be several meters tall at maturity. It is valuable in the landscape because it retains the red colors well into late Summer.

A. palmatum atropurpureum 'Murogawa'

This is a strong cultivar which brings a lot of color to the landscape.

The Spring and early Summer coloration is a striking orange-red which shades from light to dark tones. The veins are a striking green and show the tracery of their design for several weeks. As the season progresses, the tones change to a rusty green and then into a deep green by late Summer. Fall colors range from orange-reds to crimson.

The large leaves range up to 8 or 9 cm long with a spread of 10 cm. The nine (7) lobes are long ovate, tapering to a slender point, divided only a little more than half way to the center. The edges have a definite double serration which is sometimes a little deep. Green petioles are long and slender—about 4 cm.

'Murogawa' is hardy and a fairly vigorous grower but not totally upright. With age, the side branches become cascading and somewhat pendulous, and the top slows its rate of growth. The mature tree is round-topped with pendulous outer branches. Old trees grow to 3 meters, and if not trimmed will spread to 3 or 4 meters.

A. palmatum atropurpureum 'Musashino'
Syn.: 'Nomura,' 'Nomura kaede'

The rich color of this cultivar is deep purple-red. As the new leaf develops in the Spring, the surface is covered with a minute, light-colored pubescence which brings out the rich tones of purple. This pubescence soon disappears, but the basic color persists well to the end of the Summer. The underside of the leaf is purple-red with strong green overtones. At the first Fall frost, the foliage takes on a brilliant crimson hue.

The bold leaves are from 7 to 9 cm long and 8 to 10 cm wide. The seven (5) lobes are widely separated to within 1 cm of the center of the leaf. They are elongate-ovate, terminating in a long, tapering, narrow point. Margins are sharply serrated. The deep red petioles are about 2 cm long.

The tree form is strongly upright with a rounded crown at maturity. It is fairly fast-growing and not very twiggy. It will mature at 7 or 8 meters in 25 years.

This is an old and very famous cultivar which has been grown in Japan for about 300 years. It was listed as an old cultivar in some 1710 horticultural writings. It is still quite popular there and is reported to be particularly beautiful in the Fall in Hokkaido and other northern areas. It is hardy and suitable for the cooler areas of the United States.

A. palmatum atropurpureum 'Nigrum'

This selection has very dark, purple-red color which in some situations can be almost black-red. Normally, however, it is a rich purple tone reminiscent of 'Nuresagi.' There is a fine white pubescence on the very young leaves as they unfold. Late Summer tones change into brown-green mixed with dull yellow or bronze. Fall colors come as bright reds and crimsons.

The seven-lobe leaf ranges from 5 to 7 cm long and wide, although size is variable. Lobes are ovate-acuminate, ending with a sharp tip. Margins are double-serrate. Petioles are sturdy and about 3 cm long.

This is a strong grower of the A. palmatum atropurpureum type. Although vigorous, I do not believe it grows as tall as the species form. It grows rapidly when young but later slows and thickens, reaching 4 meters at maturity.

A. palmatum 'Nishiki momiji'

This small-leafed palmatum type develops strong, rich Fall colors which are normally associated with the larger-leafed heptalobum group.

The leaves are typically 5 to 7 lobed, separated about 2/3 into the center. The long, slender, lanceolate lobes gradually taper to a very sharp point. The margins are double-serrate. In both length and width the leaf measures 5 to 7 cm. Thin petioles are 3 cm long.

The leaf texture is rather thin with a basic color of pale green. The early Spring leaves unfold with a pinkish or orange-red tone which persists along the margins as the leaves mature and turn to light green.

Fall colors are an especially brilliant display of crimson to fire-red.

A. palmatum 'Musashino'

This is an upright palmatum which forms a spreading crown and reaches a height of several meters at maturity.

A. palmatum atropurpureum 'Nomura'
See: *A. palmatum atropurpureum* 'Musashino'

A. palmatum atropurpureum 'Nomura kaede'
See: *A. palmatum atropurpureum* 'Musashino'

A. palmatum atropurpureum 'Novum'

A. palmatum atropurpureum 'Novum'

'Novum' has medium-large leaves with five and seven lobes. The leaves are 6 to 8 cm long and 8 to 10 cm across. Lobes are ovate, tapering to a slender sharp point, and they are separated about half-way to the center. The points of the leaf radiate outward. The red petiole is 2 to 3 cm long.

The Spring and early Summer coloration is a light purple-red. It is a lighter tone than such cultivars as 'Bloodgood,' 'Nuresagi,' 'Moonfire,' etc. It ranges into the orange-red tones as Summer progresses. In late Summer these tones blend with green-red. Fall color is scarlet.

This is a strong upright-growing type which can reach over 7 meters. It forms a round-topped small tree which is hardy and vigorous. It is widely propagated commercially because it quickly forms a good-sized salable plant.

A. palmatum atropurpureum 'Nuresagi'
(the wet heron)

This excellent cultivar has leaves with seven lobes which radiate strongly outward. Each lobe is oblong-ovate, terminating in a long, slender tip. They unite 1 cm from the center of the leaf. The leaf looks like widely-spread fingers and measures 8 to 9 cm long and 9 to 12 cm across. Petioles are stiff and 2 to 3 cm long. The tree appears quite lacy.

The deep, rich black-purple-red tones are unusual. In Spring and early Summer they appear to have an opalescence, even a bluish overtone, in certain light. Leaves retain the dark purple-red tones into late Summer but occasionally become suffused with a slight, deep green mottling. The veins are a strong red at this time and a noticeable feature.

The bark of twigs and branches is a deep maroon color but quite overshadowed with a greyish tone. There are fine whitish vertical striations along the bark which are a pleasant addition.

This is a very hardy cultivar which is upright and vigorous. It should not be crowded in the landscape but allowed space for full development. It may reach 5 or 6 meters at maturity.

A. palmatum 'Ogashika'
See: *A. palmatum* 'Saoshika'

A. palmatum atropurpureum 'Ō kagami'
(mirror)

The beautiful purplish-red of the new foliage deepens into a shiny blackish-red as the leaves mature. It is a very strong color which lasts until late Summer when green tones blend in. Fall colors brighten to various tones of red and scarlet.

The seven lobes radiate markedly, with the two base lobes almost overlapping at the petiole like a fully-extended fan. They are elongate-elliptic with margins serrated uniformly. The lobes separate almost to the center of the leaf and are 1 cm wide where they join. The leaves are 7 to 11 cm long and wide. The reddish petioles are 3 cm long.

This is a very desirable color form and makes a delightful upright small tree probably maturing at 4 meters.

A. palmatum 'Nuresagi'

A. palmatum atropurpureum 'Ō kagami'

A. palmatum 'Omato'

This is a large-leafed type of the heptalobum group. With 5 to 7 lobes the leaves are from 6 to 9 cm long and 8 to 11 cm broad. Each lobe is ovate-acuminate and gradually tapers to a sharp point. Margins have sharp double serrations. Leaves have good substance and texture. Petioles range from 3 to 4 cm long.

Early foliage may have a tinge of orange-red, but the large leaves soon take on a rich green color. The color is durable and not very subject to sunburn. Fall colors are brilliant tones of rich red, but are not as intense as 'Ōsakazuki.'

This is a strong-growing, round-headed tree. As it matures, it will be several meters high and about as wide with good limb structure.

A. palmatum 'Ōsakazuki'
   Syn.: 'Taihai'
   Alternate spelling: 'Ohsakazuki'

This very famous cultivar is best known for its intense crimson Fall color. Some claim it has the most intense coloration of all the maples. In addition, it has very large leaves for a palmatum and is a hardy, sturdy grower. It has been listed in catalogs since the mid-1800's.

The seven-lobed palmate leaves are usually about 9 cm from the base of the petiole to the tip with a spread of 12 or 14 cm. On very vigorous young shoots the leaves may grow to 12 or 13 cm long with a spread of 17 or 18 cm. The large leaves do not make the tree coarse looking but instead lend an air of orderliness. Petioles are sturdy and about 6 cm in length. Each lobe is a broad ovate shape terminating in a narrowed tip. The edges are uniformly serrate. Leaf texture is firm. The lobes are separated about half the distance to the center of the leaf. The two small base lobes cover the petiole.

Most of the growing season the leaf color is a good rich green. It does not sunburn easily and has durable texture. Fall coloration has been likened to a burning bush. More aptly, though, it is described as intense crimson. We have observed that even at dusk the color seems to glow.

The trees will grow rapidly the first few years and then begin to slow down as do most palmatums. They become more branched and form a round-topped, small tree. They do not exceed 6 or 7 meters even in old age.

The synonym of 'Ōsakazuki' is 'Taihai.' There are two ways to write the Kanji form. Since the leaves sometimes "cup" at the base, it is termed a "saki-cup-like" leaf, or 'Ōsakazuki.'

A companion cultivar, sometimes called a sister seedling, is 'Ichigyōji.' (Some catalogs list them as synonyms.) It is just as intense a yellow or gold in the Fall as 'Ōsakazuki' is crimson. These two cultivars planted together make a brilliant Fall display.

A. palmatum 'Ōsakazuki'. Green foliage in the Spring.

A. palmatum 'Ōsakazuki'. The most brilliant of all cultivars in Fall coloration.

A. palmatum 'Rubrum'

A. palmatum atropurpureum 'Ōshio beni'

The coloration is more of an orange-red than the purple-red of similar "red" cultivars. The new growth is very bright, but as the season advances it becomes bronze to a dull reddish-green. It does not retain the bright colors as well as 'Bloodgood,' 'Nuresagi,' and 'Moonfire.' It tends to burn in hot sun locations. The Autumn color becomes a bright scarlet.

The leaves are seven-lobed and of medium texture. They measure from 7 to 8 cm long and 8 to 10 cm wide. The lobes are broadly ovate, terminating in a long, sharp point. The margins are finely serrate. Petioles are red and 3 to 5 cm long.

This is a sturdy upright-grower maturing at least 6 to 8 meters high with a spreading canopy. It is a good companion-type tree with other cultivars for color contrast.

'Ōshio beni' has been a popular cultivar in the United States for many decades. However, I feel that there may have been some dilution in this cultivar name. The name is very similar to 'Ōshū beni' which has an entirely different leaf form and is widely recorded in early literature. I can find no early references to 'Ōshio beni.'

A. palmatum 'Ōshū beni'
Alternate spelling: 'Ōsyu beni',
'Ōshyu beni', 'Ōshiu beni'

The leaves of this cultivar are separated into seven (occasionally nine) lobes which separate about ⅔ the distance into the center. Each lobe is elongate-ovate, almost lanceolate. It terminates in a slender, sharp tip. The margins are rather smooth, except for the tip portion which is slightly serrated. The lobes radiate forward, with the base of the leaf almost truncate. The leaves measure 5 to 7 cm long and wide, occasionally slightly larger. The slender petioles are greenish and 3 to 4 cm long.

The early foliage is bright red, soon changing to a maroon red. In shade the foliage tends to be greenish. In mid-Summer the mature leaves become bronzed or a green-red. Fall colors develop well and are bright red.

This cultivar will form a short, round-topped small tree of about 3 to 4 meters as it ages. It is hardy and not difficult to propagate.

This is very different from the 'Ōshio beni' being sold commercially at present in the United States.

A. palmatum 'Rubrum'

This large-leafed cultivar has seven ovate lobes separated over half the distance to the center. The lobes taper to a sharp point as in the heptalobum group, with slightly serrated margins. Leaves range in size from 9 to 12 cm broad and long, and petioles are about 4 cm.

The leaves are a dark maroon-red. The color is lighter as they first unfold but assumes the very rich tones in late Spring and into Summer. In late Summer, the leaves turn green-red or bronze. Fall colors are strong crimson.

This is a strong-growing upright tree with the crown spreading broadly as it matures. The branches are sturdy, and it is a hardy cultivar. It will reach 4 meters in height.

Some early references place this in the heptalobum group. Some equate it with 'Sanguineum,' but I find 'Rubrum' consistently darker in foliage color.

A. palmatum 'Rufescens'

The color of 'Rufescens' is rather distinctive when grown near the other "red" cultivars. The unfolding leaves are quite bright and the "rufous" or brownish color becomes strong as the leaves mature. Later in the season, the green tones predominate. Good Fall colors of orange and crimson develop.

The leaves have nine (7) lobes which separate over half way to the center. Each lobe is elongate-elliptic, gradually tapering to a slender, sharp point. Lobes are only 1 to 1½ cm wide at the middle. Margins of the lobes are sharply and distinctly toothed. The long center lobes tend to hold closely together. Leaf is about 7 cm long and 6 to 7 cm wide. The slender petioles are up to 5 cm long.

This is not a vigorous cultivar, but will make a tall bush (3 meters) after many years. Although described by Siesmayer in 1888, it is not widely known. Unfortunately, the name 'Rufescens' has been applied to different clones at different times, so there is uncertainty about some specimens in collections.

A. palmatum 'Saku' (a fence)
   The Kanji character can be read two ways.
   See: *A. palmatum* 'Shigarami'

A. palmatum 'Samidare'
   (the name given to the long rain in June)

The large leaves of this cultivar are of heavy texture—firm to the touch. When first unfolding in early Spring, the tiny leaves are almost pink. Quite soon they turn a rich green with margins a light reddish tone. During Summer, the deep green holds well without burning even in full sun. In the Fall, a gold-green center develops with the lobes turning purplish. Other combinations of gold and crimson blend in other leaves.

   Leaves are 7 (5) lobed and measure from 6 to 8 cm long and 8 to 12 cm across. The lobes radiate sharply outward and are a strong ovate, terminating in a blunt tip. Lobes join less than half way to the center, making a large-palmed leaf. The margins of the lobes are very finely serrated—almost smooth. The last 1 cm is slightly more toothed on the margin. Petioles are slender, firm, and 3½ to 7 cm long.

   This is a hardy cultivar whose twigs and young branches are thick and stiff. It will grow rapidly and upright at first but soon make a broad, short tree as it slows down. It will eventually reach 4 meters. This is a very durable yard plant which adds good color.

A. palmatum 'Sanguineum'

This name has been applied so variously by authors during the nomenclature history that its proper use is somewhat clouded.

   Primarily, it has been applied to a selection of the *atropurpureum* type of *A. palmatum*. It was selected originally as a clone with blood-red or orange-red Spring color rather than the darker or maroon-red tones. A notation by Lemaire in 1867 describes it as a "blood-red" selection.

   Since that time, some commercial nurseries apparently have propagated different forms, for variations under the name 'Sanguineum' are found in collections.

   Its growth is typical of *A. palmatum atropurpureum* in size and shape of tree and form of foliage, having 5 to 7 broad lobes.

A. palmatum 'Saoshika'

   Other cultivars carry 'Sanguineum' as a portion of the name, for example: 'Sanguineum Seigai' and 'Sanguineum Chishio'.

A. palmatum 'Saoshika'
   Syn.: 'Ogashika'

The star-shaped, bright green foliage of this cultivar is of rather thin and delicate texture. When back-lighted by the sun, it appears almost translucent. The leaves hold out horizontally, making a layered effect in older portions of the plant.

   The new foliage is a bright yellow-green, with the tips of the lobes tinged in red or carmine. This color is prominent for the first weeks, and then the leaves gradually change to a uniform light green. As Summer advances, the tones darken.

   The leaves are 5 to 7 lobed, about 5 cm long and varying from 7 to 8 cm wide. The short petioles are 1½ cm long. Each lobe radiates outward in a star-shaped pattern. The lobes are strong ovate, terminating in a sharp point. The lobes are divided midway in their length. The margins are lightly serrated.

   This is not a strongly upright plant but more of a tall, bushy shrub. When mature it is about 2 meters high. Since the twigs are angularly branched in habit, it makes a multi-branched type plant. The twigs have a bright green bark.

A. palmatum 'Sanguineum'

A. palmatum 'Saotome'

This is one of the small-leafed cultivars of palmatum, but I do not class it in with the yatsubusa type. It forms a bush-shaped plant yet cannot be called dwarf. It will probably mature at about 1 to 1½ meters.

The leaves are light green with rather thin texture. The new growth produces leaves of a very pale yellow-green with a slight hint of rusty-red on the extreme edge. They measure about 4 cm long and 4 to 5 cm across.

Each leaf is separated almost entirely to the center by five lanceolate lobes which terminate in long slender, sharp tips. The two basal lobes often have tiny spur lobes. The edges bend slightly upward, and the margins are irregularly incised.

A. palmatum 'Shichihenge'

Alternate spelling: 'Hichihenge'

This cultivar is almost identical to 'Musashino' ('Nomura') which is propagated more often. The color of the foliage is a deep purplish-red and is especially bright as it unfolds. It keeps the color well into the Summer, but will gradually fade to a deep green-red tone. Fall colors are various shades of red.

The seven lobes are strongly ovate, separated over half way to the center. They terminate in a long, sharp point. The two base lobes extend almost at right angles to the petiole. Margins are serrated. Leaves are about 8 cm long and 11 cm wide. Petioles are 4 to 5 cm long.

The lobes hold more closely together in the leaves than in 'Musashino,' almost overlapping at the base.

This is a strong-growing, upright tree which matures as a round-topped specimen. It is a good type for the large landscape setting.

There is a large tree in Tosho Gu shrine in Nikko which is about 5 meters high and 5 meters wide with a trunk 40 cm in diameter.

A. palmatum 'Shigarami'
(posts in a river or stream to which boats are tied)
Syn.: 'Saku'

The Spring foliage is a bright green, with the tips of the lobes a light purple which shades a short distance back along each margin. The contrast is quite noticeable. As the leaf matures, the entire outer half of the lobe becomes purple. In Summer, the leaf becomes solid green. This is followed by Fall colors of rich yellows and orange suffused with red.

The seven-lobed leaf is 4 to 6 cm long and 6 to 8 cm wide, with stiff petioles varying from 2½ to 5 cm long. The lobes radiate stiffly outward, with the two very small base lobes holding back along the petiole. Each lobe separates more than ⅔ into the center and is a long-ovate shape, tapering gradually to a sharp tip. The sides of the lobes turn upward from the midrib, forming a slight trough. The margins are quite smooth with only very fine serration. The foliage holds stiffly on a horizontal plane.

This small tree grows in an upright manner. However, the side branching grows laterally as it matures, and the horizontal branches give it a "layered" appearance. After many years it will reach a height of 4 meters.

The close similarity to 'Tana' has created slight confusion between the two cultivars. The narrower lobes and deeper division in the leaves of 'Shigarami' distinguish it from 'Tana.'

A. palmatum 'Shōjō'

This is a very deep-colored palmatum—almost classed as "black-red." Its foliage becomes deep purple-red, and the color holds well into late Summer, especially if given afternoon shade. In the Fall crimson tones dominate.

A. palmatum 'Shigarami'

A. palmatum 'Shōjō'

The leaves have five lobes and a truncate base. Lobes radiate openly and are elongate-ovate, terminating in a slender point. The margins are lightly serrated. The lobes join less than 1 cm from the petiole attachment. Leaves are 7 to 8 cm long and 8 to 9 cm wide and are rather thin in texture. Slender petioles are 4 cm long. Leaves are spaced openly along the newer shoots, giving the appearance of less foliage than normal.

The growth is upright and vigorous when the plant is young. It will branch laterally and at maturity become a wide, tall tree of at least 3 meters.

'Shōjō' is the name of the red-faced orangoutang which is a character in many Japanese dramas. Hence, the "red" or "Shōjō" name on several cultivars.

A. palmatum 'Sinuatum'
    See: *A. palmatum* 'Yezo nishiki'

A. palmatum 'Taihai'
    See: *A. palmatum* 'Ōsakazuki'

A. palmatum 'Taimin'
    Syn.: 'Daimyo'

This red-leafed palmatum has been known in Japan since very early days. It was apparently not an outstanding selection and did not become widely used.

However, a much sought after variegated selection called 'Taimin nishiki' ('Daimyo nishiki') originated from this clone. The old cultivar 'Taimin' has almost disappeared from cultivation, and I understand is rarely propagated at this time.

A. palmatum 'Takao'
    (the maples of Takao in Kyoto)
    Syn.: 'Takao momiji', 'Takawo momiji',
    'Oh momiji'

This cultivar is a typical palmatum (of the subsp. *septemlobum*, Koidzumi.) It is an ancient cultivar, with references back to 1690 and 1710. *Acer palmatum* is often called 'Takao momiji.' The plants with especially beautiful leaves are called 'Takao.'

Old literature describes it as being a green-leafed, 7-lobed form. Leaves are 6 to 6½ cm long and a little wider. The lobes are oblong-lanceolate, with ends tapering to a long, sharp tip. The margins are serrate.

'Takao' is known for its bright Fall colors. It is a type-tree, being upright, round-topped, and reaching 5 to 9 meters.

A. palmatum 'Takasago momiji'
    = subvariety *formosanum*

This is a geographical subvariety of *A. palmatum*, given this status by Koidzumi. It is indigenous to Formosa. It is a green-leafed, upright form. Leaves have seven lobes which are separated almost to the center. Each lobe is narrowly oblong, with the margins noticeably incised or serrated.

It is not widely used as an ornamental.

A. palmatum 'Tana'

The beautiful foliage of this cultivar is a light to yellowish green. Each lobe is tipped in a distinct purplish-red which shades back from the end and down along the margins for a short distance. This color gradually shades into the solid green of the leaf. In new leaves this marking is quite bright. As the leaf ages in the Summer, the purple disappears. In Fall, the colors become a bright combination of gold and red which dominate the landscape.

The medium-size leaves have seven (5) lobes which radiate sharply from the petiole attachment. The lobes separate only ⅓ of the leaf diameter and are broadly ovate, tapering to a blunt point. The margins are very lightly serrate and curl slightly upward.

The leaf size is 4 to 6 cm long and 6 to 8 cm wide, but leaves on young wood are much larger. The stiff petioles are 4 cm long. The foliage holds horizontally as do the new twigs, and the branches grow laterally, thus forming the characteristic layered effect of this plant.

This is an upright, strong-growing cultivar which reaches 4 meters in a few years. It will eventually become round-topped with a broad canopy.

The similarity of the purple tips of foliage and growth habit has caused some confusion with the similar cultivar, 'Shigarami' ('Saku'). The deeper indentations of the leaf distinguish the latter form. The similarity of name has also caused confusion with 'Tanabata.'

A. palmatum 'Tana'

A. palmatum 'Tsukushigata'

A. palmatum 'Tatsuta'
Alternate spelling: 'Tatsuta gawa'

An old cultivar, mentioned in literature of 1710, it has been valued for its Fall beauty. The leaves are spaced openly on the small branches and display the Fall scarlet colors to good advantage. As one Japanese reference describes, "The sun shines on all the leaves and makes the Fall foliage more beautiful."

New foliage unfolds as a very light yellow-green which soon changes to a light green. The leaves are slightly thin in texture. The petioles are long for the size of the leaf—3 to 4 cm—and flexible. Leaves are spaced openly along the new shoots and are 5 to 6 cm long and 7 to 8 cm wide. The base of the leaf is straight across (truncate), with the seven lobes joined in the center ⅓. Lobes are long-elliptic, with sharp tips and slightly serrated margins.

This plant will grow to 3 meters, with open branches and a round top.

A. palmatum 'Toshi'
See: *A. palmatum* 'Azuma murasaki'

This cultivar is not widely known but lends itself well to small and medium sized landscapes. It makes a good companion plant with the red-leafed cultivars and other flowering shrubs. Not aggressive in habit.

A. palmatum 'Tsuma beni'

A. palmatum 'Tsukushigata'
Alternate spelling: 'Chikushigata', 'Shikishigata'

This tree will attract attention in any garden. The rich purple-red or black-red leaves are spectacular.

The palmate leaves are 7 to 9 cm long and 8 to 10 cm wide. The leaf appears to be much longer than broad, however, for the center lobes are predominant. The lobes radiate stiffly and divide about half way to the center. They are ovate but come to a very sharp point. The appearance is almost star-shaped. The light-colored petioles are 4 cm long.

The deep purple-red color holds quite well all season so this remains a dark-foliage tree. However, on the shaded sides a green cast develops under the dark tones. The mid-veins of each lobe are a noticeable green contrast. The beautiful seeds are almost a chartreuse color and seem to sparkle in among the deep-toned foliage.

This strong plant forms a round-topped small tree of 3 meters or more but does not reach the full height of the species. It is one of the better dark-toned palmatums but not widely-known. The difficulty of translating the first syllable accounts for the various spellings.

A. palmatum 'Tsuma beni'
(red nail)

The outstanding feature of this cultivar is the coloration of the tips of the beautiful Spring foliage—hence the name. The light green lobes have purplish-red tips and margins blending into the light green of the leaf center. This color combination continues well into early Summer, then gradually diminishes and matures a darker green. Red colors dominate in the Fall.

The leaves are 5 to 7-lobed, separated ⅓ the distance to the center. Each lobe is quite ovate, terminating in a narrow tip. The margins are lightly and regularly serrate. Leaves are 5 to 8 cm long and slightly broader. Reddish-green petioles are 2 to 3 cm long.

This is not a fast-growing plant; it is really more of a rounded bush than a small tree. As it matures, it will reach 2 meters or more in height and width. It becomes twiggy and re-branches. It is somewhat tender and not easy to propagate.

The Spring foliage always attracts attention. It makes a very pleasant companion plant for dissectums and other shrubs.

A. palmatum 'Tsuma gaki'
  Syn.: 'Tsuma gari'

This cultivar closely resembles 'Tsuma beni' with which it is often confused. The Spring color phase is quite similar. As the foliage unfolds, it tends to droop from the petiole attachment, adding a softness to the general appearance of the plant. The color at this time is a very soft yellow-green. The tips of each lobe are shaded with a blend of tones which are difficult to describe. Colors range from a persimmon-red to a light purple-red combination. The Summer foliage is deep green. Fall colors change to a range of crimson and reds.

The leaves are 5 (7) lobed. The lobes are ovate but taper to a slender tip. They separate about ½ way to the base. Margins are evenly and lightly serrated. Leaves range from 6 to 8 cm long and 7 to 9 cm across.

This is not a tall-growing cultivar, but forms a round-shaped plant. Mature plants are 2 meters tall and wide.

Because of the similarity in name and form, 'Tsuma gaki' and 'Tsuma beni' may be confused, but they are separate cultivars.

A. palmatum 'Ukon'

The yellow-green color of this cultivar is its distinguishing feature. The new foliage is quite yellow. As the leaves mature, they become bright green with very indistinct yellowish mottling. This color is retained well during the growing season but becomes darker in late Summer. Fall colors are deep yellow and gold with red tones blended into some leaves. The petioles and young branches are also yellow-green.

The leaves are openly palmate, deeply divided into 5 (7) lobes. Each lobe is oblong-ovate, terminating in a sharp tip. The margins are strongly serrate. Lobes separate to within 1 cm of the center of the leaf. Leaves vary from 6 to 8 cm both long and wide, with 2 cm petioles.

This is not a vigorous-growing cultivar and is a little tender. It will form an upright bush form, spreading as broad as tall but is not pendulous. Old plants reach 2 meters or a little more.

'Ukon' is not widely grown, but the yellow-green tones add a nice contrast to the landscape.

A. palmatum 'Ukon nishiki'

A young plant bearing this name was added to our collection recently. The foliage looks identical to that described under 'Ukon,' and

A. palmatum 'Tsuma gaki'

we see no variegation which the term "nishiki" would indicate. However, it is unwise to judge a very young plant for certain characteristics. No reference description is available.

A. palmatum 'Umegae'
  Alternate spelling: 'Umegai'

This is a small-leafed form of palmatum with leaves ranging from 4 to 5 cm long and slightly wider. The stiff petiole is only 1 to 1½ cm. The seven lobes are separated more than half way to the center and radiate outward uniformly. The leaf base is truncate. The lobes are ovate, with a tapered, slender terminal. The margins are lightly serrate. The lobes fold gently upward from the center vein.

New foliage develops a bright brick-red which soon turns into a bright purplish-red. The main veins are a prominent contrasting green. Plants grown in full sun have bright red coloration, while shade-grown plants have more purple with green undertones. The under surface is very shiny. The color of foliage lasts well into the late Summer periods. Fall colors are quite good—mostly in crimson tones.

This is not a fast-growing cultivar, being semi-dwarf. It is upright, yet spreading, and forms a round-topped bush. It probably would not exceed 1 or 2 meters at maturity.

This cultivar has been around for about 100 years and can be found on maple lists of the late 1800's.

A. palmatum 'Umegae'

A. palmatum 'Utsu semi'

A. palmatum 'Utsu semi'

The broad, bold leaves are bright green and appear heavy in texture. The margins on new foliage are tinted purple or red. Later in the season the green becomes darker, but in the Fall crimson and purple dominate.

The seven lobes vary in width. The five center lobes are ovate, tapering to a short point. The two base lobes are lanceolate, with a sharp point, and extend outward. The lobes separate widely for the outer half of the lobe length, and the margins are finely serrate. The leaf is 6 to 8 cm long and 9 to 10 cm wide. The stiff petiole is 2 to 3 cm long.

This hardy cultivar will form a short, round-topped tree which spreads rather widely—3 meters high and 3 meters wide. It makes a fine landscape plant and adds contrasting Spring leaf texture and excellent Fall color.

A. palmatum 'Volubile'. Bright Fall coloration.

A. palmatum 'Yezo nishiki'

A. palmatum 'Volubile'
   Syn.: 'Aoba no fuye', 'Aoba fuke'

This cultivar has small, palmate, seven-lobed leaves. The two base lobes are quite small. The leaf tends to cup slightly upward from the petiole. Each lobe is elongate-acuminate, terminating in a narrow point. The margins are incised with light inter-serrations, making them prominent. Leaves vary from 3½ to 5 cm long and 4 to 6 cm wide, with thin petioles 2 cm long.

The leaf color in the Spring is a bright, yellow-green. The tone is variable but not markedly so. The foliage darkens somewhat during the Summer months and withstands full sun very well. The Fall colors are quite brilliant and range from yellow into rusty rose and on to crimson. The twig color becomes a rusty-red.

This is an upright-growing type, but delicately so. It reaches at least 4 meters at maturity. The twigs are unusually dainty. It does not grow as fast as the type species.

A. palmatum 'Waka momiji - red stem'

I carry this cultivar under this separate name, although it is doubtful that it is a true cultivar. It was sent to me for comparison by one of the leading arboreta in the United States.

In all characteristics it is identical to 'Sango kaku.' It will be retained as 'Waka momiji - red stem', however, for comparative purposes.

A. palmatum 'Yezo nishiki'
   Syn.: 'Sinuatum'

This is a brilliant cultivar in the atropurpureum group. The Spring color is a rich, bright, reddish-purple which becomes deeper as Summer advances. In late Summer, the leaves become red-bronze but in deep shade are greenish. Fall tones are brilliant carmine and scarlet.

The seven-lobed leaves are of firm texture. Each lobe is ovate-acuminate, with the ends tapering to a long, sharp point. Margins are evenly and finely serrated. The lobes separate half way to the center of the leaf. The red petioles (3 to 4 cm) are slender but not weak. The leaves are truncate and measure 5 to 7 cm long and up to 9 cm across the points.

This is an upright-growing, small tree which reaches 6 to 7 meters in 25 years. The young plant grows rapidly, then slows and thickens to form a broad, arching top. It is a hardy, sturdy selection.

DISSECTUM GROUP

Although some early authors combined them, the dissectums are separated here from what I choose to call the "deeply divided" leaf forms. Dissectums (multifidium of Koidzumi) have the lobes pinnately and/or double pinnately dissected. The "deeply divided" leaf forms (palmatisectum of Koidzumi) have the margins toothed or serrated.

Most dissectums are rounded shrub types with strongly cascading branches. Very old specimens may reach 4 meters, but this is rare. They mature more broad than tall. There is one upright cultivar. Included are the green, red, and variegated forms.

A. palmatum dissectum 'Red Filigree Lace'. An outstanding example of the dissectums. This recent introduction is probably the finest-leafed form to be developed in recent years.

A. palmatum dissectum 'Akashigata'
  See: *A. palmatum dissectum* 'Rubrifolium'

A. palmatum dissectum 'Aka washi no o'
  See: *A. palmatum dissectum atropurpureum* 'Ornatum'

A. palmatum dissectum 'Ao shidare'
  (ao = green; shidare = cascading)
  Syn.: 'Aoba shidare'

This dissectum differs slightly in the leaf form from many of the green dissectums. The leaves are of medium size. They are double dissected in typical form. However, the secondary cuts are not as deep nor are the lobes quite as long as in the better-known forms of green. The many points of each leaf seem not as sharp, giving the whole leaf a more blunt appearance in outline. The color is a slight blue-green, not the sharp green of 'Viridis.' Leaves are 6 to 8 cm long and about as wide. Each lobe, half way to the center, is quite narrow, almost just the width of the vein. The stems and branches are a pleasing green with a whitish overtone at times.

This is a cascading cultivar which becomes 2 meters high and 3 meters wide. Planted near other dissectums, the difference in color is apparent. It is quite similar to other dissectum cultivars, 'Sekimori' and 'Kiri nishiki.'

A. palmatum dissectum atropurpureum
  Red Lace Leaf Maple

The red tones, the finely multi-divided foliage, and the cascading branches make these plants among the most popular for landscape plantings. To many people this is the only form they know as "Japanese Maple," all other forms being ignored or considered "another kind of tree."

Each leaf is divided into 7 to 9 lobes; each lobe multi-dissected into pinnatifid subdivisions. This gives rise to the common term "lacy." Leaves will vary in total measurement from 6 to 10 cm long and at least as wide. Petioles are usually a slender 5 to 7 cm. Exact leaf shape and multi-divisions will vary depending upon the seedling.

The plant form is always pendulous; some become almost prostrate if not staked up the first few years. As the plant matures, it will become quite twiggy and dense. On older plants this internal excess of fine growth will die out due to shading, and the outside will form an umbrella-like canopy. Old specimens may form a mound at least 5 meters high and 6 meters across.

This form of palmatum was apparently treated as a separate cultivar in some of the older literature and carried as such in older plantings. However, as discussed under *A. palmatum atropurpureum*, it has become "diluted" in nomenclature, and we class it totally as a "group." The reason for this is that "dissectum atropurpureum" types are frequently sold from seedling-produced sources. However, some nurseries do graft from an outstanding stock plant and sell a very uniform class of dissectums. These grafts are all excellent plants for landscape use. One difficulty with seedling-producing plants is the variation in the degree of "redness" which will result. The plants may vary from a decided green cast of the foliage to the other extreme of dark maroon or black-red. All may come from the same parent seed tree. I have purchased young plants of "diss. atropurpureum" which varied from a rusty green to a very acceptable red.

A. palmatum dissectum atropurpureum. Good leaf tones remain on this specimen grown 12 years in a wooden tub. Irrigation is important.

Seedlings are usually quite slow to develop after germination. The root systems seem less vigorous than normal palmatums. Seedlings from a given stock plant may vary from typical green-leaf "palmatum type" to light-colored "dissectum type." Occasionally dissected plants of deep color occur. One cannot expect to obtain a large percentage of good red-colored dissectum seedlings even though the seed parent may be of excellent character. Seedlings normally do not come "true to type."

A. palmatum dissectum atropurpureum
  'Beni shidare'
  (red - cascading)

As the name implies, this cultivar has the typical form and color of the red dissectum group. I am not convinced that this name should have the true "cultivar" status. Instead, I understand that this is the "common term" in Japan for the red form of dissectum. This would compare to our English usage of "dissectum atropurpureum." However, I do feel that a superior clone was originally selected, and the plant material I receive from original sources is of excellent quality and color. Therefore, perhaps we should retain the cultivar status for this particular clone.

The leaf size and shape, as well as the plant form, are practically identical to that described under *A. palmatum dissectum atropurpureum*. I find the color quite uniform in the good red tones in all the plant material I have received to grow out for comparison. It will not retain the deep red, however, and will assume the bronze color in mid-Summer, as contrasted to such cultivars as 'Crimson Queen.'

Some very old specimens remain in Japan, and I understand are over 7 meters in height as well as canopy spread.

A. palmatum dissectum
  'Beni shidare variegated'
  Syn.: 'Beni shidare tricolor'

The fine double-pinnatifid leaves of this dissectum include the colors of deep green, red, white, and pink. These are blended colors, and each leaf shows a different proportion and intensity.

The base color is red green rather than the deep red of 'Beni shidare.' Blended in are sections, lobes, or filaments which have white or cream coloration with occasional small sections of pink tones. Some rare leaves are almost pure cream. All foliage darkens as the season progresses.

A. palmatum dissectum 'Beni shidare variegated'

This is not a strong-growing cultivar but will do well with extra care. It is best grown in some shade, for it will sunburn quite easily. This cultivar especially needs an even flow of moisture (not in excess) and must never be in stress. A missed irrigation will soon crisp all the leaves or occasionally cause the plant to drop them entirely.

A. palmatum dissectum atropurpureum 'Brocade'

This is another of the very fine red dissectums. The differences in many of the "reds" are hard to describe and must be seen to be appreciated. Not as dark as some of the other cultivars, this is a soft red but deep in color, lacking the "black" quality of 'Nigrum' or 'Crimson Queen.' 'Brocade' holds its color well into the Summer but will gradually turn to a green red and into bronze. It is a pleasant bronzing, not as harsh as some other cultivars or the red seedling atropurpureums.

This form cascades and eventually makes a large rounded bush 3 meters high and 3½ meters wide. The multi-dissected leaves are of medium-size range. (Leaf size and shape as described in *A. palmatum dissectum atropurpureum*.) Fall coloration is usually bright red to crimson blended softly with orange.

A. palmatum 'Chirimen kaede'
See: *A. palmatum dissectum* 'Tamukeyama'

A. palmatum 'Chirimen momiji'
See: *A. palmatum dissectum* 'Tamukeyama'

A. palmatum dissectum atropurpureum 'Crimson Queen'

The outstanding feature of 'Crimson Queen' is the persistence of the good, deep red color of the foliage. Most of the red dissectum cultivars which have excellent red color during the Spring and early Summer months will turn green or bronze. 'Crimson Queen', however, will carry the deep red color throughout the entire growing season. We have seen it endure periods of 100°F (30°C) temperatures in full sun with practically no sunburn, but under these conditions the deep red will become orange-red. Fall colors range into the extremely bright scarlet tones.

The finely dissected leaves have lobes up to 9 cm long, with the side lobes 5 to 6 cm long. Scarlet petioles range up to 4 cm. Each narrow lobe is deeply divided and notched, pinnatifid form.

This is a strong-growing dissectum cultivar which originated in the United States. It ages into a beautifully-cascading form. Under very vigorous conditions, I have seen young plants put out shoots up to 60 to 65 cm long. As the plants attain more age, the growth shoots are shorter and form a more dense growth. The tree reaches 3 meters in height and 4 meters in width.

Among the many known cultivars of red dissectums, this one is fast becoming a favorite in the United States in the commercial trade. Every effort should be made to retain its purity, and purchasers of young growing-out stock should be assured that it is the true cultivar.

A. palmatum dissectum atropurpureum 'Ever Red'

The new Spring growth of 'Ever Red' is its distinguishing characteristic. The new shoots and foliage are noticeably covered with fine silvery hairs which make the unfolding new growth look almost grey. It soon loses the pubescence and attains the rich deep red color so typical of this cultivar. Unfortunately there are many plants so labeled which are not the true 'Ever Red' but rather other forms of *A. palmatum dissectum atropurpureum*. These will not have the silvery pubescence on the newly-developing shoots, nor will these plants retain the deep red for which this cultivar is known.

The leaves have finely dissected lobes as long as 12 cm. Each lobe is deeply dissected along the edges to the midrib of the section.

A. palmatum dissectum 'Crimson Queen'

The seven dissected portions of the leaf tend to hang down, making the leaf about 10 cm wide in many cases and giving the whole plant a feathery, cascading appearance so desirable in this type of palmatum.

As the name implies, this cultivar holds the red color much longer into the mid-Summer season than many other cultivars of red dissectums. However, it will not usually hold the rich reds quite as long as 'Crimson Queen.' Planting in full sun or in partial shade will affect the length of color retention. Partial shading will prolong the deep colors. In late Summer the bronze or bronzy-green colors take over. In the Fall the rich bright red tones become prominent.

A. palmatum dissectum 'Ever Red'. The silvery pubescence of Spring growth identifies this cultivar from other similar forms.

A. palmatum dissectum 'Ever Red'

'Ever Red' is a vigorous dissectum with the typical pendulous growth habit. I have seen large old specimens which were 4 to 5 meters high and at least as wide.

This is one of the better red dissectums of the nursery trade. At least in the Western states nurseries it is the most widely used of the named cultivars of dissectum. However, at this writing both 'Crimson Queen' and 'Garnet' are gaining in popularity.

After much searching of literature, talking with experienced nurserymen in various countries, and tracing the "history" of this cultivar, I am convinced that it is, in fact, the old European cultivar 'Nigrum.' We have plants of both cultivars. Our 'Nigrum' plants came from old collections in Europe. The new growth silveriness, the tones of the red leaves, the growth habit and leaf texture, all lead me to believe that these two cultivars are synonymous. I believe that several decades ago 'Nigrum' was labeled 'Ever Red' in the United States. It is indeed well-named.

A. palmatum dissectum 'Filigree'

This is probably my favorite cultivar in the group of variegated dissectums. Its delicate texture and interesting color changes make it a conversation piece.

The basic color is light green—almost yellow green—in the Spring. It darkens as the season progresses. Entirely overlaid on the basic color is a profusion of minute dots, specks, or flecks of pale gold or cream. The leaf shape is so distinct and color so difficult to describe that personal inspection is necessary. In the Fall the leaves attain a rich gold which holds very well. The bark of the twigs and branches is a silvery green with definite white striping or elongated flecking.

Leaves are deeply dissected entirely to the center. Each of the seven lobes is delicately and deeply dissected almost to the midrib. In turn, each large serration is again toothed, making a double-dissected and very lacy leaf. The end of each dissected point is quite sharp. Lobes are up to 8 cm long on mature foliage, and the complex leaf is about 11 cm wide across the entire spread of the radiating divisions.

The growth habit is pendulous like most of the dissectums. It is compact and makes a well-rounded, cascading plant (2 meters high and 3 meters wide). Tall staking during early growth of the plant or very high grafting on a standard is desirable. The plant will then cascade as it matures.

This is a fairly recent selection. I believe that the original plant is with Joel Spingarn of Baldwin, New York. It was a chance purchase by Mr. Spingarn of a young green dissectum which developed these characteristics. He gave it the name 'Filigree.' This is the valid name and an excellent choice.

Later a plant or two appeared in the West without proper nomenclature. The name 'Silver Lace' was attached, but according to Mr. Spingarn's records and history I feel this is a misnomer.

Time has not allowed this cultivar to become distributed widely in commercial nurseries. I feel it is one of the very desirable items for landscapers as well as collectors.

A. palmatum dissectum 'Flavescens'

The distinct yellow-green of this cultivar makes it a worthwhile addition to the palmatum collection. Although the leaf form is quite typical of the dissectums, the distinct color phase of the Spring and early Summer foliage makes it quite different. The green tones of the foliage darken as Summer progresses. Fall colors are usually a good tone of yellow, occasionally tinged with orange.

The leaves are of good texture and durable. There are seven divisions of the leaf which are deeply separated entirely to the center. Each section is then serrated along the margins, giving the dissectum appearance. However, the individual lobes are not as pinnatifid as most "type" dissectums. The leaves measure up to 10 cm both in length and width.

The plant has the typical pendulous habit of the dissectum group. It is necessary to train the young plant into an upright stem so that the cascading form may develop as the plant matures to 2 meters high and 3 meters wide.

A. palmatum dissectum atropurpureum 'Garnet'

The outstanding feature of this cultivar is its color and vigor. The leaf color is the rich red-orange of the gem stone garnet. When grown in shade, the color retains a greenish cast, but in a sunny location the garnet color develops well.

It is a vigorous-growing form to 3 meters high. Under very heavy fertilization it will send out new shoots up to 1 meter on young plants. In the landscape, however, the shoots are not as long, and the plant shapes itself well. It has the pendulous, spreading habit of dissectums, and as it matures forms a beautiful, cascading, mound-shaped specimen.

The leaves are large for a dissectum, and the deep color holds well into the Summer season. Well-fertilized young plants have leaf lobes up to 12 cm long,

A. palmatum dissectum 'Filigree'

A. palmatum dissectum 'Flavescens'

A. palmatum dissectum 'Garnet'

although most are shorter. Each of the seven lobes separate entirely to the center of the leaf. The side serrations on each lobe do not cut as deeply into the center vein area as do some other red dissectums and are not as delicate. The whole leaf appears a little coarser than some other cultivars.

This plant originated with Guldemond of Holland who later sold the stock plants and propagating rights to Le Faber & Co. of Boskoop, Holland. Later, propagation rights were given to Hauenstein, Rafz CH, for Switzerland. It has become a popular cultivar with propagating nurserymen, making a good quality plant of salable size in a short time. It retains color well and is a durable landscape plant.

A. palmatum dissectum 'Goshiki shidare'

This variegated dissectum has a great variety of leaf colors. There are typical uniform dissected shapes with colors of deep green with dark red overtones. Other leaves have thin lobes twisted, curled, and almost tangled. These are deep red-green, heavily marked with pink. There are also leaves with strong white areas. All degrees of variations of the above may be present.

The leaf size averages smaller than most dissectums. Most are between 4 and 6 cm long and occasionally to 8 cm. It appears more narrow because the lobes tend to hold together (4 to 6 cm wide). On uniform leaves, the lobes separate entirely to the leaf center and are pinnately incised as are other dissectums. Many leaves have lobes much more irregularly pinnately incised.

This is a cascading cultivar as the name "shidare" suggests. It is somewhat similar to 'Beni shidare variegated' and may possibly be a synonym. However, I have no confirmation of this, and our plants are not old enough to judge adequately. It appears, from the growth during the season, to be rather dwarf.

A. palmatum dissectum atropurpureum 'Inaba shidare' (leaves of rice plant)

This outstanding dissectum differs from the others of its type in its deep color and individual leaf shape. Leaves are large for dissectum, with lobes up to 10 cm long. The base lobes hang down. The entire leaf measures as much as 15 cm in length with an equal spread between side tips. Each lobe ends in a fine tip. They measure less than 1 mm wide, broadening to 3 cm in the middle and tapering again to less than 1 mm at the base where all 7 lobes join the petiole. The lobes are dissected toward each midrib, but the many separations are not as fine as in the more common dissectum types. This gives the appearance of each lobe being more sturdy and the leaves having more substance than other dissectums. The 4 cm long petioles are bright red.

The leaves develop a deep tone of purple-red as they grow in the Spring and retain the deep color all season. They do not bronze out in the late season as do other "reds." The tips may burn in hot, direct sun, especially if the plant becomes dry. Fall colors are brilliant when they turn from the purple-red to a crimson tone. It is a "red" counterpart of 'Washi no o' (Palmatifidium).

For a dissectum this is a rather upright-growing form. Although it does cascade, it will tend to be a little more erect in appearance. It is vigorous and sturdy. The branches are not the fine, overly-delicate type which is a weakness of some dissectums.

Although not widely found in cultivation, it should become a popular landscape item when it becomes better known in the United States. It has been listed in Japan since the mid-1800's.

It presents an interesting example of Japanese nomenclature. The Japanese observed that in the rain this plant looks a little like "Ine" (rice plant), thus: "Ina ba" rice plant-like leaf; "Shidare" cascading. There was an old form of "Ine" (rice plant) which turned crimson in the Fall.

A. palmatum dissectum 'Kiri nishiki'

Most dissectums appear delicate in foliage, but 'Kiri nishiki' looks more substantial yet not coarse. The nine lobes are not as double-incised as most dissectums. Each lobe is more regularly incised pinnately, and each of the pinna is less delicately incised. Leaves vary from 5 to 8 cm long and 6 to 9 cm across the spread of the side tips. Petioles are 2 to 3 cm long.

The basic foliage color is a bright, light green. This is a strong color, and it stands full sun rather well. In the Fall the intense gold color is excellent, and occasionally it is suffused with crimson and scarlet on the tips.

This is a full cascading cultivar which is fairly strong-growing and hardy. As with other closely-allied forms such as 'Sekimori', it should be planted on a bank or grafted high in order to realize the full effect of the beautifully cascading display of branches. It will reach 3 meters high and wide. I find 'Kiri nishiki' listed in maple references back to early 1700's.

A. palmatum dissectum 'Goshiki shidare'

A. palmatum dissectum 'Inaba shidare'

A. palmatum dissectum 'Nigrum'
    See: *A. palmatum dissectum* 'Ever Red'

'Nigrum' is a purple-red dissectum which shows a silvery-grey pubescence in the Spring. This feature, plus leaf shape, bark color, and rate of growth as well as references in old literature, leads me to conclude that 'Nigrum' and 'Ever Red' are synonymous.

We have imported 'Nigrum' from Europe and grown it side by side with 'Ever Red' and found them identical.

This cultivar has been grown for many generations in Holland and England. It originated as a selection from the older cultivar 'Ornatum.' Vrugtman reports in his writing that there are at least two cultivars grown in Holland under the name 'Nigrum.'

A. palmatum dissectum 'Nomura shidare'

This may very well be a synonym for 'Shōjō shidare'. They are both deep maroon selections of *dissectum*, and the cultivars in our collection are virtually indistinguishable.

A. palmatum dissectum atropurpureum
    'Ornatum'
    Syn.: 'Aka washi no o'

The Spring foliage is an interesting red. It is more of a bronze-red when compared with other cultivars such as 'Inaba shidare,' 'Ever Red,' or 'Crimson Queen.' It is a brilliant tone and stands out well in the landscape. During late Summer it turns greenish. It assumes a prominent crimson-red color in the Fall.

The leaves are the typical dissectum combination of seven very long, thin lobes which are divided into deeply dissected side lobes, each deeply toothed. They are 6 to 7 cm long, but the total spread is only 5 to 9 cm since many leaves do not spread widely. The greenish petioles are 3 to 4 cm long.

Very old plants will be perhaps 2 meters high but create a mounded shape with a width of 3 or more meters.

A. palmatum dissectum 'Ornatum'

This is quite an old cultivar from the European nurseries. It has been popular because of the rather distinctive color tone. However, as other selections were made of deeper tones which retained color better, its popularity waned somewhat. It still makes a good color contrast in the landscape and is hardy. Many authorities regard this as a selection of *A. palmatum dissectum atropurpureum.*

A. palmatum dissectum 'Palmatifidium'
    Syn.: 'Washi no o,' 'Paucum'

This cultivar differs from other green dissectums in the shape of the leaf lobes. These have margins which are less double-dissected. The lobes are just as long and narrow, but the marginal cuts or dissected edges are not as deep. The effect is a leaf which appears a little sturdier but is just as beautiful. The rich green leaves have seven long, narrow, incised lobes. These separate entirely to the center of the leaf. The center five lobes point out, while the base lobes point back up the petiole. This gives a cascading effect to both leaves and twigs. Center lobes are 7 to 9 cm, and the spread between tips is 12 to 14 cm. Petioles are long and slender, 3 to 5 cm.

The foliage is a good green tone in Spring and Summer. Yellow, gold and crimson blend together for a very colorful Fall display.

A. palmatum dissectum 'Palmatifidium'

A. palmatum dissectum 'Palmatifidium'. The green foliage changes to a rich gold Fall color, contrasting with 'Crimson Queen' and 'Garnet' in the background.

The growth is sturdy, durable, hardy, and strongly cascading. This makes a beautiful, mound-shaped plant. Occasionally vigorous new shoots will extend upward before cascading. Older plants are often wider than tall—up to 2 meters high and over 3 meters wide.

Old literature refers to *A. palmatum dissectum* 'Palmatifidium,' and the Japanese name 'Washi no o' can be found prior to 1880. It originated as a cultivar in the early 1800's. I find the name 'Paucum' more common in parts of Europe. I saw a magnificent old plant of this cultivar at the Trompenburg Arboretum, Rotterdam, Holland.

A. palmatum dissectum 'Paucum'
See: *A. palmatum dissectum* 'Palmatifidium'

A. palmatum dissectum 'Pendula Julian'

The leaves of this cultivar are not quite as finely serrated on the deep-cut lobes as some other dissectums. In fact, some of the older wood produces leaves almost lanceolate, with deeply cut side-toothed margins, making it approach the form of 'Palmatifidium.'

The deep purple-red color holds well into the Summer, gradually changing to a rusty green with a reddish undertone. In the Fall, the crimson-orange combinations are quite vivid.

Leaf size is about average for a dissectum, being up to 8 to 10 cm both long and wide. The normal seven lobes radiate outward in good fashion. Petioles are firm and 2 to 3 cm long.

It is quite pendulous, and young plants must be staked early to reach the desired height. The cascading is outward, then downward. It is a very hardy form. We have seen older plants survive -18°C (0°F) and heavy coats of ice.

Henry Hohman had this in his collection for many years. I believe he originally brought it from the Yokohama Nurseries in the 1930's. There is a beautiful 30-year old plant growing in Oregon which came from Mr. Hohman's nursery.

A. palmatum dissectum 'Pendulum angustilobum atropurpureum'

As the long name implies, this is a "pendulous, narrow-lobed, dark purple" form of foliage. It is a selection out of the *dissectum atropurpureum* group. Wada includes it in his catalog of 1938 as one of eight forms of "Pendulum."

The leaves are a strong, dark red with a noticeable undertone shading of green. The mid-veins are quite green. Lobes radiate strongly and make a leaf 10 cm long from petiole attachment to 15 cm wide. They are not as double-dissected as many cultivars but more regularly pinnatifid.

By mid-Summer, it changes to a definite bronze. It becomes quite bright in the Fall with yellow and scarlet combinations.

This is a strong, hardy, pendulous cultivar. It is not very different from many seedling selections of *A. palmatum dissectum atropurpureum.* However, I retain it in the collection because of the many questions which arise from numerous references in old literature.

A. palmatum dissectum atropurpureum 'Red Filigree Lace'

The leaves of this outstanding new cultivar must be seen to be appreciated. Description will hardly do it justice.

The uniform color is a deep purple-red or maroon. The foliage retains this color extremely well throughout the entire growing season. In the Fall, it becomes a bright crimson.

The dissectum-type leaves are seven-lobed. However, each lobe is extremely lacy, being much more delicately dissected than the normal type. The lobes are extremely pinnatifid, with the center of the lobe being no wider than the vein (1 mm or less in width). The dissected side portions are equally fine and interspersed with sharp, tooth-like sub-divisions. The side points on each lobe are sometimes 1 and 2 cm long but still only 1 mm wide. As these interlock, they add to the delicate tracery of the leaf pattern. With these finely double-dissected lobes lying close together, the effect is certainly filigree-like.

A. palmatum dissectum 'Pendulum angustilobum atropurpureum'

A. palmatum dissectum 'Red Filigree Lace'

The leaf measures 6 to 8 cm long and at least 7 to 9 cm between the extended fine tips. Petioles are stiff and about 2 cm long.

The growth has the pendulous habit of the dissectums and is sturdy in spite of the fineness of some of the small twigs. The overall effect is one of extreme beauty. Rate of growth is not quite as fast as other "red" dissectums.

In my opinion this is the most beautiful and unusual new introduction to the dissectum group.

The parent plant of this cultivar is owned by John Mitsch, Mitsch Nursery, Aurora, Oregon. As I understand its history, this was a chance seedling grown by Will Curtis of Sherwood, Oregon, from seed of a dissectum in his garden. As a yearling seedling, it was given to William Goddard of Victoria, British Columbia. Mr. Goddard cultured and nurtured the plant for a number of years and finally sold it to Mr. Mitsch. It is very fortunate that this plant was not lost, for it adds greatly to the magnificent series of palmatum cultivars.

A. *palmatum dissectum* 'Roseo-marginatum'
Syn.: 'Roseo-pictum'

As the name denotes, the margins are colored red or rust-red as the leaves first unfold. The basic color of the leaf is green. This color pattern is often found in seedling-produced dissectums. In many cases, the reddish tones are faint and not predominant. As the Summer foliage matures, the red edge usually disappears, leaving the normal green of palmatum dissectums. Grown in full shade, the reddish colors rarely or faintly develop. Fall foliage is the yellow or orange-yellow of other green dissectums.

Leaf shape and size are typical of green dissectums. Plant shape and habit also make it a typical cascading, round-topped large shrub (2–3 m.).

I have seen old plants of this cultivar which showed very little of the "roseo-marginatum" character.

In 1867 Lemaire gave this plant a separate status.

A. *palmatum dissectum* 'Rubrifolium'
Syn.: 'Akashigata'

The typical dissectum leaves are a different red than most of the "purple-reds" of this type. It is more brown-red or rust-red, with the green main veins showing in each dissected lobe. This color is retained well into the Summer and then changes to a rich, dark green. In the Fall the leaves become a rich gold with occasional crimson edges.

The leaves are about normal size for dissectums and typically double pinnatifid. Length varies from 7 to 10 cm. Petiole length is about 5 or 6 cm. The bark on this cultivar is a powdery green with minute white striations.

This is a fairly strong-growing dissectum type which develops the typical dome shape to 3 meters high. It will grow fairly fast at first and become pendulous with maturity. It is one of the lesser known cultivars.

Although Pax in 1902 attributed the name 'Washi no o' to this red dissectum, we find most of the older Japanese literature describes 'Washi no o' as the green colored 'Palmatifidium' or 'Paucum.'

A. *palmatum dissectum* 'Seiryū'

It is unusual to see an upright-growing form of the dissectum maples. All other dissectum cultivars are of the cascading or weeping form. This green "laceleaf" offers a pleasing contrast when planted in company with the other more conventional dissectum forms.

The foliage is a pleasing bright green. Each leaf is lightly tipped with reddish tones as it first unfolds. This soon fades to a uniform light green. The leaves are slightly smaller than most of the other cultivars of green dissectums. They range from 4 to 5 cm long and are slightly wider. The seven lobes are pinnately dissected but not as finely cut as typical dissectums. It is more multi-dissected than the 'Washi no o' or 'Palmatifidium' types. The short, stiff petioles are 1½ to 2 cm long. The bark is a dark brown-green.

Fall colors are quite spectacular and range from strong gold to light yellows with a suffusion of crimson in most leaves.

The upright growth is quite strong but not overly vigorous as is the case with some of the large-leafed palmatum types. The new

A. palmatum dissectum 'Seiryū'

shoots are stiff, not willowy, and will grow as much as ½ meter per year. Young vigorous plants will exceed this rate. A more mature tree will become multi-branched and gradually thicken without becoming excessively twiggy.

I have not seen specimens of 'Seiryu' which were older than about 20 years. Older plants might reach 4 meters in height in fertile locations.

This is a delightful addition to the landscape and quite different from the usual cascading form expected of dissectum maples.

A. palmatum dissectum 'Sekimori'

The leaf shape and color set this cultivar apart. Also, the bark is a delightful bright green which lasts quite well in the older branches and limbs. The green has a faint whitish overcast and has distinct lengthwise, white striations.

The deep green leaves have 9 lobes. They are of medium size—7 to 9 cm long. The lobes tend to hang down slightly and fold together to make the width 8 to 9 cm. Petioles are 5 cm.

Each of the nine lobes is deeply but uniformly pinnatifid, but not as finely or unevenly cut as the normal dissectums. This gives the leaf an appearance of more substance. It does not have the coarse cuts of 'Palmatifidium' ('Washi no o'). The basal ¼ of the lobe is only the width of the mid-vein. The lobe develops the dissected portion on the outer ¾ length. To me, the lobes look more "feathery," while other green dissectums look "lacy."

This is a strong, hardy plant. Growth on young plants can be vigorous, forming a nice-shaped bush in a short time. The cascading branches go out and down. By training the top shoots, the plant can reach more height from which to cascade more beautifully. Planting on a slope enhances its beauty. Fall colors develop one of the best bright yellow-gold combinations of the green types. It reaches a height of 3 meters and a width of 4 meters at maturity.

A. palmatum dissectum 'Shōjō shidare'

The basic color of the leaf is a deep maroon—brighter in the new foliage and darkening as the leaf matures. A dark, rich green tone is suffused down the center of each lobe and the sub-lobes. The two-tone color combination gives this plant a unique appearance. Petioles are deep maroon, as are the young twigs and branches.

The leaves are 7 to 9-lobed, pinnately dissected with irregular serrations on each pinnate sub-lobe. Some of the sub-lobes are long and slender. On leaves of new wood, the lobes are occasionally restricted between the pinnate lobes to only the mid-rib width. These in turn have minute side lobes extending out for 1 to 3 mm. Leaves vary from 4 to 7 cm long and 5 to 7 cm wide. Petioles are slender but firm and are 2 to 3 cm long.

It has the cascading form of all dissectums. It should be grafted high or staked up for a few years to get some initial height so that the beauty of the cascading form can be seen.

This cultivar is very beautiful but as yet is little-known. It is a little tender and not easily propagated.

A. palmatum dissectum 'Sotoyama'
See: A. palmatum dissectum 'Toyama'

A. palmatum dissectum 'Sotoyama nishiki'
See: A. palmatum dissectum 'Toyama nishiki'

A. palmatum dissectum 'Takiniyama'

This excellent form of dissectum has deep maroon foliage in Spring and early Summer. Its leaf shape, coloration, and growth habit are all identical to 'Tamukeyama.' The plant was added to our collection several years ago, and as it matures its characteristics lead me to believe it is synonymous with 'Tamukeyama.' I have found no record of 'Takiniyama' in past literature.

The similarity in nomenclature to 'Tamukeyama' and 'Takinogawa' may have caused confusion in past years.

A. palmatum dissectum 'Tamukeyama'
Syn.: 'Chirimen kaede',
'Chirimen momiji'

This cultivar has the multi-dissected leaves of the dissectum type, but the pinnatifid cuts

A. palmatum dissectum 'Sekimori'

A. palmatum dissectum 'Tamukeyama'

are not quite as deep as such forms as 'Ever Red' or 'Crimson Queen.' There is a little more width to the center of the lobe, making each appear slightly bolder. The 7 to 9 lobes radiate outward, terminating in an extremely fine tip. Leaves are 7 to 9 cm long and as much as 11 cm across. The red, stiff petiole is 3 to 4 cm long.

The new foliage is a deep crimson-red when unfolding, but soon changes to a very dark purple-red. It is an excellent color tone which holds very well but will sunburn slightly in full sun. Fall colors are bright scarlet. The bark of the twigs and young branches is a deep maroon-red, overcast with a whitish tone.

This is a hardy plant and is strongly cascading. It is an old cultivar, having been listed as early as 1710. The Japanese record old plants, 50 to 100 years old, which are up to 4 meters tall.

A. palmatum dissectum 'Toyama'
Alternate spelling: 'Sotoyama'

This is a very old name in Japanese Maple literature. It is applied to *A. palmatum dissectum atropurpureum* or individual selections thereof. I find one reference indicating that it is a synonym for 'Ornatum'. There is also a reference applying 'Toyama' to a form of *A. buergerianum.*

A. palmatum dissectum 'Toyama nishiki'
Syn.: 'Yamato nishiki'
Alternate spelling: 'Sotoyama nishiki'

The basic leaf color is purple-red to greenish-red, variegated to a greater or lesser degree. Some leaves lack variegation; others are completely pink as they first open in the Spring. Most markings are pink or white and insert into portions of the lobes or blend into the leaf in endless variation. Each leaf is a different pattern. When grown in shade, the colors are more intense and will hold better into the heat of summer. The leaves sunburn easily.

The foliage is typical dissectum, with 7 to 9 lobes, double-dissected, pinnatifid, and lacy. However, these finely divided leaves appear to droop more than other dissectums because slight distortions occur at or near the variegated areas. They are 6 to 8 cm long and wide, with 3 to 4 cm petioles.

This is not a strong-growing cultivar and is rather tender. It should be grafted high or staked when young to get more height. It is difficult to propagate and is not common in collections.

I find this cultivar very similar to 'Beni shidare tricolor.' The two cultivars show completely overlapping leaf characteristics. Both are equally difficult to propagate. The amount of pink in the variegation is quite variable. Old plants of both cultivars vary considerably within the plant and from year to year.

A. palmatum dissectum 'Toyama nishiki'

A. palmatum dissectum variegatum
Syn.: Polychromum, Ornatum variegatum, 'Friderici-Gulielmi' (several spellings)

The leaves on this dissectum are about normal size for the type, ranging from 7 to 10 cm long and from 8 to 12 cm across the feathery lobes. The much-divided seven lobes are separated entirely to the base attachment. Each lobe is extremely pinnatifid; each cut reaches into the main vein of the lobe.

The basic leaf color is deep green and is lacking the red present in 'Toyama nishiki' or 'Beni shidare tricolor.' Variegation is almost entirely white, although pink markings do occur. The white portions may be an entire side of a pinnatifid lobe or only an occasional fleck. Where variegations are strong in a leaf, that lobe portion will curve slightly, giving the entire foliage a lacy but uneven look.

A. palmatum dissectum variegatum

This is not a strong grower and needs protection from the hot sun. It will cascade beautifully when grafted on a high standard or staked up in its formative years.

It is not as vigorous as other dissectums and is difficult to propagate.

A. palmatum dissectum 'Viridis'

The term "viridis" has come to mean any green form of dissectum palmatum just as "atropurpureum" encompasses all the red forms. In old literature, the original Latin description was "Folia viridia," from whence came the general term "viridis." The Japanese name for the green form of dissectum is 'Ao shidare,' or 'Aoba shidare.' I suspect there was a form or cultivar specifically named 'Viridis,' but today, at least in the United States, it has come to mean any good green dissectum.

The foliage is the "type" for dissectums, being mainly 9 (7)-lobed. Each lobe separates entirely to the petiole attachment. Lobes are multi-dissected, or strongly pinnately formed, so that each lobe is extremely narrow with the deeply cut side separations again re-cut. Some descriptions state "deeply and doubly serrated in pinnate form." Leaves range from 6 cm long and 7 cm wide on older wood to 10 cm long and 12 cm wide on younger wood. While these dimensions are large, the leaf is not "gross" but has the delicate tracery of the typical "dissectum" form. Petioles usually are about 4 cm long.

A. palmatum dissectum 'Viridis'

The bright green foliage holds color well through the Summer. In extremely hot sun, the tips of the leaves may burn. Partial shade will keep the foliage bright all season. In the Fall, the delightful gold colors dominate, with occasional splashes of crimson.

This is also the growth form "type" for this group. It is strongly cascading, and the long, drooping branchlets form a dome-shaped plant at maturity. It needs to be grafted high on a standard or staked during the young formative years so it can attain some height from which to cascade. Very old trees (75 to 100 years) reach a height of as much as 4 meters.

A. palmatum dissectum 'Washi no o'
(eagle's tail)
See: *A. palmatum dissectum* 'Palmatifidium'

A. palmatum dissectum 'Waterfall'

The leaves are typically dissectum but they are slightly larger than those normally seen in the 'Viridis' group. They range from 7 to 12 cm long and 8 to 12 cm wide. The lobes hold together closely and have a cascading tendency. There are 7 to 9 multi-dissected lobes. Each lobe is narrowly pinnatifid and re-incised. The distinguishing feature of this cultivar is that the leaves have a longer and more flowing appearance as they cascade down the outside of the mature plants. Petioles range from 3 to 4 cm long.

The foliage is a good, bright green which is retained well all season. The plant stands full sun quite well. The Fall colors are brilliant golden tones, suffused with crimson blends.

The branch development is strong and sturdy. Branches on the top of the plant will slowly add height to this cultivar as it matures. However, young plants should be staked, or grafted quite high, to attain height. The side branches cascade strongly. This is a hardy and beautiful cultivar.

I saw the original "mother" plant at the Willowwood Arboretum at Gladstone, New Jersey which was 3 meters high and 4 meters wide. Dr. Ben Blackburn discussed the origin of this plant. It was a selected seedling named by Henry Hohman in the 1920's. Its beautiful cascading character gave it value as a separate cultivar. It is now quite popular in the United States nursery trade.

A. palmatum dissectum 'Waterfall'

DEEPLY DIVIDED GROUP

The foliage of this group of cultivars is composed of 5, 7, or 9 lobes which separate entirely to the center of the leaf. This is the "palmatisectum" of Koidzumi. The lobes are predominately elongate-lanceolate. They are closely allied to the dissectums, but the lobe margins are not pinnately incised. Most of these leaves are deeply toothed to moderately serrated.

In many cases these types of cultivars have cascading branches, such as with 'Omurayama.' They make medium-size trees, but they do not grow in a stiff, upright manner, nor are they the low bush-type of the dissectums.

A. palmatum 'Omurayama'. The cultivars with deeply divided leaves are often medium-size specimens with cascading outer branches. Most of them are also notable for their brilliant Fall coloration.

A. palmatum 'Aratama'

This cultivar is reported to be a bud-sport of 'Komurasaki,' a very fine, deep purple cultivar.

The red of 'Aratama' is a brighter tone, lacking the "purple" of the parent. The color is deeper in the center of the lobes, shading toward the edges. The underside of the leaf has an overshading of green on the red base color. Fall colors are bright red.

Leaves are 5 to 7-lobed and measure 6 to 7 cm long and 5 to 6 cm wide. The lobes are elongate-ovate, restricting at the base. They are separate almost entirely to the center of the leaf, and the lobe ends taper to a very sharp tip. The margins are sharply toothed.

This is a hardy, upright tall shrub form which grows to 3 meters.

A. palmutum 'Beni kagami'

A. palmatum 'Azuma murasaki'
(The purple of the East) or Azuma could mean an old name for Tokyo in this context.
Syn.: 'Toshi'

The deeply divided reddish lobes of the foliage distinguish this cultivar. The "red" is of unusual tone. There is a slight purple hue in the red, but the entire leaf has an undertone of green showing through. New foliage has a "dusty" appearance due to a covering of fine pubescence which soon disappears. As mid-Summer arrives, the leaves alter to a deep green with a reddish cast to the surface.

Leaves are 7-lobed, measuring from 5 to 7 cm long with a spread of 9 cm. Each lobe separates widely from the rest, is long ovate-lanceolate, and has definite toothed margins. Petioles are bright red most of the season. The underside of the leaves develop a bright, shiny, green, smooth surface.

This is not a tall-growing cultivar. The short tree form will reach 6 meters and become rather round-topped. Early growth is fairly rapid but will slow down as the years pass. Outside limbs will make a cascading form in time.

The color tones of this choice tree contrast well with the other red-leafed forms. It is different enough to make good contrast in landscape plantings.

A. palmatum 'Beni kagami'
(the red mirror)

One of the deeply divided red forms of palmatum. In Spring the leaves are orange-red to purplish red, depending on location and shade cover. It is not the deep black red of other cultivars. The leaves have green undertones when grown in deep shade. The palmate leaves are divided into long, narrow ovate lobes. The divisions do not quite reach the center of the leaf. Leaves are 6 to 8 cm long and slightly wider. Petioles are 2 to 3 cm long and bright red. Edges of lobes are double serrate.

This is a fairly strong grower, of a spreading small tree form and not a stiff upright shape. It is quite graceful.

It is reported to be a seedling selection from *A. palmatum* 'Nomura kaede.'

A. palmatum 'Burgundy Lace'

This is a striking American cultivar of the "ribbon-leaf" group of Japanese Maples with red coloration comparable to Burgundy wine. The leaves are deeply divided with separation of the lobes completely to the center of the leaf. Lobes hold together closely, making the leaves appear longer than broad. Leaves are 10 cm long and 8 to 9 cm wide. Each lobe is ovate-lanceolate, coming to a very gradual and sharp point. The lobe is up to 1½ cm wide in the middle and narrows to a tiny 1 mm at the base. Lobes are sharply-toothed along the entire margin.

Spring and early Summer coloration is the typical burgundy red, but as the season progresses it will turn bronzy or greenish. It will sunburn in full, hot sun.

This is a spreading-type, small tree (4 meters high) which develops a wide (5 meters) canopy when given room. While upright, it is classed in the shorter tree group. Hardy and beautiful, it makes an excellent contrast with other upright palmatums. It will fit into smaller landscape plantings with judicious pruning.

A. palmatum 'Chitoseyama'

This is one of the deeply-divided red forms of palmatum. The leaves have slender lobes which separate to the center of the leaf. Lobes are long, narrow, ovate-lanceolate. The leaves measure up to 8 cm long, and lobes are about 5 mm to 1 cm broad. The edges are partly double serrate with many sharp teeth. New leaves are often pale crimson but open to a rich purple-red. However, it will not color well in deep shade. As the season progresses, the bronze green to dark green color appears in Summer foliage. Fall colors are rather bright crimson.

This is a cascading type but not as fully drooping as some cultivars. Older plants make a mound-like tall shrub, not an upright tree 3 meters tall and broad. This is an excellent cultivar of the older type and found quite widely in collections and some nurseries. It is often used as a specimen in containers and occasionally for bonsai.

A. palmatum heptalobum 'Elegans'

Like most members of the heptalobum type, the glory of this cultivar comes with a burst of color in the Fall. It is a bright orange tinged with red. It starts in the Spring with its newest leaves a yellowish color which then turns to a dark green.

The leaves usually have 7 (5) deeply divided and widely separated lobes. The lobes are up to 7 cm long and 1½ cm wide at the broad midpoint. They are broadly lanceolate with the edges distinctly serrated. The leaf is divided entirely into the center, and the lobes are very narrow at the base. Petioles are strong and 3 cm long.

This is a stocky-growing, low tree which tends to become as wide as it is tall. Old specimens reach heights of 3 meters or a little more. The branches grow in a sturdy manner, and like many of the heptalobum group, are thicker than other types of palmatum.

This is a good, hardy, trouble-free plant and is useful when a short tree type is desired for background planting.

A. palmatum heptalobum 'Hessei'
Syn.: A. palmatum heptalobum elegans atropurpureum

This is a deeply-divided, red-leafed form of palmatum. Its leaves are normally composed of 7 lobes, long and narrow, and divided almost to the center of the leaf. Each lobe is elongate lanceolate with the margins toothed. Lobes are 8–9 cm long and hold closely together thus making the leaf appear longer than wide although the spread is to 7 cm to the side tips. Leaves droop slightly and give the plant a ribbon-leaf effect.

Leaf color from Spring to early Summer is a very rich purple-red. Later in the heat of Summer it changes to bronze. Fall color is quite a brilliant crimson.

A. palmatum heptalobum 'Elegans'

A. palmatum heptalobum 'Hessei'

A. palmatum 'Chitoseyama'

Spring growth has a reddish-brown or deep rusty appearance. As Summer develops, the colors change to a rich, deep green. Fall colors appear with bright crimson tones which make this a very conspicuous plant in the garden.

Not a tall upright tree (reaching 3 meters), yet a vigorous grower which will broaden with age. It is hardy and useful in landscaping for its good Fall color.

A. palmatum 'Matsu kaze'

A. palmatum laciniatum
  See: *A. palmatum* 'Tsuri nishiki'

A. palmatum 'Masumurasaki'

This is a very intense red cultivar, showing best when in full sun. The red does not have the green undertone of many similar cultivars but shades more toward purple. When grown in full shade, the leaves have almost a black-red tone with deep green shading in the center of the lobes. Petioles and veins are also bright red.

The leaf has seven lobes, separating ⅔ the distance into the center of the leaf. Each lobe is ovate-acuminate but with an elongate tip. The margins are double serrate. The leaf is 5 to 7 cm long and 6 to 8 cm wide. The red petioles are 1 to 2 cm long.

The color is difficult to describe adequately. When grown close to similar cultivars, its unique color is apparent.

A. palmatum 'Matsu kaze'
  Alternate spelling: 'Machi kaze'

This is a deep-cut red form of palmatum which makes a handsome landscape plant.

The leaves are 7 to 8 cm long and deeply separated with seven long, narrow, elliptic-ovate lobes. The lobes tend to remain together rather than radiate outward, thus making a total spread of only about 8 to 9 cm. Each lobe is double-serrate and tapers to a long, slender point. Lobes join in the center about the last 5 mm before the petiole attachment. Petioles are long and slender—about 4 to 5 cm.

The Spring color is a spectacular bronze-red to purple-red. The bright green veins add a special effect. The leaves develop a rich green in Summer and then turn a rich carmine and crimson in the Fall.

The growth habit of this cultivar is vigorous. While some shoots may be ½ to 1 meter on fast-growing young plants, growth on older wood is much shorter. It does not grow upright but soon becomes a broad plant of 2 meters with gracefully cascading, pendulous branches, maturing at 4 meters.

This is a striking addition to the landscape but is not suitable for the small alpine or rock garden planting because it needs space to spread in order to display its unique "weeping" look.

A. palmatum 'Miyagino'

Fall color is the outstanding feature of this cultivar. It turns a crimson color which is flecked with gold or orange.

The leaves have 7 lobes with the two base lobes quite small and narrow. Each lobe is a narrow oblong, with the base gradually tapering to just the width of the midrib and the outer end gradually tapering to a long, narrow point. The lobes are widely separated and radiate outward. Bases of the lobes join only at the leaf center. The leaves are about 6 cm long and up to 7 cm across. Petioles are slender and about 3 cm long.

The green leaf holds good color all Summer and is pleasing in the landscape.

This is a medium-strong growing plant which becomes a wide, tall bush-type rather than a strongly-upright tree up to 4 meters.

A. palmatum 'Mure hibari'

The leaves of this cultivar are deeply divided into 7 lobes which are narrow elongate-lanceolate and taper to a long, slender point. Lobes separate to the center of the leaf and radiate sharply outward. The margins are deeply and prominently double-serrate. The edges of each lobe are slightly curved up, or trough-shaped. Leaf size is about 4 to 5 cm long and 5 to 6 cm wide. Petioles are 2 to 3 cm long.

The basic leaf color is a light green. Margins of new leaves are tinted with a bright brick-red. In the Fall, yellow to crimson blends appear.

This medium-strong grower forms an upright plant of 4 meters. It is quite vigorous and hardy.

One Japanese writer described the leaf shape as "like a crystal of snow" and unique. It is indeed a beautiful cultivar but is little known.

A. palmatum 'Nana segawa'

The leaves of this cultivar are deeply divided by seven lobes which radiate gently from the center. The lobes are elongate-ovate and terminate in a long, narrow, sharp point. The basal portion of the lobe narrows to 3 or 4 mm, making an open pattern to the leaf center. The margins are sharply toothed—sometimes double-serrate. The leaves measure 5 to 7 cm long and about 8 cm wide. The green petioles are about 2 cm long.

The Spring foliage opens with a crimson color which soon changes to purplish-red. In early Summer as the green tones begin to develop, the veins turn a contrasting green. By mid-Summer the entire leaf is greenish. The tree is bright crimson in Fall. It will reach 3 meters at maturity, growing as a tall, spreading bush.

A. palmatum 'Nicholsonii'

The best feature of this cultivar is its Fall coloration.

The leaves are seven-lobed and vary from 6 to 8 cm long and 7 to 8 cm wide. However, the leaf appears longer because the three center lobes are especially long and narrow. Each lobe is elongate-ovate and narrowed at the base. They join together about 1½ cm from the petiole. The margins are double-serrate with sharp points. The lobe terminates in a fine point. Petioles are red and about 3 cm long.

Spring foliage is a good red—slightly purple. A deep, rich green color develops during the Summer and is followed by the beautiful crimson of the Fall.

'Nicholsonii' is a medium-strong grower which reaches 2 to 3 meters in height and width and becomes multi-branched. This fairly hardy cultivar was first described by Schwerin in about 1893.

A. palmatum 'Mure hibari'

A. palmatum 'Nana segawa'

A. palmatum 'Nicholsonii'

A. palmatum 'Nomura nishiki'

The notable feature of this cultivar is the Fall coloration. The combinations of orange and red are very bright and pleasing. In the Spring the leaves unfold a bright red, suffused and shaded with green undertones. As the leaves mature, they become more green.

The leaves have five or seven lobes, widely separated almost to the center. They are elongate-ovate with a tapering point. The margins are faintly serrated. Leaves measure 5 to 6 cm both long and wide. The strong petioles are 4 cm long.

I have observed a 25 year-old tree here in Oregon which came from Henry Hohman. It has reached about 4 meters in that period of time.

A. palmatum 'Ogon sarasa'
(gold calico cloth)
Alternate spelling: 'Ogona sarasa'

The color combination and leaf shape identify this interesting plant. Early leaves have a brick-red color which blends over the deep green base color. It is not a sharp marking as in variegations, but appears as if the red were brushed over green. Each leaf will vary in intensity. Also, the green mid-veins are in sharp contrast to the darker lobe color. In mid-Summer, the leaves become solid green. The Fall colors are bright, in many shades of orange and crimson blends.

This is not a large-growing plant but forms a tall shrub as it matures at 4 meters.

A. palmatum 'Omurayama'

Each leaf of seven lobes is 6 to 8 cm long and 8 to 9 cm across, with a truncate base. It looks longer than this, for the three center lobes are large and long, and the two base lobes much smaller. The lobes are elongate-elliptical, gradually tapering to a narrow point. The bases are joined within 1 cm of the center. Lobes curve up from each side, forming a rounded trough-shape.

A. palmatum 'Omurayama'

'Omurayama' is an excellent example of the cascading type of palmatum. As it attains the height of a tall shrub or small tree, the pendulous branches become willowy and form a long curtain around the perimeter of the plant. This is not to be confused with the cascading form of the dissectum group which is always a low spreading shrub.

The leaf consists of seven long, slender lobes which are held closely together. The leaves are 7 to 8 cm long and spread to 7 cm. They tend to hang down, and the closed slender lobes emphasize the pendulous effect of the branches. Long slender petioles are 5 to 6 cm. Lobes are lanceolate or elongate-elliptical, tapering to a slender point. They separate almost to the center of the leaf. At the base they are less than 1 cm wide, making the leaf appear open in the center. The margins are deeply toothed with fine serrations between.

The new, unfolding foliage has a bright orange cast to the edges, but the leaves soon become a uniform brilliant green. Fall colors are quite spectacular gold and crimson combinations.

Young plants are vigorous and upright; later they show the true pendulous character. The long willowy shoots start upward, then bend out and down. The leaf nodes are quite far apart on this long, slender growth. At the same time enough shoots continue upward to give more height. A mature tree becomes quite rounded with long cascading side branches.

In 20 years the tree will reach 3 to 5 meters in height with a canopy spread of 4 to 5 meters.

A. palmatum 'Ōshū shidare'
Alternate spelling: 'Ohsiusidare,'
'Ohshiushidare,' 'Ohsyu shidare'

This old and famous cultivar has long been a favorite in Japan. It is attractive as a small, round-headed tree with cascading form. Pendulous branches form on the outside of the plant and descend gracefully to the ground. Mature trees will reach at least 3 meters but will be even broader.

The foliage is a strong purple-red or maroon. The seven lobes radiate markedly and are separate almost entirely to the center of the leaf. Each is elongate-lanceolate, narrow at the base and tapering to a long, slender tip. The margins are narrowly double-serrate. Leaves measure up to 7 cm long and 9 cm wide. Petioles are supple and 3 cm long. There is a greenish cast to the underside of the leaf. The Fall tones will develop into strong crimson.

This interestingly shaped cultivar is comparable to other pendulous forms such as 'Omurayama.' This is not, however, the type of cascading growth found in the dissectum group.

A. palmatum 'Ōshū shidare'

A. palmatum 'Sazanami'

The sharp-pointed foliage creates the unusual texture of this plant. The leaves are seven-lobed and rather small (3–4 cm long and wide.) Margins are distinctly small-toothed and sharp. Leaf lobes are separated over half the distance to the center. The base of the leaf is almost truncate, with petioles 1½ cm long.

The Spring color is an interesting light orange-red, with the center veins a contrasting very light green. The color becomes a rich green during the later Summer months. Fall colors are strong gold blends.

This is a rather slow-growing but hardy cultivar. It will form a large, compact bush-type, reaching 2 meters or more.

'Sazanami' is not common in collections at present but is a delightful plant for the effect of the leaf shape. The Japanese point out that the shade pattern of the leaves on the ground is most delightful.

A. palmatum 'Sazanami'

A. palmatum 'Sherwood Flame'

These beautiful leaves are a rich reddish-purple color similar to burgundy. This color remains very strong until the end of Summer, fading but very little to the red-green tones. It holds color better than most similar cultivars of this leaf type.

The leaves are seven-lobed. Each lobe divides entirely to the center of the leaf. They tend to hold together slightly so that the leaf appears longer than wide. The leaf measures 7 to 8 cm long and about 8 cm across. The lobes are an elongate-lanceolate, quite narrow at the base attachment, with the outer end tapering to a very long and sharp point. The edges are deeply and regularly incised. Petioles are red and 4 cm long.

A. palmatum 'Sherwood Flame'

This is a vigorous small tree which makes a pleasant round-topped form. The largest I have seen is about 4 meters high and 3 meters wide. Young plants grow rapidly at first, and then begin to broaden slightly and branch out. It is an excellent landscape specimen tree, adding color in the Spring and retaining the deep tones for the Summer.

This is almost identical to 'Burgundy Lace' during the Spring months. However, 'Sherwood Flame' will not fade and turn greenish-brown or bronze in mid-Summer. I have seen large plants of the two growing side by side at Wil-Chris Acres in Sherwood, Oregon, and by mid-Summer the contrast is quite noticeable.

This cultivar was selected and developed by Mr. Will Curtis of Wil-Chris Acres, Sherwood, Oregon, and was reportedly a seedling selection of 'Burgundy Lace.'

A. palmatum 'Shigure bato'

A. palmatum 'Shinonome'

A. palmatum 'Shigure bato' (late fall rain)

These beautiful leaves are seven-lobed, with the two base lobes very small. Each lobe is extremely elongate, broadened in the middle but gradually tapered to a very long, narrow tip. The base ¼ of the lobe quickly narrows to 2 or 3 mm wide as it joins at the petiole attachment. Tips of lobes tend to turn down. The margins are deeply and irregularly incised with serrations between. They almost approach the lobe shape of 'Palmatifidium' ('Washi no o,') but are not quite so incised.

Leaf measurement ranges from 4 to 6 cm long and 5 to 6 cm wide. The leaf has a very "feathery" appearance. The thin petioles are 2 to 4 cm long. The new foliage develops with a brilliant red tone which lasts into late Spring. During the Summer leaves turn green which is lighter under shade. Fall colors range from gold to crimson.

This is not a rapid-growing cultivar. Although it is upright, it will reach only 2 meters or less at maturity. It is tender and not easily propagated.

A. palmatum 'Shigurezome'

This cultivar is not widely known even though it has been listed since the early 1700's. However, it is still being propagated in Japan.

The leaves are seven-lobed, separated to within 1 cm of the center of the leaf. Each lobe is strongly ovate but ends with a long taper into a sharp tip. The margins are smooth to faintly serrate.

These are medium-sized leaves of 4 to 5 cm length and 6 cm width. The petioles are about 3 cm long and reddish brown.

Leaf color starts in the Spring as a bright purplish-red. As Summer progresses, it becomes green with a reddish cast to the tones. Fall colors are good reds. The small branches have a brown-red bark.

This is a hardy plant which grows erect but is not as tall a grower (4 meters) as other standard upright palmatums.

A. palmatum 'Shinonome'

The Spring foliage of this cultivar is a bright orange-red which turns a deeper red as it matures. These are very noticeable color tones when compared with other "red" cultivars. In the Summer the leaves become green with a deep red overtone. This accentuates the green of the mid-veins.

The leaves are 5 to 7 cm long and about 7 to 9 cm wide. The petioles are slender and red and 3 to 4 cm long. The seven lobes are separated completely into the center of the leaf. They are elongate-ovate, drastically narrower at the base than in the center. The outer end tapers to an elongated, sharp point. The inner third of the lobes have rather smooth margins, while the outer margins are markedly toothed or serrated. Young branches grow vigorously, and the leaf nodes are spaced far apart. It has an open habit of growth.

This is an erect plant which grows rapidly when young, but with age the shoots become shorter and more branched. It does not become a tall tree for a palmatum but will reach perhaps 3 or more meters.

It is not a well-known cultivar but offers a nice contrast when planted in large plantings. Well-grown container plants make a fine display.

A. palmatum 'Shiranami'

Although this cultivar is mentioned as far back as 1710, it is not well known or widely distributed.

The leaves are 7 (5) lobed, medium size, and deeply divided. Each lobe is elongate-ovate, constricted at the base, with the terminals tapering to an elongated point. Lobes unite less than 1 cm from the center attachment. The inward half of the margin is almost smooth, while the outer half is sharply toothed. Each lobe has a slight longitudinal upward roll from the mid-rib. The leaf is 7 to 8 cm long and about the same width, with the lobes radiating outward. Petioles are 1½ to 2 cm long.

Spring foliage is bright red with green undertones. This gradually changes to green during the Summer months. The Fall colors are tones of yellow.

This is not a rangy-growing plant but forms a tall bush with lateral branching to a height of 3 meters.

A. palmatum 'Shōjō nomura'

This little-known cultivar is a distinct color form of the 'Shōjō' and 'Nomura' *palmatums*. In early Spring, the foliage is a good purple-red. As the leaves mature in the Summer, there is an undertone of green, but it is strongly overshadowed with a bright orange-red. These tones are both solid and mottled and give the plant a distinctive appearance.

A. palmatum 'Suminagashi'

The leaf is divided almost entirely to the petiole attachment by seven lobes which radiate strongly. Each lobe is oblong-ovate, constricted at the base, and tapering to an elongate, sharp terminal. The margins are strongly incised, with fine serrations between. Leaves measure from 5 to 7 cm long and 6 to 9 cm across, with red petioles 3 cm long. This forms a rather cascading type of small tree up to 3 or 4 meters high.

This cultivar was sent to me only recently, and I have not found a full description of this particular form in literature.

A. palmatum 'Suminagashi'

This is a large-leafed cultivar. The lobes usually number seven (9). Two very small basal lobes sometimes appear on some of the largest leaves. Lobes are strongly elongate-ovate, dividing almost to the base, and are well separated. The lobe can vary from ½ cm at the base to 2 cm in the middle. The outer end tapers gradually to a thin, sharp point. The outer margins are double serrate; inner margins are smooth.

Leaves will range from 7 to 9 cm long and 10 to 12 cm spread at side points. The petioles are red and about 4 cm long.

The Spring color is a bright purple-red. As the leaves go into early Summer, they become almost a black-red or very deep maroon. From mid-Summer and into Fall, the colors gradually change to a deep green-red and brown-red. It holds color a little better when given afternoon shade. Fall tones are crimson.

This is a strong-growing cultivar, vigorous in growth, and semi-upright. It forms a small tree up to 4 meters high and is an excellent landscaping type.

A. palmatum 'Takinogawa'

This cultivar name has a confused status. It is applied to a cultivar of *A. palmatum* in several early references, including some with clear illustrations. However, I also find the name applied in certain early nursery catalogs to *A. japonicum*. In addition, specimen plant material has been sent to me from old collections in the Eastern United States and Europe, all of which are *A. japonicum*. I will describe the *A. japonicum* types under that species section. I consider the placement of this cultivar in *A. palmatum* as the better designation.

The colors of the seven-lobed leaves are distinct. The new foliage has a bright brick-red or rust color as a strong over-tone on the light-green leaf. This color develops best in the sun. Heavily-shaded plants will remain a light green. The color of the foliage stands out in contrast with other cultivars. During the Summer months, the intensity will diminish. In the Fall these colors take on a mottled pattern, and the reds will become stronger.

Lobes separate almost to the center of the leaf and are elongate-ovate, terminating in a long, narrow tip. The margins are finely serrated. The base of the leaf is truncate, and the petiole is 2 cm long and stiff. The leaves are 7 cm long and 8 to 9 cm wide and extend horizontally instead of hanging down.

This is a fairly hardy type plant which makes a round-headed, tall shrub to 4 meters when approaching maturity.

Refer to this name also in the japonicum section.

A. palmatum 'Tanabata'
(Festival of the Stars, July 7)

Because of similarity of name, this cultivar has occasionally been confused with 'Tana'. However, they are very different.

'Tanabata' foliage has seven lobes completely separated to the center of the petiole attachment. The lobes are elongate-elliptic, terminating in a long, narrow tip. The base of the lobe is extremely narrow, and the margins are serrated.

Leaves measure 5 to 6 cm long and are very slightly wider. The lobes tend to lie close together.

This is a bright purple-red type which becomes redder as the leaves mature in the Summer. Fall colors are strong, varied red tones.

The plant is a fairly strong grower which starts upright, but as it becomes older develops slightly pendulous outer branches, becoming 5 meters high and 5 meters wide.

Name similarity occasionally leads to clouding of a cultivar status. In this case, the names 'Tanabata' and 'Tana' are similar, while the plants 'Tana' and 'Saku' are similar. If careful records are not kept, these plants could easily become mixed.

A. palmatum 'Trompenburg'

This cultivar was selected at the Trompenburg Arboretum, Rotterdam, Holland, and is finding popularity wherever grown.

The unusual leaves are 7 to 9-lobed, 6 to 8 cm long and 9 to 12 cm across the widespread side tips. The lobes separate distinctly to within 1 cm of the center of the leaf. They radiate laterally and evenly from the petiole attachment, giving the appearance of fingers extended from a hand. Petioles are 2 to 3 cm long, stiff, and a good red color.

Each lobe is oblong-ovate. However, the edges roll down and under ¾ the length of the lobe, almost forming a tube. The remaining ¼ of the lobe flattens to display the prominent deep-serrated margin which is hidden in the curled-under portion. Lobes turn slightly downward on the outer end of the mature leaves. This extraordinary leaf gives an unusual and pleasing effect to the whole tree.

The color is also an outstanding feature. The foliage is a rich, deep purple-red. It lasts exceptionally well into late Summer. Even in full sun the leaves do not burn but later change to a deep reddish-green and

A. palmatum 'Trompenburg'

bronze. The Fall coloration of crimson completes a colorful year.

This is an upright-growing cultivar—strong but not unruly. The mother plant at the Trompenburg Arboretum shows a tendency to broaden as it grows older. The branches begin to extend laterally, with the finger-like leaves reaching outward and down. As it becomes more widely distributed, it will surely become a favorite for landscaping. I estimate its mature size to be 4 to 5 meters high and 3 to 4 meters wide.

A. palmatum 'Tsukubane'
(the ridge of Mt. Tsukubo)

These deeply-cut red leaves have seven lobes, divided about ⅔ the distance to the base of the leaf. In the center the lobes hold closely together but radiate out at the ends. Lobes are elongate-ovate, but taper to a long, slender terminal with edges regularly and delicately serrated. The base of the leaf is truncate. Leaves range from 4 to 8 cm long and 5 to 9 cm wide. The vigorous growth on newer shoots can produce even larger leaves. The petioles are 3 to 4 cm long. The thin leaves are almost translucent.

The Spring foliage is light red with a green cast to the center of the lobes. This quickly changes to a deeper brick-red tone, maturing as a deep greenish-red. The green mid-viens are quite prominent. By late Summer the leaves are rich green with a slight tint of dark red. Fall color is brilliant crimson.

A tall, upright-growing tree—fairly vigorous—it will branch sideways and form a broad-topped, small tree up to 5 meters at maturity.

This is not a widely-known cultivar but has distinct color tones to add to the landscape. It was popular in the early 1800's.

A. palmatum 'Tsuri nishiki'
Syn.: *A. palmatum euseptemlobum laciniatum* (Pax), *A. palmatum laciniatum*

The interesting leaves are 7-lobed, occasionally 5 or 9. Lobes are widely separated, almost entirely to the center of the leaf. They spread slightly and are sometimes twisted at various angles. The lobes are narrow, almost lanceolate, and terminate in a long, tapering, sharp point. The margins are conspicuously toothed or rough-serrated. Leaves vary widely from 7 to 12 cm long and 6 to 11 cm across, but the lobes are less than 1 cm wide. Petioles are 4 to 6 cm long.

The leaves are deep green with a light tinge of red on the margins. They become darker during the Summer months. The Fall colors are quite brilliant with yellow, orange-gold, and crimson blended together. The leaves are of firm texture and are not easily sunburned.

The twigs and branches develop an angular framework as the tree matures. It grows to a sturdy, short, hardy tree of 3 to 4 meters.

A. palmatum 'Tsuri nishiki'

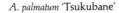

A. palmatum 'Tsukubane'

A. palmatum 'Ueno homare'

This is a small-leafed form of green palmatum. The bright green leaves are five-lobed and deeply separated to the center of the leaf. Each lobe is elongate-ovate, terminating in a long, slender tip. The margins are deeply toothed, with the finer serrations between giving a "feathery" appearance to the leaf. Leaves measure 4 to 5 cm long and wide. The stiff petioles are 3 cm long. The lobes do not extend uniformly but are on different planes, which gives a non-uniform appearance to the foliage.

This little-known cultivar was only recently added to the nursery, so I have not been able to evaluate it nor describe it fully. No reference has been found in literature which might expand the description.

A. palmatum 'Wou nishiki'

A. palmatum 'Yūgure'

A. palmatum 'Wou nishiki'

These interesting leaves are deeply divided into 7 (5) lobes which are widely separated. Each lobe is elongate-lanceolate and separated almost entirely to the center. The lobes taper from the center to a long, sharp terminal. The margins are deeply incised, almost pinnatifid, with light serrations between the deep cuts. The base of the leaf is cuneate. Leaves measure from 4 to 6 cm long and 5 to 6 cm wide. The reddish petioles are thin and 2 cm long.

New foliage is a bright—almost yellow-green. The margins of the leaves are strongly tinted with bright rose which shades into the leaf. The center of the lobes usually remain green. As the Summer progresses, the rose tints fade out, and the leaves become a bright, light green. They take full sun quite well but will bronze in extreme temperatures. The Fall color becomes variable bright crimson tones.

An upright-growing plant classed as a tall shrub of about 3 meters, it tends to be almost fastigiate and produces many small branches and twigs.

A. palmatum 'Yūgure'

This is an old cultivar which is found in Japanese literature as early as 1710.

The leaves have seven deeply separated lobes which are oblong-ovate, terminating in a short, sharp point. The inner ⅓ of the lobe constricts to only 5 mm wide. They unite about 1 cm from mid-leaf. Margins are lightly serrated. The leaves are 6 to 7 cm long and 8 to 9 cm wide, with 4 cm petioles.

The new foliage is crimson and later turns to a rust tone. In Summer, green tones are suffused into the reddish leaves. The Fall color becomes a variable red-crimson hue.

This is a hardy, upright form with quite slender branches. Young plants grow vigorously, but as they mature the growth rate slows and a 2 to 4 meter, round-topped tree is formed.

Unfortunately, there is confusion in this cultivar. I have received specimen materials from two nurseries and an arboretum, all of which are small-leafed, green palmatum type. This material must have been mistakenly labeled at one time. In fact, I believe it has resulted from understock overcoming the small original graft. Descriptions in old Japanese literature as well as more recent illustrations in their publications, leave little doubt about this reddish-leaf cultivar.

LINEARILOBUM GROUP

In this section I have placed the distinctive cultivars with the long, narrow lobes in the leaf. There are not many cultivars in this group, and several are identical though carrying different names. However, the leaf group is so distinctive it demands separate treatment. Both the green and red color forms are included.

A. palmatum 'Aka no hichi gosan'
  'Aka shime no uchi'
  See: 'Shime no uchi'

This is a synonym for 'Shime no uchi.' The name is quite descriptive. Thus: Aka = red, no = of, hichi = 7, go = 5, san = 3 (red leaves with 7, 5, and 3-lobed leaves). 'Shime no uchi' is an alternate way to read the Kanji writing of this name. 'Aka shime no uchi' emphasizes the red character of the leaf.

A. palmatum 'Aka shime no uchi,'
  'Aka no hichi gosan'
  See: 'Shime no uchi'

A. palmatum 'Ao no hichi gosan,'
  'Ao hichi gosan'
  See: 'Shino buga oka'

This literally means "green, 3–5–7 leaves."

A. palmatum 'Ao shime no uchi,'
  'Ao hichi gosan'
  See: 'Shino buga oka'

This cultivar is the green linearilobum counterpart of 'Aka shime no uchi.'

A. palmatum 'Ao shime no uchi shidare'

This plant is quite similar to 'Shino buga oka' except that it is more pendulous in habit. The branches tend to droop and give a round bush effect in contrast to the other members of the linearilobum group which tend to be upright.

The deep green leaves are mostly 7-lobed, each lobe very long and narrow like a blade of grass. Lobes are about 3 to 5 mm wide and up to 8 cm long. They turn yellow in the Fall, sometimes to a deep gold.

There are many cultivars of the linearilobum group which are quite similar but show fine differences. All are finely separated in their characteristics but overlap in description. A single leaf from one plant could appear to belong to another cultivar. It is necessary to observe the entire plant to see the differences.

A. palmatum linearilobum 'Atrolineare'. Greenish Summer tones replace the red leaves of Spring.

A. palmatum linearilobum 'Atrolineare'
  Syn.: *A. palmatum linearilobum atropurpureum, A. palmatum filifera purpurea*

One of the red forms of the linearilobum group.

The foliage is dark, black-red when in its prime in the early season. It may "bronze" out later in the season, especially in full sun. The leaf has five lobes, widely separated, very narrow, and separate completely to the base, joining at the petiole. The center vein is green. Lobes of leaves on mature wood are 7 to 9 cm long. Each lobe is 2 to 5 mm wide. Foliage on current year wood is much more coarse. The leaves may be even semi-palmate on vigorous new shoots. Leaf lobes may be 1 to 1½ cm wide and 9 to 10 cm long. As the wood matures, the foliage takes the characteristic "string-like" lobe shape.

It has an upright-growing small form and is quite twiggy. It might be classed as a tall shrub rather than a small tree, reaching a height of 3 meters. A very desirable form, contrasting with the more round-headed types of cultivars in the linearilobum group, such as 'Red Pygmy' and 'Villa Taranto.'

Refer to 'Shime no uchi' for taxonomic discussion.

A. palmatum 'Filifera purpurea'
See: *A. palmatum linearilobum*
'Atrolineare'

We carry this cultivar in our collection under this separate name. However, we are quite certain that it is identical with *A. palmatum linearilobum* 'Atrolineare'. Henry Hohman carried it in his collection under this name, but in the last lists he sent me he did not list 'Atrolineare.' He may have considered them synonymous also.

A. palmatum 'Koto no ito'

This cultivar approaches the linear-leaf form of palmatum. The leaves have 5 (7) narrow lobes of rich green color. They are lanceolate, gradually tapering to an elongate, sharp point with margins almost smooth. Their length is normally about 5 to 7 cm, and the radiating lobes spread about 8 cm. On mature wood and small twigs, leaves are much finer; while on new growth some leaves exceed these measurements, and the lobes are much wider. Petioles are fairly short for the leaf—about 2 to 3 cm. New leaves unfold with crimson tones but soon turn green. The leaf base is almost truncate with the lower lobes extending straight out.

Although an upright-growing form, it does not exceed 3 meters in very old plants. It usually makes a tall shrub of 2 meters in 10 to 15 years. As it is densely branched, it can become twiggy. The bark is a good bright green. Fall colors range through the various shades of yellow. This plant is hardy.

A. palmatum form *linearifolium*
See: *A. palmatum* form *linearilobum*

A. palmatum form *linearilobum*
Syn.: *linearifolium*

This is a form of the species from which such cultivars as 'Ao hichi gosan,' 'Shino buga oka,' and 'Koto no ito' have been selected. While in many cases it is treated with cultivar status, I believe it is botanically proper to refer to it as a form of the species.

The green leaves are usually 7 (5) lobed. Each lobe is a long, narrow, strap-like section of the leaf, normally from ½ to 1 cm wide. Each leaf is separated entirely to the center and petiole attachment. The center lobe is usually 5 to 8 cm long, depending on the vitality of the plant and the age of the wood on which the leaf is growing. New shoots often have larger leaves, and the lobes broaden non-typically. Petioles are about 4 cm long.

These are upright plants. Old specimens may reach 4 meters—perhaps more. They tend to become twiggy in older age but will respond well to pruning and shaping.

Some authors regard 'Scolopendrifolium' as a synonym, while others disagree. I tend not to agree, for all the 'Scolopendrifolium' I have seen as older plants have much broader lobes on the leaves. Also, I note that 'Scolopendrifolium' growing in several locations in the United States tends to be more vigorous. Some arboreta carry this form under the name *linearifolium*.

Refer to 'Shime no uchi' for taxonomic discussion.

A. palmatum linearilobum atropurpureum
(*A. palmatum linearilobum purpureum*)
See: *A. palmatum linearilobum*
'Atrolineare'

A. palmatum 'Koto no ito'

A. palmatum, form *linearilobum*

A. palmatum 'Red Pygmy'

This is one of the cultivars of the linearilobum group. The red or bright red-maroon leaves are 7 (5) lobed. Each lobe is a long strap-like section of the leaf measuring from 5 to 9 cm long but only 2 to 4 mm wide along the entire length. The lobes separate entirely to the center of the petiole attachment. The total spread of all lobes forming the leaf is 10 to 14 cm from tip to tip. The petioles are 2 to 3 cm long. The entire effect of these delicate leaves is lace-like. On one and two-year old wood of a vigorous tree the leaf size is large and the lobes are broad with toothed margins, while leaves on older wood tend to be quite a bit smaller.

It should be noted that on current year wood, when the growth is vigorous, the leaves almost approach the typical palmatum form. Some people think the cultivar is reverting and prune off this vigorous growth, which is a mistake for it produces typical cultivar foliage the next season.

The Spring and early Summer coloration of red-maroon holds quite well through the hot weather. In late Summer it deepens into a more purplish tone. In direct sun it will "bronze" somewhat late in the season. However, the color holds much better and sunburns less than the older standard cultivar 'Atrolineare.'

I saw the mother plants at Firma C. Esveld in Boskoop, Holland, where D. M. VanGelderen originally recognized the value of this form. He named, propagated, and introduced it into the European trade. It was awarded a Certificate of Merit in 1969.

Older plants tend to broaden and become round-topped rather than upright and rangy as do other forms of linearilobum such as 'Atrolineare.' Some 20 to 25 year old plants are 1½ to 2 meters across and less than 2 meters high.

This is an excellent cultivar, superior to 'Atrolineare.' I believe it will increase in popularity as it becomes more widely known. It makes a delightful contrast in shape and tone when combined with other forms.

A. palmatum 'Scolopendrifolium'

These large leaves appear delicate because of the five long, narrow lobes. The lobes are only ½ to 1 cm wide in the middle. They narrow markedly at the base, and the outer end tapers gradually to a long point. Margins rarely serrate but are faintly

A. palmatum 'Red Pygmy'

irregular. Leaves vary from 7 to 8 cm long. The five lobes tend to close together slightly and make the leaf about 10 cm wide. Petioles are 3 cm long and reddish on top.

The bright green foliage has a soft tone until Fall when strong yellow colors appear.

This is a strong-growing, upright tree. Very old specimens will reach about 5 meters. It can become twiggy inside, but the plant still remains an open, round-topped type.

I find some authors group 'Scolopendrifolium' with 'Linearilobum,' while other separate them. In 1902 Pax had them completely separate. The lobes are normally wider in 'Scolopendrifolium' than

A. palmatum 'Scolopendrifolium'

in 'Linearilobum.' Also, the lobe number is usually five in the former and seven or more in the latter. 'Scolopendrifolium' seems to be the more vigorous plant.

The common names used in retail nurseries in the United States are "strap-leaf" and "finger-leaf" maple.

A. *palmatum* 'Scolopendrifolium rubrum'

This is the red form of the narrow-lobed palmatum. The color is quite good in Spring and early Summer and then turns a bronzy red-green later in the season. Fall colors are reddish.

Not as strong-growing as its green counterpart 'Scolopendrifolium,' it makes an upright, tall bush of up to 2 meters, which becomes rather twiggy.

The leaves are five-lobed (rarely 7) with the base lobes very small. They range from 6 to 8 cm long and about 9 cm between points of side lobes. Each lobe is long and slender, the center being only ½ to 1 cm at the broadest point. The base is even narrower than the middle, and the outer end tapers to a long, slender but rather blunt point. Petioles are about 3 cm long, red, and fairly stiff.

There may be some questions as to synonymity with 'Filifera purpurea.' The differences in lobe number and width give me reason to doubt that they are identical.

A. palmatum 'Scolopendrifolium rubrum'

A. *palmatum* 'Shime no uchi'
Syn.: 'Aka no hichi gosan',
'Aka shime no uchi'

The long, narrow lobes of the linearilobum type are deep red, or purple-red, in the Spring and early Summer. In the full sun of late Summer the leaves turn reddish-green or bronze. Crimson color tones dominate in the Fall.

Leaves have 3, 5, or 7 lobes, but usually 5. They are from 5 to 7 cm long and about 6 cm wide. Each lobe is rarely over ½ to 1 cm wide. Juvenile foliage has much wider lobes. Margins are slightly serrate. Petioles are about 3 cm long.

This cultivar grows more slowly than the similar 'Atrolineare.' The Japanese state that 'Shime no uchi' rarely exceeds 1 meter in height, but I find it grows a little taller than this. It has an upright but twiggy growth habit.

Koidzumi assigns the name 'Shime no uchi' to the entire subvariety status, *linearilobum*, of the variety *palmatipartitum*.

If this is followed with fidelity, the separation of cultivars and forms would be as follows:

subvariety *linearilobum* = 'Shime no uchi'
  form *lineare* (*linearilobum, linearifolium* of some authors), green foliage.
  'Shino buga oka', Syn.: 'Ao hichi gosan', 'Ao no hichi go san', 'Ao shime no uchi'
  form *atro-lineare* ('Atrolineare') red foliage.
  'Aka shime no uchi',
  Syn.: 'Aka no hichi gosan'

In the nursery trade in Japan, the major reference of 'Shime no uchi' is to the "red" linear-leaf form as an inclusive name.

A. palmatum 'Shime no uchi'

A. palmatum 'Shino buga oka'
Syn.: 'Ao no hichi gosan',
'Ao shime no uchi'

The leaves are the long, slender-lobed form of *linearilobum*. The foliage is 3, 5, or 7-lobed, usually 5. Juvenile foliage has rather broad lobes. Each lobe is "strap-like" and not more than ½ to 1 cm wide. The leaves are 5 to 7 cm long and about 6 cm wide. The lobes tend to hang down, giving a cascading appearance. The margins may be smooth or lightly toothed. Petioles are 2 to 3 cm long.

The bright green foliage holds color well all season. As Fall approaches, the color changes to a pleasant yellow.

This is an upright-growing plant but not tall. It rebranches readily to form twiggy growth. In good cultural situations, it can reach 2 meters or more. It is well adapted to container growing for the patio as it is a shrub type which is easily shaped. It also provides interesting effects when used in bonsai culture.

A. palmatum 'Villa Taranto'

This excellent cultivar is a recent introduction from Europe, named after the Villa Taranto in Italy. It was propagated and introduced by Firma C. Esveld of Boskoop, Holland.

The leaves are normally five-lobed. Each lobe is the long, narrow, parallel-sided form of *linearilobum*. Lobes are rarely more than 5 mm wide, except for foliage on fast-growing new shoots. Leaves measure 7 to 9 cm long and 8 to 10 cm between the ends of the side lobes. The center lobes are longest and create a total lacy effect. The stiff petioles are 2 to 3 cm long. The margins of the lobes are smooth.

A. palmatum 'Shino buga oka'

The bright tones of the foliage are green, with a light reddish overtone creating an unusual color effect. I was impressed by the brilliance of the older stock plants which I saw in Holland. It is unique in color and is between the green and the purple forms of the *linearilobum* cultivars. In the Fall our specimen plants turn a pleasing gold.

This is a hardy cultivar which will not become a fastigiate tree but rather a dome-shaped plant of 2–3 meters. Its growth habit is very similar to 'Red Pygmy.'

A. palmatum 'Villa Taranto'

DWARF GROUP

Most of the cultivars represented here belong to the "yatsubusa" group. This term is used in Japanese horticulture to denote the slow-growing or compact varieties and cultivars of plants.

Some are variegated, most are green-leafed, but I include here mainly those which mature at about 1 meter or less. They are also characterized by having the leaf nodes closely arranged on the twigs and usually tending toward profuse multi-branching. This usually results in plants which are rather dense.

A. palmatum 'Beni komachi'

A. palmatum 'Beni maiko'

A. palmatum 'Beni komachi'
(the red, beautiful little girl)

This is a dwarf type plant with very unusual leaves of brilliant red. Each leaf is five-lobed, separated entirely to the center—almost to the petiole attachment. The lobes extend widely and openly, the basal two extending backward. Each lobe is long and narrow, lanceolate, but not parallel-sided. The outer half gradually narrows to a very sharp terminal. The margins are irregularly but markedly toothed or incised. Lobes curl sideways, or down, or both. The sides of the lobes bend slightly upward, almost forming a shallow trough at times.

The overall leaf measurements vary from 3 to 5 cm long and wide on the smaller foliage to 5 to 7 cm on the larger leaves. However, even though the lobe may be as much as 3 to 5 cm long, it is never wider than 3 to 5 mm.

The new foliage, which is delicate-appearing at first, is a bright crimson. The intense color begins to darken as the leaf matures, and older foliage is a greenish-red. The margins remain edged in crimson. In the Fall the colors again become a scarlet tone.

The growth is fine, never gross, and mostly of a multi-branched, twiggy nature. Occasionally long shoots occur, adding height to the plant. However, the total growth is short and lacy and forms a small bush. Mature plants are up to 1 meter tall.

This is a very choice plant, not widely known as yet, and rather difficult to propagate.

A. palmatum 'Beni maiko'
(red, a dancing girl)

This is one of the very brilliant, scarlet-red small palmatum types. As the foliage unfolds in the Spring, it is a fire-red or scarlet tone. As they mature, the leaves appear rather thin in texture and fade into a pinkish-red with a very slight green undertone. During the Summer the foliage becomes a greenish red with the main veins remaining red as do the petioles.

The leaves are irregular, even though typically five-lobed palmate. Each lobe separates about half way to the center and tapers to a blunt point. Margins of the lobe are serrate. Lobes tend to curve sideways. Smaller leaves on the plant tend to be even more irregular and more intense in coloration. Mature leaves measure from 3 to 6 cm in length and width. Petioles are 1 cm long.

While classed as a dwarf type, this plant will occasionally produce shoots up to 60 cm long. Older growth tends to remain multibranching and rather bushy. I would not expect old plants to exceed 1½ to 2 meters.

This can be compared with other brilliant scarlet types, such as 'Shindeshōjō.' I feel it is not quite as brilliant. However, the irregular leaf shape adds to the interest. In Japan it is classed as more brilliant than such cultivars as 'Chishio' and 'Seigai.'

This is an exciting plant, especially when planted with contrasting foliage plants. Very adaptable to container culture.

A. palmatum 'Chiba'
  See: *A. palmatum* 'Kashima'

This is a "yatsubusa" or dwarf form of palmatum.

A. palmatum 'Chichibu'
  See: 'Kotohime'

This is one of the very dwarf forms of palmatum.

A. palmatum 'Coonara Pygmy'

Our Australian friends have selected an excellent little dwarf form which they have named 'Coonara Pygmy.' This was selected by Mr. Arnold Teese, Yamina Rare Plants, Victoria, Australia. I place this in the group termed "yatsubusa" along with the other dwarf palmate leaf forms.

It is a beautiful little selection with bright green leaf tones. The leaves vary, as do most yatsubusa, having very tiny leaves on older wood and larger (more palmate) leaves on the new shoots. On mature wood the leaf nodes are very close together, creating a dense cover of foliage along the twigs. The tendency to multi-branching adds to the compact formation of foliage clusters. The twigs and branches are thin but stiff.

Most leaves on the old wood measure about 2 cm in length and width. New growth produces foliage 3 to 4 cm across. The leaf is five-lobed and is rather typically palmate. The lobe is broad-ovate, acuminate, with a sharp tip. The margins are incised—sometimes bluntly so.

This forms a small, round bush and is a fine addition to the dwarf series of palmatums.

I found it of particular interest that we were able to exchange scions for grafting during the growing seasons. Since it is mid-Summer in January for Mr. Teese, and mid-Winter for me, getting propagating material at the proper time seemed a problem. However, Mr. Teese sent a few terminal shoots, 2 to 5 cm long, in full leaf which he had cut during the summer "resting period" following the first flush of growth. I grafted the first of February, and the plants all put out two more growth periods that season. Indeed, that must have seemed like a long year to those plants!! Grafting in July with dormant scions from Australia would probably have worked as well but would have given the new plants only a short half-season.

A. palmatum 'Goshiki kotohime'

A. palmatum 'Goshiki kotohime'
  (a multi-colored form of "dwarf old harp"—an endearing term)

This beautiful little plant is the variegated form of the excellent dwarf 'Kotohime.' The basic color of the foliage is a rich green with each leaf varying in amount of variegation. Some are completely marked with tiny flecks or speckles; others are solid green. The markings are always minute, often overlapping, and are white, cream, light yellow, pink, and red. The individual tones are subdued, but the total effect is quite brilliant in the Spring. The newest growth tips are often quite pink as they develop but soon assume the normal variegation. As the Summer approaches, the leaves take on a darker green color.

The foliage is quite small for palmatums, measuring 2 to 3 cm long and wide. Each leaf has five lobes radiating outward and divided ⅔ toward the base. The lobes are wide at the base, tapering quickly to a sharp point. The margins are incised. The leaves are not flat but are irregular, falcate, or slightly crinkled.

A. palmatum 'Coonara Pygmy'

98

Leaves measure 2 to 3 cm in length and are 2½ to 3½ cm across the two side points. Petioles are very slender and 1 to 2 cm long. Leaves on older wood are always smaller. Vigorously grown plants produce larger foliage.

As they open, the new leaves are a very light yellow-green with margins a brick or rust color, thus making the new growth very noticeable. Fall colors are mostly in the yellow tones.

This is a very shrubby grower as are all the yatsubusa group. It is difficult to predict the size on maturity for this depends upon fertility and culture. It can be forced in the landscape or retarded in container or bonsai. We have seen a specimen of this cultivar which was probably 20 years old and over a meter high. But, we have had this same cultivar in a container for 10 years, and it is only about 40 cm tall and wide.

'Kashima' lends itself very well to rock garden culture. As do other similar yatsubusa forms, it takes well to shaping and pruning. It is hardy and sturdy, and will tolerate some drought when reduced growth is desired.

A. palmatum 'Katsura'

A. palmatum 'Katsura'
(a wig)
Syn.: 'Katsura yatsubusa'

This delightful dwarf form is quite striking in its Spring growth. As the leaves develop, they are pale yellow-orange. The margins shade into a brighter orange. The color is difficult to describe accurately, but it is rather bright. As the season progresses, the leaves turn into a rich green. Fall colors are bright yellow and orange tones.

'Katsura' is a small-leafed cultivar with most leaves about 3 cm in both dimensions. Occasionally on vigorous new growth individual leaves will reach a length of 4½ cm. The five lobes are lanceolate, tapering to a long point. The division between lobes almost approaches the center but retains a small center area before the 1 to 1½ cm petiole attaches. Sides of the lobes are shallowly toothed. The center lobe always is longer, and the leaves tend to turn downward, giving a distinct appearance to the plant.

This is a small growing form with the leaf nodes and twigs quite close together so that the foliage is dense. The upright growth will quickly broaden with side branching. It will not attain a height of more than 1½ meters at maturity. Repeated pruning will make a more compact plant. It adapts well to bonsai culture.

A. palmatum 'Kiyohime'
Syn.: 'Kiyohime yatsubusa'

Although its leaves are quite small, 'Kiyohime' has foliage slightly larger than some of the others in the yatsubusa group. Leaves on a vigorous plant reach 4 cm long on the middle lobe and 3 cm across the points of the side lobes.

Each leaf is five-lobed with the center lobe being noticeably longer. Lobes are ovate-lanceolate, tapering back from the wide point to the base where all lobes join, a distance of ¾ into the center of the leaf. Lobes point sharply, and the margins are toothed. Lobes tend to turn downward, making a slightly falcate form. Petioles are a rich green and 1 to 2 cm long.

A. palmatum 'Kiyohime'

Early Spring leaves are beautiful. The edges are tinged in an orange-red which is lightly and delicately shaded into the center of the light green leaf. The rich green foliage dominates the Spring season. Fall colors run into the yellow-orange range following a Summer of rich green.

Of the several yatsubusa types, 'Kiyohime' probably will grow more vigorously than other forms. Yet in containers and bonsai culture, it will dwarf down as well as the others. Side-branching ability is good on the shoots, especially with some pinching back of Spring growth. This is a sturdy, vigorous plant. For landscaping it is valuable as a dwarf with a little more size and vigor than some others. It would be possible to obtain a 2 meter bush in about 10 years. It grows densely and forms a roundish bush. Rarely do they put up a strong center leader but rather branch and rebranch.

A. palmatum 'Kotohime'
　　Syn.: 'Tokyo yatsubusa,' 'Chichibu,'
　　'Chichibu yatsubusa,'
　　'Kotohime yatsubusa'

This is one of the smallest leaf-forms of the palmatums. On mature wood many of the leaves will only be 1 to 1½ cm long and wide. On newer wood they may reach dimensions of 3 cm.

These leaves have five lobes, although much of the time they appear to have only three as the two basal lobes almost disappear. The center lobe is always prominent, with the two side lobes angling outward. The lobes are ovate, bluntly acuminate, with margins deeply toothed (for the size of the lobe). Petioles are very short, less than 1 cm—often 2 mm.

The new leaves often come out a bright rose or orange-red. This is heaviest on the edge of the leaves and shades into the light green of the center. Mature foliage is a bright, light green. Fall colors are the light tones of yellow blended with orange.

This is a sturdy little plant for its type. It tends to grow upright with much side-branching which rounds out the shape. Each branch will send out side branches in profusion so that it becomes quite dense. The leaf nodes are spaced very close together, thus giving a dense cover of leaves.

'Kotohime' is useful planted along with other yatsubusa forms in such special places as alpine gardens. It is also popular with bonsai specialists and can be trained into a very tight bun shape. In bonsai containers there will be a profusion of delightfully small leaves.

A. palmatum 'Mikawa yatsubusa'

The leaves on this little dwarf overlay each other like shingles on a roof. They are of light green color, paler when first unfolding, and are of thin texture. The outer leaves have very bright red tips on the fine serrations of the margins.

The leaves are 4 to 6 cm long and 5 to 6 cm wide. The seven lobes are separated ⅔ the distance to the center. Each is oblong-ovate, with a long, tapering point. The margins of the lobes are finely incised. The base of the leaf is truncate or sub-cordate, making all the lobes point "forward."

The leaf nodes are very close together, and the new shoots are very short and stubby. This makes for a very dense leaf covering on the twigs. The growth is multi-branched, forming a compact little plant.

This dwarf cultivar has slightly larger leaves than other yatsubusa forms.

A. palmatum 'Kotohime'

A. palmatum 'Mikawa yatsubusa'

A. palmatum 'Mizu kuguri'

The Spring color of this cultivar is unusual for the palmatums. The undercolor is light green, but the entire leaf has an over-shading of a pinkish-rose to a light brick-red color. The effect is not harsh but a rather gentle over-all brushing of color. Later in the season the leaf tones proceed into a deeper green.

The typical palmate leaves are 7-lobed and regular in shape. Edges have fine, sharp-toothed margins. The lobes are ovate but taper to an elongated, narrow tip. Leaves measure 5 to 7 cm long and 6 to 8 cm wide. The petioles are 1½ to 2 cm in length.

This becomes a bushy plant rather than a tall tree form, reaching 3 meters.

A. palmatum 'Murasaki kiyohime'

A. palmatum 'Ryūzu'

A. palmatum 'Murasaki hime'

As the name implies, this is a dwarf, purple-leafed cultivar. This plant grows to a rounded shrub, probably not exceeding 1 meter.

The leaves are 5 to 7-lobed, divided almost to the center. Each lobe is oblong-lanceolate, terminating in a long, slender tip. The inner margins are smooth, while the outer half is sharply toothed, each tooth finely serrated. Leaves measure 5 to 6 cm long and wide.

The color of deep purple shades to a green-red inside the plant where shaded. Color tones vary within the plant. This cultivar seems a little delicate and not vigorous.

A. palmatum 'Murasaki kiyohime'

Another of the dwarf cultivars in the "yatsubusa" group, this plant is most desirable but not widely known.

The foliage is deeply divided into five lobes which radiate openly from the center. The base is almost truncate. Each lobe is lanceolate, tapering to an elongate, sharp terminal. The margins are incised on the outer half of the length, smooth within. Lobes separate almost entirely to the center of the leaf. The center lobe is very prominent, especially in the new leaves where it is often dominant. Mature leaves measure 3 to 5 cm long and 4 to 5 cm wide. The foliage is often smaller than this, especially in container culture.

The new foliage is a very light yellow-green but heavily marked around the margins with a broad area of bright purple-red. This is heaviest on the edges, shading gradually into the leaf blade. As the leaves mature, they become a solid green. Often there is a very light speckling of minute white markings within the green. Fall colors become gold or blends of orange.

As a dwarf type, it is not a vigorous grower although it is hardy. It tends to be multi-branched and twiggy, as are most of this type. It is excellent for alpine plantings, container growing, and bonsai culture. It tends to be upright, reaching heights of 1 meter as it gets older.

A. palmatum 'Ryūzu'
(dragon's head—ornament)
Syn.: 'Tatsugashira'

This delightful dwarf is a compact little shrub which is popular for bonsai as well as for rockery plantings. The leaf nodes are closely spaced on the twigs, and it forms a multi-branched structure. The leaves are tightly spaced and overlapping.

The new leaves have a faint shade of pink overlaying the pale green. This soon disappears, and the mature leaf is light green. The margins are very prominently serrated. The tips of these serrations are often bright brick-red, but the color does not come into the leaf. The texture of the leaf is rather thin.

The leaf has five (occasionally seven) lobes which radiate openly. When seven-lobed, the two base lobes are very small. Each lobe is ovate, but gradually tapers to a long, sharp point. The edges of the lobes bend slightly upward, almost making a shallow trough. The leaf measures 3 or 4, occasionally 5 cm long and broad. The stiff petioles are only about 1 cm long.

It may reach 1 meter at maturity.

A. *palmatum* 'Sekka yatsubusa'
Syn.: 'Yatsubusa Sekka'

As in other yatsubusa types, the leaves of this cultivar are quite small. 'Sekka' differs from others in having narrower lobes. The five lobes are ovate with a gradually tapering tip. The lobes are separated almost to the leaf center. The margins are very lightly serrated, and the tiny tip of each serration turns slightly upward. Often the two base lobes are so small that the leaves appear only three-lobed. Leaf size is from 2 to 3 cm long and 3 to 5 cm wide since the side lobes extend sharply outward. Petioles are 1 to 2 cm long.

This dwarf plant has a deep green color. The new growth is edged with rust color. It takes full sun quite well. The Fall colors range into the yellow tones.

The leaf nodes are close together, and the foliage is rather bunched. New growth is fine but not willowy, short, and multi-branched. It is hardy and offers another choice of small shrub for rock gardens, bonsai, and small plantings. This cultivar is not widely known or easily propagated.

A. *palmatum* 'Tamahime'
Syn.: 'Yatsubusa Tamahime'

The tiny leaves of this dwarf are a light green as they unfold, soon becoming a rich green. The green color holds well into the Fall, when red, crimson, and some yellow leaves appear. This is a good form for Fall color. The leaves are rather lustrous from Summer into Fall.

The five-lobed leaves are 3 to 4 cm long and wide and of thin texture. Lobes are ovate, terminating in an abrupt tip. The margins are toothed and, at times, prominent for so small a leaf. Lobes

separate over half way to the base. Red petioles are quite short—1 to 2 cm long.

This is a compact-growing, multi-branched, small form of yatsubusa. It is popular for bonsai work. Leaves can be reduced to less than 1 cm with repeated pinching and other bonsai cultural methods.

A. *palmatum* 'Tatsugashira'
See: 'Ryūzu'

A. *palmatum* 'Sekka yatsubusa'

A. *palmatum* 'Tamahime'

A. palmatum 'Tsukomo'

A. palmatum 'Tsukomo'

This delightful dwarf can only be termed "stubby." Even young plants will grow only 5 to 10 cm per year. Older plants grow 5 cm or less on the terminals. The leaf placement is very thick since the buds are closely arranged on the shoots. It is multi-branching and makes a dense, dwarf mound 1 meter high. The stems are very stiff and upright.

The bright green foliage is five-lobed, some with very tiny pairs of base lobes. The new leaves unfold a bright, "rusty"-red. As the leaves are more developed, they become a light red-green, maturing to a rich, deep green. This effect is quite beautiful as the shoots develop, and all these color phases appear from the terminal to the base. In the Fall the yellow gold tones are very strong.

The leaf lobes are ovate, but gradually taper to an elongated tip. The margins are sharply double-serrate and conspicuous. The entire leaf tends to stick out stiffly laterally. The stiff petioles are 1 to 2 cm long and green. Leaves vary from 3 cm long and wide to as much as 6 cm. On young plants, the large leaves form on the lower half of the current growth. Leaves on the older wood are always smaller.

This is a very choice and delightful dwarf. It is extremely difficult to propagate, and new grafts grow very slowly.

A. palmatum 'Yatsubusa'
Alternate spelling: 'Yatsufusa'

'Yatsubusa' is included here as a cultivar since the name has been used in this manner for many years. In proper use, however, "yatsubusa" is a Japanese botanical designation for "dwarf." There are "yatsubusa" in species of other genera. This could be compared to our term "dissectum" embracing all the selections and cultivars of this type. There are many named clones of "yatsubusa" which are therefore designated with the cultivar status, such as 'Kotohime yatsubusa.'

I have seen several types of plants labeled 'Yatsubusa' in various collections and arboreta. These vary in the size of plant, leaves, and rate of growth, although each is truly a "yatsubusa."

Palmatum "yatsubusas" may be generally described as:

Small size leaves which are 5 to 7-lobed, typically palmate. The lobes are short ovate, usually separated about half the distance to the center of the leaf. The lobes terminate in a sharp point, and the margins are usually distinctly serrate. The leaves will measure from 2 to 4 cm long and about as wide. The center lobe is usually more prominent. Petioles are stiff and 1 cm long.

The basic leaf color is light green. The new foliage unfolds with a shading of red along the margins, which is rather typical of many green palmatum seedlings. This red soon fades out into the solid green of Summer. Fall colors are a mixture of yellows or reds, sometimes on the same plant.

The "yatsubusa" group all form small, compact, shrub-like individuals. Some selections grow more upright, while others tend to grow laterally. All selections are popular for bonsai work, having the dwarf character as well as the ability to produce large numbers of tiny side branches, thus making a dense plant.

I have seen 10 to 12 year-old "yatsubusa" which were almost 1½ meters tall with fairly coarse leaves, along with plants of equal age which were less than half that size in leaf and plant structure. Both belong in "yatsubusa."

A. palmatum 'Yatsubusa'

VARIEGATED GROUP

In this section are grouped all the cultivars with foliage containing variegations of color. In most cases this feature is evident in the Spring and Summer foliage. Also included are those few cultivars which variegate only in the Fall. Most of these plants are upright-growing and of medium height, although those like 'Versicolor' reach full tree height of 8 meters.

I have omitted the variegated dwarfs and dissectums which are in their respective sections.

A. palmatum 'Aka shigitatsu sawa'

A. palmatum 'Aka shigitatsu sawa'
  Syn.: 'Beni shigitatsu sawa'

This is the red-tinged form of 'Reticulatum' or 'Shigitatsu sawa.' The leaves, however, have the lobes slightly longer and more deeply separated than in 'Shigitatsu sawa.' The leaves are 7 (9) lobed and separate ⅔ the distance to the center. They are elongated and taper to a sharp point. Leaves are 4 to 6 cm long and 6 to 9 cm wide. The leaves on young growth may be much larger. The margins of lobes are wavy and sharply toothed.

As the new buds first open, the bud-sheaths and new leaves are maroon. When fully opened, the typical leaf has quite dark veins with all inter-spaces the light basic yellow green of 'Shigitatsu sawa.' The entire leaf is strongly overtoned with pink or red, however, which is the feature of this cultivar. This color holds very well into the Summer when the whole leaf darkens somewhat and develops a strong green tone within. Clearance between lobes is rather wide.

This is not as strong a growing plant as its green counterpart. It will become a tall shrub, somewhat brushy (3 meters). It is hardy, but it does not propagate easily. It is rather rare in nurseries and collections. It makes a very interesting specimen plant because of the unusual color form and combination.

A. palmatum albo marginatum (Pax)
  See: *A. palmatum* 'Matsugae'

A. palmatum 'Aocha nishiki'
  (yellow green brocade)
  Syn.: 'Seicha'

Usually listed with the variegated types, I find this cultivar to be rather "shy" in its display of color. Our stock plant is reticent about producing markedly variegated leaves. Older plants I saw in Europe were not strong in variegation either.

A. palmatum 'Asahi zuru'

The medium-size leaves are of pale green tone and measure 5 cm to 6 cm wide and are slightly longer. The 5 to 7 lobes graduate to a sharp point and separate about half the distance to the center of the leaf. The variegations are creamy yellow and in small sections on the leaf. Occasionally the light areas occupy almost the entire leaf. However, most of the leaves are not variegated.

This plant will eventually form a short, broad tree of nearly 2 meters. It is not a strong, vigorous grower and is not a bold plant in the landscape.

A. palmatum 'Aokii'
  See: 'Versicolor'

A. palmatum 'Argenteo marginatum'

This is another example of a name being applied to more than one cultivar. I find the name 'Argenteo marginatum' applied to 'Higasayama' as well as to 'Matsugae.'

I have received plant material from various sources under these names, and 'Argenteo marginatum' grows out to match exactly both of these two other cultivars. Therefore, we can expect to find this name attached to different plants in different localities.

I believe it should be identified as a designation for cv. 'Matsugae.'

Also see discussion on related and overlapping misnomers under cultivars 'Roseo marginatum', 'Higasayama', and 'Kagiri nishiki.'

A. palmatum 'Asahi kaede'
  See: *A. palmatum* 'Asahi zuru'

A. palmatum 'Asahi zuru'
  (The rising sun maple)
  Syn.: 'Asahi kaede'

One of the dependable cultivars with sharply defined and clear variegations. The white portions have distinct and sharp margins in the green leaves. The green portions are a rich green. Leaves vary considerably in markings on each plant. Some of the smaller leaves are almost entirely white. Leaves vary from entirely white to completely green with only one small patch of white. Some leaves will have only minute flecks of white or pink. Solid green leaves occur and are usually larger in size than the variegated ones. Quite often the new growth in the Spring is a light pink which later turns white.

The typically-shaped palmatum leaves vary from 3 cm wide and long to large leaves of 8 cm in width and length. Normally the five-lobed, good-textured leaves are symmetrical, but a percentage have the lobes sickle-shaped when containing white sections. Petioles range up to 6 cm long and vary from pink in some leaves to green in the normal-colored leaves. Twigs and small branches are dark green.

An upright, but spreading, round-headed small tree, it will grow rather fast as a young plant. As it becomes older, the growth slows down and becomes more compact. I have seen trees 3 to 4 meters tall and 3 meters wide. Multi-stemmed trees are quite striking in appearance.

New growth occasionally is typical palmatum, but as the wood becomes two-years old and older, the variegations develop well.

A hardy form, desirable in landscaping for many situations. As with all variegants, afternoon shade will prevent excessive leaf-burn.

A. palmatum 'Aureo variegatum'

The new foliage in the Spring is not strongly variegated, being a rather uniform light green tone. However, the stronger variegation comes in the Fall. Small and indefinite markings of yellow or gold appear in the green background color. The variegation is not brilliant but discernible.

The foliage is five-lobed, truncate base, and good texture. Each lobe is oblong, gradually terminating in a slender point. The lobes separate to within 1 or 2 cm of the base. Margins are finely serrated on the outer half of the lobe. Petioles are firm and slightly reddish in color. Leaves measure 5 to 6 cm long and about 6 cm wide. Petioles are 2 to 3 cm. It is an upright-growing tree but does not get as tall as the species type. The older trees I have seen are broadened at the top, not overly twiggy, and about 4 meters high.

In searching through literature, I find this term applied to more than one cultivar. Several years ago we received propagating wood from two collections and have seen some 25-year old trees of this cultivar. I have to admit that I have been disappointed at the lack of "aureo" and "variegatum" characteristics!

A. palmatum 'Beni schichihenge'
  (red and changeful)
  Alternate spelling: 'Beni shishihenge'

The outstanding feature of this cultivar is the coloration in the variegated leaves. It is similar to 'Kagiri nishiki' and 'Butterfly', but the markings are orange rather than pink.

Each leaf varies in size and shape, some 5-lobed and 7-lobed, and are up to 6 cm in length and spread. Some lobes are very slender and uniform while others are contorted and of different widths. Basic coloration is green, or bluish-green, with strong white margins. The white is overlaid or blushed with pink-orange, a distinct color. Occasionally the entire lobe is orange. Petioles are crimson and are 2 to 3 cm long.

The plant grows upright to 2 meters but is classed as a tall shrub. It is not a strong-growing tree type but tends to be twiggy.

This cultivar is highly desirable and attracts much attention but is still rather rare.

A. palmatum 'Beni shigitatsu sawa'
  See: *A. palmatum* 'Aka shigitatsu sawa'

A. palmatum 'Beni schichihenge'

A. palmatum 'Beni tsukasa'
    Alternate spelling: 'Benino tsukasa'

The remarkable color tones of this plant make it a very noticeable cultivar. As the foliage first appears, the small leaves are a bright yellow-red or peach tone. As they mature, the color changes to delicate shades of pink and red with greenish undertones. Some leaves will show strong green vein colors through the blend of red-pink. Further into Summer, the foliage darkens somewhat and many leaves take on a faint variegation. This pattern is of minute flecking with tiny light-colored dots.

The leaves are 5 to 7 lobed. When seven, the base lobes overlap the petiole attachment. Lobes are separated about half way and are ovate lanceolate with double serration on the margins. These taper quickly to a slender point. Small leaves of older wood will be 2 cm long and 3 cm wide. However, leaves on the new, vigorous shoots will be at least twice as large. The thin petioles are 1½ to 3 cm long.

This is a willowy, slender-twigged plant but not cascading. Occasionally young shoots will grow quite vigorously, but normal growth is rather shrubby and makes a small plant up to 1½ meters at maturity. Usually it will make a lower shrub than this.

This cultivar makes a fine accent plant in small landscapes and lends itself very easily to container growing.

A. palmatum 'Butterfly'
    Syn.: 'Kochō nishiki' (butterfly, variegation); 'Kochō no mai' (butterfly, type of dancing girl)

This is a very spectacular small-leafed variegate. The leaves are variable in shape—rarely are any two alike. They are usually 5-lobed; some are 7. Each lobe is different—some short, some long, and most of them irregularly shaped on leaves of older wood. Leaves on new growth have lobes which are more uniform. The slender lobes are long (2 to 5 cm) and narrow (½ to 1 cm) and are separated almost to center of leaf. Petioles are short (1 to 3 cm).

The variegation is basically a cream color on a bluish to pale green. Sometimes an entire leaf is cream colored, but most often this color appears on the edges of lobes or an entire lobe. Quite often the variegated portion of the lobe is sickle-shaped. Noticeable in the Spring are the pink markings which border the white or cream portions. In Fall coloration, the white areas become a striking magenta, lending an entirely new quality to the appearance.

Seeds are extremely tiny, not over 2 mm in diameter. They are often cream colored.

A. palmatum 'Beni tsukasa'

A. palmatum 'Butterfly'. Typical twiggy, upright growth.

A. palmatum 'Butterfly'

Growth is normally short and twiggy, making a dense, large shrub or very small tree of 3 to 4 meters. It is stiffly upright. Occasionally a plant in very good culture will put out a shoot 40 to 60 cm long. New shoots and twigs are very delicate and slender. It is difficult to graft because of the very small diameter of the scions.

One of the most desirable cultivars of the variegated group. This dainty and attractive tree always brings comments from visitors.

A. palmatum 'Chirimen nishiki'
(a colorful type of paper)

This is a variegated form of green palmatum with a basic foliage color of deep green. Irregular markings of yellow are predominant. These are often light areas involving an entire lobe. Other markings are indistinct little areas of a subdued white-green. There are occasionally flecks of light yellow. It is a very delicate variegation on a very delicate type leaf. Many leaves are entirely green.

These unusual leaves measure from 3½ to 4½ cm long and up to 4 cm wide. They are five-lobed and separated to within about 1 cm of the center. Each lobe is very elongated, linear-lanceolate, acuminate. The margins are very irregular, wavy, incised, sometimes with small side lobes which are short and round. Foliage on leaves of new wood is more regular (palmate) with lanceolate lobes and very incised margins. Petioles range up to 3 cm long and are thin.

This is not a strong-growing plant. Rapidly growing young trees will grow 30 to 40 cm but slow down as the plant gets older. It is a shrubby type of plant—rather delicate and not easily propagated. This is a very choice cultivar which is not very widely known or found in many collections.

A. palmatum 'Cristata variegatum'
See: A. palmatum 'Higasayama'

A. palmatum 'Daimyo nishiki'
See: 'Taimin nishiki'

A. palmatum 'Hamaotome'

This is one of the newer cultivars to come from Japan. It is considered a variegated form, since the foliage is quite variable.

New leaves are very pale yellow-green or whitish-green. The lightest tones are in the center of the leaf, gradually becoming darker toward the outer portions of the lobes. It is not a sharp color division but a soft blending of tones. As the leaves become more mature, they will gradually darken to a light green, but some still retain the undertone of yellow.

The texture of the leaf is rather thin. There are five, sometimes seven, lobes. When seven, the two base lobes are extremely small. The lobes separate almost to the center of the leaf. Each lobe is ovate-lanceolate with a long, slender terminal. The margins are finely serrate. The size varies from 5 to 7 cm long and up to 7 cm spread of side tips.

This cultivar is a medium-size shrub type, growing to about 2 or 3 meters. It is hardy, not fast-growing, and relatively easy to propagate.

A. palmatum 'Hanaizumi nishiki'
(flower-like variegated, type of yellow)
See: 'Kasen nishiki'

A. palmatum 'Hanazono nishiki'
(flower garden)

This shy variegate is beautiful when carefully grown. Heavy fertilization will suppress the variegations.

The leaves are a base color of pale green and range from 3 to 6 cm in size, normally five lobed. Variegations are mostly the Kiri Fu (cut in) type with some additional irregular marking. Colors range from pink to cream, the pink being predominant when leaves first develop in the Spring. Twigs also have faint pink markings in the bark.

The ''pink'' cultivar 'Karasugawa' is more widely known. This lesser known cultivar is not strong-growing and will rarely exceed two meters.

A. palmatum 'Harusame'
(spring rain)

This one of the variegated forms of palmatum and is best known for its Fall coloration when the red color develops dusted with yellowish-brown markings (Sunago Fu). Most of the year the leaves are a normal light green, but this cultivar is an example of the type worth waiting for to see its Fall display.

A. palmatum 'Chirimen nishiki'

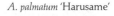

A. palmatum 'Harusame'

Foliage is 5 to 7 lobed, palmate, with length and width about 5 cm. Lobes are deeply separated almost to the center and are lanceolate-ovate. Petioles are about 4 cm long.

As an upright, bushy, small tree, it will not reach much more than two meters with considerable age.

Occasionally this cultivar will throw a white variegation in the leaf during the early growing season. I mention it for I find it amusing. It is so infrequent that it could not be called a character. Some years we have had only two leaves on the whole tree so variegated.

A. palmatum 'Higasayama'
(from Mt. Higasa)
Alternate spelling: 'Hikasayama'
Misnomers: 'Roseo marginatum,' 'Cristata variegatum,' 'Rosa marginalis,' 'Argenteo marginatum,' 'Albo marginatum,' 'Shinn's #2'

This cultivar is one of the variegated forms which has unusual-shaped leaves. It is found in maple lists from Japan since the early 1800's. Many names were applied as it worked its way around the world. These different names were probably used because of its different foliage traits at different times of the year.

One widely-used name in the United States is 'Roseo marginatum.' This confusion is unfortunate, for the true cultivar 'Roseo marginatum' ('Kagiri nishiki') is so outstanding and beautiful in its own right. Other names have been applied to depict certain traits. I saw large specimen trees of 'Higasayama' in Holland and England which were several decades old. These mature plants strengthen my opinion of the veracity of this nomenclature.

Most leaves will range up to 6 cm long with overall width of 5 cm. They average about 3 to 4 cm. Leaves are divided ⅔ down to the obtuse base. The seven leaf divisions are slender, elongate, tapering to a sharp point, with the margins strongly toothed. Usually the lobes curl upwards; however, many lobes are slightly twisted or curve downward, making the aggregate appearance quite unique.

A. palmatum 'Higasayama'

A. palmatum 'Higasayama'. Spring buds are spectacular as they unfold.

Leaf color is so changeable it is difficult to describe. Starting in the early Spring, the buds unfold with leaflets pale cream, tightly curled and with the elongated sheath a brilliant crimson, giving the whole effect of two-toned popcorn. This remains until the unique leaf unfolds and equals the blossoming effect of some shrubs. The veins are bordered in dark green, especially the broad band on each mid-rib. Borders of each of the seven divisions are cream colored, and the striping continues on down into the leaf center. This color is quite pale in early season and changes to a light cream-green as the season advances. For the first month or so the leaves also have strong pink tones on the margins overlaying the cream color and lightly bordering the edges of the lobes. This undoubtedly gives rise to the confusing misnomer of 'Roseo marginatum.' The color fades and disappears as the season progresses.

In the Fall the cream colored portions take on an orange to dark yellow and occasionally red tone.

The growth on older wood is quite twiggy. Twigs are closely spaced, and the nodes are close together. This is one reason this cultivar is so popular for bonsai work. When suppressed in pots, it is quite dense and lends itself to shaping. As 'Shinn's #2' it is quite popular for bonsai in California.

Under good growth conditions in the ground, however, long shoots will occur which are up to 1 meter in length. The new foliage on these shoots will almost always be non-typical of the cultivar. Instead they are regular palmate, flat, dark green, and most often have five lobes. They are up to 8 cm long. These new non-typical shoots will revert to the normal 'Higasayama' by the second year and need not be pruned off. The trees can be quite vigorous—up to 6 meters high in old specimens.

These are hardy plants which lend themselves well to landscape use. The unique growth habits and foliage make them most attractive. Light shining through the variegated leaves gives a very unusual effect which is very pleasing.

A. *palmatum* 'Iijima sunago'

The colors of this dark-leafed variegate make it an unusual addition to the landscape. The large leaves are up to 11 cm in length and 14 cm broad from tip to tip.

The seven lobes are each broadly ovate acuminate with edges having a fine-toothed, double-serrate form. The lobes divide about 2/3 into the center of the leaf. The leaves have a good texture—not thin—and are durable. Petioles are up to 5 cm long.

Spring growth develops as a rich red, slightly on the orange side. This is a durable color which lasts into the Summer. At this time, the feature for which it is named develops. The leaves become a rich purplish-brown—a rather unique color. Sprinkled in are the tiny and irregular green spots, sometimes rather obscure, but with the appearance of "sand-sprinkled" markings, thus the name Sunago. "Sunago-fu" is the type of variegation called "sand-sprinkled." These colors intensify as late Summer and Fall colors develop. The mid-ribs of each lobe of the leaf remain a distinctly contrasting green.

This is a strong-growing tree type which remains upright but does not reach extreme heights. It probably matures about 6 meters and forms a round-headed tree. The branches are sturdy and not willowy.

A. palmatum 'Iijima sunago'

A. *palmatum* 'Kageori nishiki'

This name is used in two ways. It is listed as a synonym for 'Shikageori nishiki' in some references.

Also, I have received plant material labeled 'Kageori nishiki' which is identical to 'Kagiri nishiki' (also spelled 'Kagari nishiki'). The close similarity of names may have lead to misspelling in the transliteration from various nursery sources around the world.

This is a small bushy tree, probably not reaching much more than 4 meters even in older plantings. It will not form an open type small tree but more of a bushy type. It is a hardy cultivar and well worth its place in any landscape.

A. palmatum "Kingsville variegated"

This is another of Henry Hohman's selections which is worthy of a place in Japanese Maple collections. It probably should have a true cultivar status, although I don't believe Mr. Hohman ever registered it.

The basic leaf color is a deep green or blue-green. Variations of color patterns are irregular, and variegation is mostly white. However, there is often a noticeable amount of pink, and occasionally on young leaves the pink margins are almost entire. The leaf margins are quite different from either 'Butterfly' or 'Kagiri nishiki.' Fall coloration changes the white portions to a brilliant rose tone.

Leaves are five-lobed and irregular. Each lobe is long and narrow with very irregular dentate margins. The leaves range from 2½ cm long on some of the older wood to as much as 5 cm on vigorous new shoots. Petioles grow from 1 to 2 cm long.

I have not seen an old plant, but from the growth rate and performance of our stock plants, I could easily assume that the mature plants will be more like 'Kagiri nishiki.' The habit is somewhat twiggy on older wood. I find it a delightful companion to some of the other variegated forms.

I assume that this could have been a seedling selection out of 'Kagiri nishiki' ('Roseo marginatum') or 'Butterfly' ('Kochō nishiki') both of which Mr. Hohman had as stock plants. However, he did not indicate the parentage of this selection. The character is somewhere between these two cultivars.

A. palmatum 'Kochō nishiki'
(variegated butterfly)
See: A. palmatum 'Butterfly'

A. palmatum 'Kochō no mai'
(dancing butterfly)
See: A. palmatum 'Butterfly'

A. palmatum 'Komon nishiki'
(small figures on cloth)

This is another of the variegated forms of palmatum. The leaves of this cultivar are about 3 to 5 cm long and 4 to 5 cm wide. Leaves on older wood tend to be even smaller. Petioles are short, (1 to 2 cm long) thin, and light green.

The lobes vary from 5 to 7 and each lobe is ovate-acuminate—widest at the base and center and gradually tapering to a point. The margins are toothed. Lobes join about ⅔ the distance to the center of the leaf.

The basic color of the foliage is a bright pale green, but in the Spring the new leaves have a rose-tinted edging which blends almost to the center of the lobes. Occasionally the new tones are almost pink. As the leaves expand fully in late Spring, they take on the variegated character of "Sunago Fu" or sand-dusting. This denotes that the very tiny yellow or white specks or spots are dusted onto the leaf. The specks rarely join together to make a larger white area. This is a very subtle and beautiful form of variegation. The leaves take on bright crimson tones in the Fall.

This is not a large-growing plant but cannot be classed as a dwarf. Container grown it makes a fine-leaf, small plant, and lends itself to bonsai culture. They can attain a height of 2 meters or more when planted in a good location in a rock garden.

A. palmatum 'Koshibori nishiki'

This variegated leaf form of palmatum has a basic color of a light, bright green. Its new leaves are edged with orange. The variegation consists of extremely fine dots and flecks of yellow on the green. It is of the "Sunago Fu" or sand-dusted form. The minute dots are irregularly,

A. palmatum 'Komon nishiki'

A. palmatum 'Koshibori nishiki'

indiscriminately, and often quite thickly scattered all over the surface. The five lobes are long ovate with the tip not extremely sharp. The margins are shallowly dentate. Lobes radiate out from the center giving a definite palmate appearance. Occasionally they are irregularly curved. Branchlets are crimson. Fall colors graduate through the yellows into the orange tones.

Leaves vary from 2 to 2½ cm long to 3 cm wide on mature foliage of older wood. Some leaves will be as much as 5 cm long and 6 cm wide.

This short shrub is of twiggy, slightly cascading habit and makes a dense but lacy plant. It is a cultivar of dwarf stature with small foliage and for best appearance should not be over-fertilized. It will probably reach 2 meters or a little more at maturity. It is a desirable small landscape plant and also adapts very well to container growing.

A. palmatum 'Marakumo'
Alternate spelling: 'Marakum'

The new leaves on this cultivar show a bright pinkish or light orange coloration, shading from the margins to the center of the lobes. The basic leaf color is pale green. It is made even lighter by the great profusion of extremely fine dots of white or cream which are sometimes so thick that they merge, forming almost a solid area. A translucent effect results from the very dense, fine stippling of the thin leaves. Fall colors range into yellow and light gold.

Leaves are 5 to 7-lobed, 5 to 7 cm long and 6 to 8 cm wide. Usually they are the smaller size. Petioles are 3 cm and quite red. Leaf lobes divide ⅔ the way to the center and are oblong-ovate, tapering to a slender point, thus forming a basic palmate-shaped leaf. The margins are quite toothed. Leaf texture is rather delicate but not weak.

Because it is not very vigorous, 'Marakumo' forms an upright bush of 3 meters rather than a tree. It is somewhat tender and needs at least afternoon shade. It is not easily propagated. Although a very desirable variegated form, it is not widely known.

A. palmatum 'Masukagami'
Alternate spelling: 'Masukaga'

This variegated cultivar is not widely known. I find it one of the most interesting among those which are subtly marked.

These are five-lobed (7) leaves, separated openly and deeply—almost to the center. Each lobe is elongate-ovate with the terminal elongated to a very sharp tip. The margins are prominently incised with serrations between. Leaves vary from 5 to 7 cm long and 5 to 9 cm across.

The new foliage appears crimson when first unfolding, occasionally showing strong pink tones. These colors lessen, but the reddish shades persist along the margins into late Spring. The mature leaves are a basic green color but are often so heavily marked as to appear almost white-green. The extremely fine dots of white or yellow often merge to form more solid areas of light color. The stippling effect is almost lacking in some leaves, but most foliage is very strongly marked, making the leaves appear pale.

This cultivar does best with light shade protection. It is a hardy plant and is a medium-growing cultivar, eventually making a tall shrub type of 4 meters.

A. palmatum 'Matsugae'
(the pine branch)
Syn.: albo marginatum (Pax), argenteo marginatum

This variegate is one of the older cultivars and a very satisfactory landscape plant.

Basic leaf color is a deep green—almost a bluish green. The variegation is of several types: Fukurin Fu (along the edges of the lobe); Fukurin kazure (irregular); or Hoso fukurin (shallow margins). The markings are white or cream but in the Spring are overlaid or blended with a deep rose. The colors lessen somewhat in the late Summer, but Fall intensifies the deep rose color in all the variegated areas.

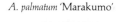
A. palmatum 'Marakumo'

A. palmatum 'Masukagami'

A. palmatum 'Matsugae'

A. palmatum 'Nishiki gasane'

A. palmatum 'Ōgino nagare'

The leaves are very irregular, each leaf being slightly different from the next. They are basically five-lobed with each lobe separated almost to the center. Lobes are long and narrow, slightly wider half way to the apex, terminating in a slender point. Each lobe is about ½ to 1 cm at its widest point. Edges are deeply and non-uniformly notched, toothed, or a combination of the two forms. Lobes are sometimes sickle-shaped, especially where there is heavy variegation. Sometimes individual lobes will be broad, almost elongate-ovate. Leaves are 3 to 4 cm long, with a spread across the lobes of 4 cm. The two basal lobes tend to point out at right angles to the petiole which is 1½ to 2½ cm long and quite slender.

This cultivar is about "half-way" between 'Butterfly' ('Kochō nishiki') and 'Kagiri nishiki' (roseo marginatum). The general appearance is similar to 'Kagiri nishiki' but close comparison of individual leaves will show minor differences. And, there is a greater depth of color in 'Matsugae.' It is a little more open and less twiggy than 'Butterfly.'

This is perhaps a more vigorous plant than 'Kagiri nishiki' and will grow a little taller—up to 3 or 4 meters. It is a hardy plant, can take full sun, and responds well to shaping.

A. palmatum 'Naruo nishiki'

While this is classed as a variegated cultivar, I have plants from two sources which show very little tendency to color. My plants are only a few seasons old, which may account for the lack of variegation.

In one of the early descriptions, the palmate-type leaves are described as first unfolding with light green color. As the leaves mature, there appears a faint creamy-white shading or variegation.

This is an upright-growing plant but not fast-growing. It tends to form a round-headed tall shrub up to 3 meters.

A. palmatum 'Nishiki gasane' (overlapping variegations)

This is a very different type of pattern than found in other variegated cultivars. It is termed the "Hoshi fu" or star-like type. The deep green leaf is speckled and flecked with gold. In most cases the spots occur in varying amounts and concentrate along the margins. Some markings are tiny and separate while others merge to form "blotches." Occasionally the variegation will occupy almost the entire leaf. When first unfolded, the heavily variegated new leaves have an apricot color shading from the edges into the center. This tone soon fades into the clear gold color of the mature leaf.

The palmate leaves have seven (5) ovate acuminate lobes, terminating in a long, slender tip. The lobes are separated ⅔ the distance to the center of the leaf and radiate openly. The two base lobes are very small. The margins are incised and serrate. Leaves measure from 5 to 7 cm long and 6 to 8 cm wide. On older wood, the leaves tend to be quite closely arranged on the small twigs. The petioles are 4 to 5 cm long.

This is an upright-growing tall shrub or small tree which matures at about 2 or 3 meters. The growth slows considerably after the first few years, and the plant begins to thicken and become twiggy.

As with many variegated cultivars, 'Nishiki gasane' especially needs protection from hot afternoon sun to prevent severe burning of the gold variegations. The cultivar 'Sagara nishiki' is almost identical.

A. palmatum 'Ō ginagashi'

This is a rare cultivar of the *Matsumurae* type. The rather large leaves have 7 to 9 deeply separated lobes. Kobayashi describes it as one of the newer variegated forms of palmatum.

I have not grown this cultivar but include it here for reference purposes.

A. palmatum 'Ōgino nagare'

The foliage is a light green with indistinct flecks of lighter green scattered in the tissue. These are not the bright variegations of other cultivars; all markings seem subdued. Occasionally, pale spots of cream or white appear, but these, too, are suppressed. New foliage unfolds with a tint of rose along the margins, but this soon disappears. The Fall colors become a little more prominent in shades of yellow and deep gold.

The leaves are five-lobed, each lobe being ovate-acuminate. The lobes separate about half way to the center, and the tips radiate sharply. The margins are double serrated, alternately deep and shallow, making a feathery edge. The leaves measure 5 to 7 cm long and 6 to 9 cm wide.

This is a strong-growing short tree which is delicate in appearance but hardy. It may reach 5 meters or more.

A. *palmatum* 'Orido nishiki'

This is one of the better variegated palmatum types. The leaves are 5 to 7 lobed, separated half way to the center. The lobes radiate outwardly. They are ovate but with doubly-serrated margins and a long, tapering point. Leaves measure 5 to 6 cm long and 6 to 8 cm wide. Very small leaves occasionally occur on twigs on very old wood. Petioles are slender and from 3 to 6 cm long.

The basic color is a rich, deep, shiny green which holds very well into the Fall.

The variegations are extremely diverse. The new Spring foliage is bright pink, white, cream, or a combination of these and may include various sized areas of green. Sometimes new leaves are entirely white. However, the main impression of Spring growth is often "pink." Leaves coming from twigs and branches of older wood have white or cream markings which will vary from a single tiny spot to irregular flecks, small area, blends, half-lobes, or any combination in between. Leaf portions which are strongly variegated will curve or be sickle-shaped. The bark of new shoots is sometimes pink or pink-striped. Many combinations of color occur on the same plant. This cultivar does not produce as much non-variegated foliage as do some others such as 'Versicolor' ('Aokii').

'Orido nishiki' is vigorous but does not become rangy. It will become an upright, round-topped tree of 5 or 6 meters in 15 or 20 years.

A. *palmatum* 'Reticulatum'
See: *A. palmatum* 'Shigitatsu sawa'

A. *palmatum* 'Roseo marginatum'
See: 'Kagiri nishiki'

This name has been applied to several cultivars. The name is also spelled various ways: Rosa marginatum, roseo marginata, etc. In the United States, 'Higasayama' is being sold under this name. 'Roseo marginatum' should rightfully be applied to the variegated cultivar 'Kagiri nishiki.'

A. palmatum 'Orido nishiki'

A. *palmatum* 'Ryūmon nishiki'

The green foliage of this variegate has white or yellowish, irregular areas composed of small markings. The new growth in the Spring develops with pinkish or reddish tones. Sometimes the new growth (including new twigs) is quite pink but less so than certain other cultivars. Later the leaves tend to become dull and the variegations are not as pronounced.

The medium-size leaves are flat-surfaced and usually about 5 cm long and broad. The lobes are 5 to 7, rather irregular, and not uniformly separated or divided, so that they vary somewhat in size.

This is an upright-growing small tree or tall bush, probably not exceeding 3 meters at maturity. The growth is rather twiggy and multi-branched.

A. *palmatum* 'Sagara nishiki'
Syn.: 'Yamato nishiki'

The foliage of this beautiful cultivar has variegations of pale yellow in the light green base color. As the new leaves unfold, there is an overshading of pink on the yellow margins. This soon fades as the leaf matures. The pattern is much the same as on 'Nishiki gasane'.

The leaves are mainly five-lobed (rarely 3 or 7), and the lobe is more broadly ovate and the base of the leaf more truncate than on 'Nishiki gasane'.

A. palmatum 'Sagara nishiki'

This cultivar is very similar to 'Nishiki gasane' except for the lighter variegations and leaf shape. The plant size, shape, and growth rate are the same. This cultivar needs semi-shade to protect the beautiful colors in the Summer months.

A. palmatum 'Seicha'
See: A. palmatum 'Aocha nishiki'

A. palmatum 'Shigitatsu sawa'
Syn.: 'Reticulatum,' 'Shigitatsu'

The leaf is "reticulated" with a network of prominently-colored green veins with light yellow or yellow-green interspaces. In the Spring and early Summer, the contrast is very prominent. This unique marking is bright and holds well, especially when the plant has protection from the hot sun. In mid-Summer, the leaf darkens, and the yellowish interspaces become greener. In the Fall, the leaves change to a red, or rich red-green tone, which is quite different from other cultivars.

The leaves can vary in size, depending upon the fertility, vigor, and location of the plant. They will vary from 6 to 8 cm long and 9 or 10 cm wide to lengths and widths of 12 to 14 cm. Slender petioles are 5 or 6 cm long.

The leaves have 7 (9) lobes which join about half way to the center. Lobes are ovate, tapering to a long, sharp point. Margins are sharply and quite regularly toothed. The leaf is inclined to cup slightly upward from the center while the lobes radiate sharply outward.

This is a fairly hardy plant but not as tough or as vigorous as some other old cultivars. It appreciates some protection from the hottest sun. It is a small, open-growing tree and will grow up to 4 meters tall with a spread of perhaps 3 meters.

Japanese consider it tender, dwarf, and best grown in containers. Here in the Northwest, it is a vigorous small tree suitable for gardens.

The name appeared for the first time in an old publication called "Seki Hin Binran." It has appeared many places in literature since the early 1800's.

Hideo Suzuki writes that the name "Shigitatsu sawa" means "snipes, quacking, fly up from a swamp." The poetic beauty of many of the cultivar names is fascinating and adds to the joy of the study.

'Shigitatsu sawa' is also the name of a place in Sagami-Ōiso. In the Genroku Era (200 years ago) the poet, Michikaze O yodo, lived there and called it Shigitatsu sawa. Quoting from an old poetry book by Priest Saiygo: "In the evening, in Fall, at Shigitatsu sawa, even a person whose heart is vacant, feels sad."

A magnificent plant!

A. palmatum 'Shikageori nishiki'
Syn.: 'Kageori nishiki'

The purple-red foliage has a brownish overtone which distinguishes this cultivar. The indistinct brown tones are often suppressed in new foliage and then later become apparent, although never strong. As Fall colors develop, the difference becomes more pronounced.

The leaves are seven-lobed, but the two base lobes are very small and sometimes lacking. Lobe shape is oblong-ovate. Lobes separate ¾ the distance to the center and terminate in long slender points. The outer half of the lobe has deeply serrated margins, while the inner half is smoother. The leaf is 7 to 8 cm long and 9 to 10 cm wide, with red petioles 3 cm long.

The plant is fairly hardy and strong-growing for its type and matures as a broad bush form up to 3 meters tall.

This cultivar is not widely known. Its status appears to me to be somewhat confused. I have retained use of the name 'Shikageori nishiki' although Koidzumi puts it in the taxonomic "form" 'Kageori nishiki.' This latter name has been confused with 'Kagiri nishiki' ('Kagari nishiki'). Further, plant material received under the name 'Kageori nishiki' has had green foliage. I have also seen descriptions in some nursery catalogs which call it a green-leaf plant with red-marked leaves. However, based on old descriptions, I feel that the brownish-red foliage form is correct.

A. palmatum 'Taimin nishiki'
Syn.: 'Daimyo nishiki'

This variegated red-leafed form of palmatum has foliage of medium size, 6 to 7 cm long and slightly wider. The seven lobes

A. palmatum 'Shigitatsu sawa'

are shallowly separated (about half way to the base) and are ovate-acuminate with the margins slightly serrated. The red petioles are 2 to 3 cm long.

There are different descriptions of this cultivar in old Japanese literature. One description has the new foliage unfolding a bright red color. Then, as the leaves mature, pink variegations appear which gradually change to brick-red markings. Another description gives the color as dark purple (when the leaves open in the Spring) with vermillion spots appearing and no green areas. Still another writer mentions the variegations turning brown on a reddish background.

I refer to the old descriptions in literature because the plants in our collection do not go through any of these changes. Instead, they remain solid colors of purple-red. They are still very young plants imported from collections overseas and have not begun to mature. I have found with other variegated clones that it sometimes takes a few seasons for the markings to become evident.

Also, old references indicate that the variegations tend to disappear when grown with too much fertility. I know this to be true with other variegants which I have forced. Withdrawal of fertilizers has brought them back in later seasons. Perhaps this will be true of 'Taimin nishiki.'

All references mention the difficulty in propagation. I have also experienced this with several other cultivars, such as 'Tsukomo.' Some clones do not heal well in grafting. 'Taimin nishiki' is classed as a very tender plant and is rare in nurseries.

I reserve judgment on the plants grown here until they become more mature.

A. palmatum 'Tama nishiki'

The bright green foliage is marked with white and yellow combinations in irregular and varied patterns. This type of variegation is the "Chiri fu," or "dust variegation" pattern. These are not bold markings, but rather subdued under most conditions. In the Fall, the markings become brighter, with rose tones coloring the white and yellow portions.

The leaves are regularly palmate, with the seven lobes deeply separated almost to the center of the leaf. Each lobe is irregular where the variegations are strong and becomes sickle-shaped or curved in those areas. The variegated leaves are 3 to 4 cm long and wide with short petioles of 1 to 2 cm. Leaves with no variegation are larger—5 cm or more long and wide. The lobes are a long elliptical-ovate but curled on the variegated portion. They narrow to long, sharp points, and the margins are serrated.

This is a little-known cultivar, not widely distributed. I find it in Japanese catalogs from 1930 into the 1960's. It is a slightly delicate, upright-growing plant up to 2 to 3 meters.

A. palmatum 'Ukigumo'
(floating clouds)

Among the variegated cultivars, this is one of the most outstanding forms. The pastel tones blend in subtle combinations unlike others which are more bold.

The basic leaf color is a light shade of green. The least variegated leaves have a faint shading of pink on the edges made up of very minute dots. Most of the leaves are marked in varying degrees by white and pink spots, sometimes merging into large areas. Other leaves are totally white or pink. None of the coloration is garish; it is soft.

The leaves measure from 4 to 5 cm long and across. The five lobes radiate openly and separate almost to the center of the leaf. They are oblong-ovate acuminate, ending in a sharp tip. The margins are finely and regularly serrate. The lobes that are highly colored do not lie flat but may curl downward or sideways. Occasionally they are twisted or undulate.

This is not a rapidly growing plant, although it is vigorous for its size. The twigs are rather short and slightly multi-branched, forming a semi-dense plant. It becomes a tall-shrub type, probably reaching a height of 1 to 2 meters after many years.

A. palmatum 'Ukigumo'

A. palmatum 'Ukigumo nishiki'

I have received several plants of this cultivar carrying the "nishiki" on the label. After growing them beside the cultivar 'Ukigumo', I find them identical. This is probably one of the instances where part of a cultivar name may have been omitted as plants were transported.

A. palmatum atropurpureum 'Variegatum'

The typical leaf shape of *palmatum atropurpureum* measures 9 to 11 cm long and 10 to 12 cm or more wide. They are 7-lobed with the lobes mostly ovate tapering to a strong, prominent point. The lobes are well separated over half way to the leaf center. Petioles are strong and up to 6 cm long. An upright-growing plant, attaining the stature of a small tree.

Early sources describe crimson variegations in the purple-red leaves. I have seen this cultivar several places and was never strongly impressed with the leaf coloration most of the year. The Fall coloring does redeem it somewhat with scarlet and crimson variegations, more correctly described as mottling.

We have received this plant from two different sources. Our plants show basically a reddish green leaf during most of the year followed by the good Fall tones.

This cultivar is listed back as far as the late 1800's and has been introduced several times. I see evidence that perhaps several different clones have been given this same designation.

A. palmatum 'Versicolor'
Syn.: 'Aokii', Albo variegatum, argenteo maculatum, discolor versicolor, roseo maculatum, variegatum

This is one of the more widely distributed cultivars of the American commercial nurseries. It is a strong-growing, hardy form and will make an upright tree exceeding 7 meters in 25 to 40 years. The top will form a broadened canopy typical of the palmatum species. Young wood has a bright green bark which darkens as the tree matures, and the new growth progressively becomes more multi-branched.

The leaves are typically palmate, deep green in color, with a varied pattern and amount of marking. The white portions consist of streaks, flecks, and blotches and are quite prominent in some leaves. Where variegations are large, that portion of the lobe will be sickle-shaped and curve laterally but not under. Occasionally pink colors are noticeable, but not in the profusion of some other cultivars, such as 'Orido nishiki.'

Leaves are 7 (5) lobed and are ovate acuminate. The tips are elongate, and the margins are double serrate, in most cases quite shallowly. Leaves are 4 to 6 cm long and 5 to 8 cm wide, attached to long, thin petioles (4 to 6 cm).

Many nurserymen feel that this cultivar will "revert" to normal, unvariegated palmatum type as it matures. I have seen 40 year old trees which have not reverted and hold the variegation quite well. However, I have also seen young trees with most of the foliage unmarked. High rates of fertility may cause lack of variegation. Culture factors which encourage extremely fast growth often adversely affect color of foliage, leaf shape, and amount of variegation. This may be especially true in 'Versicolor.' To assure using the best propagating wood during the dormant season, it is advisable to tag or mark the outstanding variegated branches while foliage is present. By selecting the best scion wood, it is possible to continue the best form of the cultivar.

A. palmatum 'Waka momiji—variegated'

This is a variegated form of palmatum. The typical palmatum leaves are seven-lobed. The separation is slightly over half way into the leaf. Each lobe is oblong, terminating in a long, slender, prominent tip. The margins are lightly serrated. Lobes radiate outward, but the three middle lobes appear longer. Leaves measure 4 to 5 cm long and 5 to 7 cm across the side lobe tips. The red petioles are 4 cm long.

The foliage has a yellowish-green cast. The variegation is white and varies from a few flecks to entire portions of the lobe but is often entirely absent. In Spring, some of the new foliage may be pink but not strongly marked. The stems of this cultivar are quite red during the growing season, in contrast to the green twigs of 'Versicolor' and 'Orido nishiki.'

This cultivar is carried under a separate name, although I am not positive of the veracity of the status. I cannot find descriptions of this cultivar in old literature. Its variegation intensity is between that of 'Versicolor' and 'Orido nishiki.'

This is a vigorous, upright-type, small tree. It will form a round-topped plant, probably reaching well over 7 meters after 25 years.

A. palmatum 'Yamato nishiki'
See: 'Sagara nishiki', 'Toyama nishiki'

UNUSUAL FEATURE GROUP

Those cultivars which have noticeably unique features are placed in this grouping. The foliage may be green, red, or variegated, but it is non-typical. Such features as bark color and texture also separate these cultivars as unusual. Some are short plants, such as 'Shishigashira' while others may be quite tall, as is 'Koshimino'. They originate from seedlings which have occurred at rare intervals, or have arisen as bud-sports or mutations. Observant horticulturists are constantly searching for the unusual forms of *A. palmatum*, since the species seems to have an inclination to produce a multitude of variable forms.

A. palmatum 'Akaji nishiki'
   Syn.: 'Seigai', 'Bonfire'

The brilliant scarlet foliage is the most attractive feature of this cultivar. The leaves are palmate and five-lobed. Each lobe narrows rapidly to a sharp point, and the margins are slightly toothed. Most leaves are 4 cm wide and 5 cm long. In the older more twiggy growth the leaves will be at least a cm smaller. The lobes divide at least half way to the center of the leaf.

The buds open in the Spring with a brilliant show of bright crimson. This will remain about a month. During early Summer the leaves change to a bronze tone and continue into the green of Summer. Fall colors become prominent again in the flame red tones.

This is a hardy cultivar and will eventually make a small upright tree or large shrub (4 meters). It occasionally puts out strong upright shoots when in good culture. The predominant growth, however, is multi-branched with short internodes. Because of its tendency to produce short, twiggy growth, this cultivar is quite popular for bonsai use. It tends to be difficult to propagate.

This cultivar is synonymous with 'Seigai.' It is found listed both ways in early literature. It should not be confused with the similar cultivar name 'Seigen.' In California a cultivar named 'Bonfire' has increased in popularity. After close comparison of characteristics and assessing the history, I conclude that this is identical to 'Akaji nishiki.' This should not be confused with the similar name 'Akikaji nishiki' which is a variegated form of *Acer truncatum*.

A. palmatum 'Arakawa'
   (rough bark)
   See: *A. palmatum* "Rough Bark Maple"

A. palmatum 'Bonfire'
   See: 'Akaji nishiki'

This is an American name which is quite popular in California. As far as I can find, it is a name originated many years ago by a California nursery which is no longer in business.

All characteristics are identical with the cultivar 'Akaji nishiki' which is also known as 'Seigai,' and I believe it is synonymous with these cultivars.

A. palmatum 'Chishio'
   Alternate spelling: 'Shishio'
   (two kinds of Kanji are written)
   Syn.: 'Mosen'

This is one of a large group of maples which have brilliant crimson Spring foliage. During the Summer months it turns a normal green. Then in the Fall it develops orange-red tones of varying intensity depending on the season.

A. palmatum 'Bonfire'

A. palmatum 'Chishio'

Leaves are palmatum type mostly five-lobed, occasionally seven. They are 5 to 6 cm long and wide, divided ⅔ to the center. Each lobe is rather narrow, ovate-lanceolate, and slightly toothed on margins. The petiole is thin and about 3 cm long.

'Chishio' is not a large tree and probably will not exceed 3 meters in a very old tree. It grows as broad as tall. The twiggy habit is typical as with most of this Spring-colored group.

The intense crimson new growth and new leaves make this plant as colorful as a flowering shrub. Compared to others such as 'Shindeshōjō,' 'Corallinum,' and other similar types, we describe the color as having a tinge of orange in the scarlet rather than red-scarlet. Since it is one of the more hardy group, it is a desirable landscape plant for small-size tree situations.

It is reported that there was, in the ancient days in Japan, a cultivar called 'Yashio' which looked much like 'Chishio.' The latter was newer and more colorful, so 'Yashio' seems to be lost to horticulture at present.

A. palmatum 'Corallinum'

A. palmatum 'Corallinum' ('Coralliformis')

The Spring foliage is the most outstanding feature of this cultivar. The color is difficult to describe, but I would class it as a shrimp-pink. It is very distinct and attracts much attention. It is a thrill to see this plant in its Spring and early Summer glory. During the Summer the foliage turns a good tone of green, and some leaves are slightly variegated with minute flecks or speckles of light tones. The new growth which comes in late Summer or early Fall is scarlet.

The leaves are near typical palmatum, mostly five-lobed, occasionally seven. From leaf base they are 4 to 5 cm long and are 5 to 6 cm wide. The leaf is divided about half way to the base. Lobes are broad, tapered ovate, very slightly toothed. Many of the leaves develop a slight crinkling, not lying perfectly flat in a plane. The petioles are slender and about 4 cm long.

We had the privilege of seeing the fine specimen plant of Mr. Harold Hillier at the Hillier Gardens and Arboretum, Jermyns House, Ampfield, near Romsey, England. Viewed during the first week in June, it was in its glory of rich pink tones. In our opinion it rivaled many flowering shrubs. His older plants are about as broad as tall and are about 1½ meters high. It has twiggy growth habit and makes a dense plant. Extremely old plants probably do not exceed 2½ meters under most conditions.

Unfortunately the cultivar name 'Corallinum' has also been applied to the Coral-bark palmatum, 'Sango kaku' ('Senkaki'). While 'Corallinum' will have some Winter bark tone, it must not be confused with 'Sango kaku.' When discussing this synonymity with Mr. Hillier, he remarked, "Why, they are as different as cheese and chalk!" I found this remark most descriptive and one I will not soon forget!

A. palmatum 'Corallinum' growing at the H. G. Hillier Arboretum, Jermyns House, Ampfield, Hampshire, England.

A. palmatum 'Crispa'
  See: 'Okushimo'

While the name 'Crispa' is found in old literature and catalogs for many years back, it is confusing. Unfortunately it has been applied to other cultivars of maples. Also, it can be confused with the name 'Crispum' which is one of the synonyms for 'Shishigashira.'

Therefore, with this cultivar as with some others which have many synonyms, I personally prefer to use the Japanese nomenclature.

A. palmatum 'Decompositum'
  See: 'Koshimino'

A. palmatum 'Deshōjō'

This is one of the bright-foliage palmatums in the Spring. At the early leaf stage the new foliage is a brilliant carmine red. It is a very bright-colored plant for a short period of time, but the color does not hold as long as other related cultivars.

The leaves are palmatum-shaped with lobes separated about half the distance to the base. Lobes radiate from the center and are sharply tapered to a point with fine serrations on the edges. Leaves range up to 5 or 6 cm wide and long. Petioles are thin and up to 4 cm in length.

The basic color of 'Deshōjō' the rest of the year is a good tone of lighter green. There are different selections of 'Deshōjō.' Some forms do not have such brilliant Spring coloring. However, we have received plants with the label " 'Deshōjō', good form" which do have the characteristic striking scarlet color. But even these do not retain the brilliance into the early Summer as do some other cultivars.

The portion of the name 'shōjō' can become confusing. Thus:
  'Shōjō' is an older standard form of one of the red palmatums.
  'Deshōjō' as described above is the base for other selected cultivars.
  'Shindeshōjō' is a newer selection and more brilliant than 'Deshōjō' ("shin" meaning new or newer).
  Other forms of varying red shades include 'Kondeshōjō' and 'Ima deshōjō'.

This is an upright form which makes a rather tall shrub which is usually as wide as high (3 meters). It takes its place as an outstanding ornamental companion plant for smaller gardens. Quite desirable in the group of "brilliant new growth" types.

A. palmatum 'Ganseki momiji'
  See: *A. palmatum* 'Rough Bark Maple'

A. palmatum 'Garyū'

My dictionary states "Garyū—One's own style or manner." This is certainly a suitable name for this cultivar. The foliage is most distinctive.

The leaves appear small and delicate, even though measurements seem larger. The small type leaves are 2 to 4 cm long and wide. The larger leaves measure 6 to 8 cm long and 6 to 9 cm across. This is misleading since the lobes are so long and slender that the leaf appears much more delicate than indicated. Each leaf has three, and occasionally five, lobes which separate

A. palmatum 'Garyū'

A. palmatum 'Deshōjō'

entirely to the center. They form a "T" or a cross. They are elongate-lanceolate, narrow at the base, tapering gradually to a narrow tip. While the lobe may measure 5 or 6 cm long, it is not over 1 cm in width. However, it is not the parallel-sided point of the linearilobums. The margins are complex—deeply incised to lobulate or combinations of both. The lobes do not lie flat but twist sideways, curl up or down or become slightly sickle-shaped. This occurs between leaves or even on the same leaf. The entire appearance of the foliage is rather disorganized, but it is attractive.

The colors also vary. Basically, the foliage is medium to light green. New foliage has a definite red overtone. Some older foliage also assumes a red tone in full light.

This is a compact dwarf which tends to produce indefinite direction to the twigs, much as with the foliage. It is semi-prostrate in habit but also has some shoots growing erect. The nodes on the twigs are very close together. I have not seen a mature plant but could assume that it would reach 1 meter in height and width after many years.

A. palmatum 'Hagoromo'
(dress worn by Japanese angels—drama)
Syn.: 'Sessilifolium,' 'Decompositum,' 'Kakuremino'

This is one of the unusual leaf-forms of palmatum. I describe the distinct leaf of this green cultivar in common terms as "having five feather-type divisions, joined with a stem." More specifically, the leaf is divided completely to the base which is attached without petiole (sessiliform). Each leaf blade is broadly lanceolate with the base quickly tapering to a petiole-like attachment. Margins of each lobe are incised. Each portion has a different plane of attitude, twist, and curve, as does each leaf on the twig, thus giving an overall very feathery and non-uniform foliage cover. Each leaf segment is approximately 5 to 6 cm long and 3 cm wide.

Foliage color is dark green. The twigs on older wood are very short and become dense in habit. However, frequent new shoots elongate, and terminals shoot 6 to 35 cm or more. Very vigorous growth may occur under heavy fertilization.

Fall colors are a blend of yellows and oranges in light tones.

Our plants, while not old, do not grow as vigorously as 'Koshimino.' Perhaps this is the main distinction between these two cultivars. Japanese authorities state that 'Hagoromo' does not grow very vigorously. The tallest trees reach about 1 meter. Some of ours exceed this. However, to date we have not seen the 4 to 5 meter height of 'Koshimino.'

A. palmatum 'Hazeroino'

The leaf shape of this cultivar is almost identical to A. palmatum 'Hagoromo' (see for leaf description). However, the primary difference is the variegated coloration. The leaf is occasionally white-flecked with cream-colored irregular spots. This is not a strong color variegation nor does it appear on all foliage. If the plant is too highly fertilized, the variegations are masked for a growth period or two. Every effort should be made to keep the plant in good vigor but not overstimulated.

This is not as strong growing as the non-variegated forms 'Hagoromo' and 'Koshimino.' It will eventually reach a height of 1 to 2 meters.

A. palmatum 'Issai nishiki momiji'

This is a very dwarf plant with extremely rough bark. It develops the bark characteristic within a year or two of propagation, becoming more rough each season.

A. palmatum 'Hagoromo'

A. palmatum 'Hazeroino'

'Issai nishiki momiji' is not actually a cultivar name in the strict sense. It is a horticultural designation in this instance. "Issai" indicates that the characteristic develops in "one year" or a short period of time. 'Nishiki' used in this context is a horticultural term for "rough." "Momiji" is a word for maple.

The description for this cultivar is found under "Pine Bark Maple."

A. palmatum 'Kakuremino'
    See: A. palmatum 'Hagoromo'

A. palmatum 'Koshimino'
    Syn.: 'Decompositum'

The foliage, Fall coloration, bunchy habit on old twigs, etc. are all very similar to 'Hagoromo.' However, I carry this cultivar under a separate name. The leaf shape is basically the same as 'Hagoromo' (see for description), and I admit that they could be synonymous.

Japanese nurserymen list 'Hagoromo' as slow-growing, rarely reaching 1 meter in height. We have received plant material from various sources, and 'Hagoromo' never grows as vigorously as 'Koshimino.' Our stock plants of 'Koshimino' have reached a height of 5 meters very quickly. A ten-year old tree is about 6 meters tall and is slender. Another of the same age is only about 3 meters but multistemmed and quite broad. Our plants of 'Hagoromo' show no tendency to be so vigorous. This lends weight to my assumption that they are different cultivars. Other authors indicate that they may be synonymous, but grown side-by-side the comparison leads me to believe they are separate cultivars.

A. palmatum 'Koto ito komachi'
    (old harp string—beautiful little girl)

Of the many thousands of seedlings I have produced, including those by hand hybridization, this is the most unusual. The original was a chance seedling I germinated many years ago.

The plant is extremely dwarf. The original seedling remained very tiny the first three years. It was not until I grafted the tiny tips onto vigorous understock that I began to get any size at all. The most growth I have been able to force on any one graft in a season has been about 15 cm. Most grafts make an annual growth of 5 or 6 cm. The shoots are sturdy, for the size, and the leaf nodes are very close together—often only a few mm apart thus making the foliage quite dense.

A. palmatum 'Koshimino'

A. palmatum 'Koto ito komachi'

Leaves usually have five extremely long, narrow lobes. Many have only 3 lobes. Each is only 1 mm at the widest point, down to ½ mm at the base. There is often very little more than the mid-rib. The lobe is narrowest on the inner half of the length with margins not toothed but slightly wavy. Each lobe is about 5 cm long. Lobes join only at the petiole which is quite fine and 1½ to 2 cm long. The total spread across the two side lobes is 11 cm. The leaves do not lie on the same plane and each one has a different curl to the lobes.

It seems hardy (survived -10°C) and also takes full sun. I constantly marvel that it grows at all since the leaf surface is so small it can manufacture very little food. However, since I have been culturing these plants, they all seem to thrive very well.

We were pleased to have Mr. Hideo Suzuki of Japan view this plant and suggest the name which we have assigned to this cultivar. While he visited our nursery, he suggested the name 'Koto ito komachi' (old harp string—beautiful little girl). The leaves are like harpstrings, and it is our "beautiful little girl." "Komachi" is also a horticultural term for dwarf.

This is extremely difficult to propagate since any scion wood is measured only in mm or at the most 2 cm.

It is a delightful plant for alpine gardens or areas in landscaping calling for small to medium-size upright plants. It can be pruned with excellent results. Japanese gardeners report it as slightly tender.

A. palmatum 'Maiko'

The foliage of this interesting cultivar is yellow-green to a bright green. It is the five-lobed type, but the leaves are decidedly non-uniform. They vary from 3 to 5 cm long and 3 to 7 cm wide. Some

A. palmatum 'Kurui jishi'

A. palmatum 'Maiko'

A. palmatum 'Kurui jishi'
(crazy lion—fictional)

This delightful cultivar has deep green leaves with the edge of each lobe tightly rolled upward and inward. The leaf almost appears star-shaped. There are 7 lobes but the two basal lobes cup upward, making the leaf appear to have 5. Each lobe is long and gradually pointed and gives the appearance of a pointed tube as the rolled edges almost meet in the center. Edges of the lobes are dentate, but this is lost because they roll inward. The tips are extremely sharp and are often hooked. Lobes join about ¾ the distance to the center, giving a small center palm to the leaf. The leaves are very similar to 'Okushimo' but are usually smaller. Petioles are red and 1½ to 2½ cm long.

The deep rich green of the foliage turns a delightful yellow in the Fall.

'Kurui jishi' is a more dwarf type than 'Okushimo.' It is a slow, upright grower to 2 meters. The leaf nodes are quite close together and make for a very bunchy growth habit and dense cover of leaves. Side shoots develop frequently for a tight growth habit. Normal growth is up to 15 cm per year.

lobes are quite narrow (not over 4 mm wide) but are 4 cm long, with margins deeply and irregularly incised, even lobulate. Some leaves will have this type of lobe combined with more typically triangular-ovate shape, tapering to an elongate blunt tip. A few leaves will have typical palmatum shape but with very deeply incised margins. All these variations can occur on the same plant. The cultivar is similar to 'Mama,' but the foliage is smaller and even more irregular. The red petioles are stiff and 2 cm long.

Fall colors are pleasing yellows of different intensities. The plant will make a tall shrub type up to 2 meters. After the vigorous growth of the early years, it will broaden and become multi-branched as it matures.

I have received propagating material from different sources to grow for comparison. These were labelled 'Maoka' and 'Maioka.' I have grown them side by side with 'Maiko', and they appear identical. This is an example of how misnomers can be created by carelessness in writing labels.

A. palmatum 'Mama'
(doing as one pleases)

The leaf description of this cultivar is very difficult because there are no two leaves alike. I was told that a translation of "Mama" is "any which way," or "doing as one pleases." (I suppose that in today's vernacular this could mean "doing your own thing"). The foliage does just this!

The bright green foliage is classed as five-lobed. There the uniformity stops. Some leaves have seven lobes or as few as three. The foliage has the following shapes: five long narrow lobes separated entirely to the center with margins irregularly incised, appearing wind-tattered; three broad lobes, separated shallowly, with two lobes long, narrow, completely separated, with very "tattered" margins. Other leaves will have all these combinations or any variation conceivable. Each leaf is slightly and interestingly different. The whole effect is a rather lacy appearance.

Leaves may reach a maximum of 7 to 8 cm in both measurements. However, most of them will be from 5 cm down to 3 cm. Petioles are 2 to 4 cm long and are bright red.

The bright green of the Summer foliage turns to a beautiful blend of yellow-orange combinations in the Fall.

This is usually a well-branched plant—even "twiggy." Occasionally strong shoots develop. It matures at about 3 meters as a tall bush form. It is still rather rare in nurseries.

A. palmatum 'Mejishi'

The Japanese designate two forms of the well-known cultivar 'Shishigashira'. These are 'Mejishi' and 'Ō jishi'. 'Mejishi' is the female "lion" (the mythical lion of Japanese drama.)

'Mejishi' is the designation for the more widely distributed form, 'Shishigashira', and is the more upright form of the two.

A. palmatum 'Momenshide'
Syn.: 'Yushide'

The leaves of this cultivar look very much like 'Hagoromo,' but the lobes are not deeply incised. Also, 'Momenshide' is a smaller plant.

Leaves have practically no petiole (only a few mm long) and are attached almost directly to the twig. They are normally 5 (3) lobed. Each lobe is oblong, ovate, tapering to a blunt point. The margins are only slightly cut or toothed and irregular. They taper abruptly the last cm to the width of the main vein so that each appears to have

A. palmatum 'Mama'

its own petiole. Lobes do not lie flat but twist slightly on different planes. The leaves are 3 to 5 cm long including about 1 to 1½ cm of bare "petiole-like" base. Each lobe is from 1½ to 2 cm at the broadest point but with lobes overlapping the leaves may appear to be only 4 or 5 cm wide. The entire effect is "feathery" foliage.

The foliage is reddish in the Spring but soon changes to a deep, rich green. The veins are somewhat prominent and give a slight "textured" look to the surface. In the Fall the bright yellow colors add to the beauty of the garden.

This cultivar assumes an upright bush shape and will probably not reach more than 1 or 2 meters in maturity. It tends to be twiggy and takes pruning and shaping very well.

The Japanese have found this cultivar rather tender. It is regarded as a bud-sport from 'Hagoromo.' It is occasionally found on older plants of 'Hagoromo' starting as a small shoot of new growth. It is difficult to propagate.

A. palmatum 'Momenshide'

A. palmatum 'Mosen'
See: *A. palmatum* 'Chishio'

A. palmatum 'Nishiki gawa'
See: *A. palmatum* "Pine Bark Maple"

A. palmatum "Nishiki sho"
(a botanical term for rough bark)
See: *A. palmatum* "Rough Bark Maple"

A. palmatum 'Okushimo'

A. palmatum 'Ō jishi'
Syn.: 'Yu jishi'

The well-known cultivar 'Shishigashira' is separated into two types by the Japanese. 'Ō jishi' is the male "lion" (the mythical lion of Japanese drama.)

This form is more compact than the more widely-known form. The leaves are more closely arranged on the stems, the leaf nodes being very close together. The rate of growth is limited (perhaps only 2 to 5 cm), making a very dwarf, multi-branched, compact little shrub. The leaves are slightly larger than 'Shishigashira', but in all other respects are much the same.

A. palmatum 'Ō jishi'

A. palmatum 'Okushimo'
Syn.: 'Crispa'
Misnomers: 'Crispum', 'Shishio', 'Chisio', 'Cristata'

This very desirable cultivar has three outstanding features: the odd-shaped leaves, the sweeping upright growth habit, and the beautiful gold Fall color.

The foliage is a rich green color. Each of the seven (5) lobes is separated about ⅔ into the center and radiates stiffly outward. The lobe is lanceolate and tapers to a sharp, stiff point. The most noticeable feature is that the margins of each lobe roll upward, almost forming a tapering tube. It makes the leaf appear as though it has five to seven round segments for lobes. Margins of the in-rolled lobes are slightly and bluntly notched. The ends of each lobe bend inward and upward. Leaf size is 4 to 5 cm long and 3 to 4 cm wide. The stiff petioles are 3 to 4 cm long.

The shape of the tree is unusual—stiffly upright (vase shaped), not the round-headed or umbrella form of so many other palmatums. It is sturdy, erect, and vigorous, and often reaches 8 meters or more at maturity. In young plants new growth can shoot up 1 meter or more in a season. However, it readily fills in with multi-branched small shoots which are only 5 to 6 cm long. It forms compact bunches of leaves and fine twigs. This quality adapts it to bonsai use, and it will assume a compact habit under this culture.

Another feature of this cultivar is its Fall foliage color. The intense yellow and gold tones seem almost fluorescent at times. In our plantings the colors still seem vivid when it is almost dark in the garden.

This cultivar is very desirable for landscaping and is increasing in popularity in the United States. While it can become a larger-size plant with adequate space, it can also be kept confined to smaller plantings with pruning and shaping. It is unfortunate that there has been some confusion in the nursery trade created by applying alternate names. This beautiful tree has been recorded since the early 1700's. As it was introduced into other countries, the Japanese name was not always used. The old taxonomic descriptions put it in the *A. palmatum*, subvariety *crispum*, and included the Japanese name 'Okushimo.' Unforutnately, the terms "crispum" and "crispa" were used indiscriminately both for this and other cultivars. I prefer the early Japanese cultivar name of 'Okushimo.' (One source translated this name as "The pepper and salt leaf"!)

A. palmatum 'Okushimo' has this typical vertical growth habit.

A. palmatum "Pine Bark Maple"
  Syn.: 'Nishiki gawa'

A rough "pine-like" bark is the outstanding feature of this cultivar. It has been likened to the bark of the Japanese Black Pine. The older the plant, the rougher the bark. It becomes quite corky with coarse, longitudinal, irregular creases in the thickened bark. This feature does not appear in young propagates, but begins to develop within 2 or 3 years. In an old plant the bark becomes very thick and convoluted. This is much more pronounced than in the cultivar "Rough Bark Maple."

The normal palmate leaf usually has seven lobes. The two base lobes are very small. The elongate-ovate lobes taper to a long point and separate over half way to the center of the leaf. The margins are strongly toothed for this size leaf, which is 4 to 5 cm both long and wide.

The Spring colors are light green, edged with a light shading of red. Mature leaves assume bright green color and turn to a strong yellow in the Fall.

This plant is upright but bushy and matures as a tall shrub form of 1 meter. It is shorter than the similar "Rough Bark Maple." It has become popular in Japan for bonsai training and lends itself well to frequent pruning and shaping.

A. palmatum "Ribescifolium"
  See: *A. palmatum* 'Shishigashira'

A. palmatum "Rough Bark Maple"
  Syn.: 'Arakawa', 'Ganseki momiji',
  "Nishiki sho"

Normally the cultivars of Japanese Maples are chosen for some outstanding feature of the foliage. However, in this case, it is the interesting bark. It is quite roughened and corky, with longitudinal creases and also short cracks and irregularities across the surface. It is not as deeply fissured as the "Pine Bark Maple." New propagates do not show this feature for 3 to 5 years, at which time the roughening begins and develops more rapidly each year. The word "nishiki" usually indicates a variegated leaf. However, in this context "nishiki sho" refers to the rough bark feature.

The green foliage is typical palmatum in shape. The 5 or 7 lobes are narrow-ovate, tapering gradually to a long, slender point. They radiate outward and are separated ¾ the distance to the attachment of the petiole. Margins are double serrated. Leaves range from 4 to 7 cm long and 5 to 7 cm across the extreme tips. The red petioles are slender and 3 to 5 cm long.

This is a vigorous, upright palmatum type plant which matures at over 5 meters. Young plants can produce shoots over 1 meter in a season. However, it will also dwarf well for bonsai use and make a very interesting plant. The rough bark is prominent even when the plant is dwarfed.

A. palmatum 'Sango kaku'
  (Coral Tower)
  Syn.: 'Senkaki' (Coral Bark maple,
  Cinnabar Wood maple)

The brilliant coral color of the bark is the outstanding feature of this maple. At times the color becomes almost fluorescent. The younger the wood the stronger the color. It has long been a popular cultivar in the nursery trade, and the demand is due mainly to this striking coloration. The brilliant tones brighten in the Fall and then intensify as Winter approaches. It is especially striking in winter snow.

The foliage is typically palmate. The leaf is 5 to 7 lobed, ovate acuminate, tapering to a sharp point. The margins of each lobe are double serrate. Most leaves are from 4 to 5 cm long and 4 to 6 cm wide. On the strongest growing new shoots the foliage is at least 1 cm larger in each dimension.

A. palmatum 'Pine Bark Maple"

A. *palmatum* 'Sango kaku'. The Winter bark coloration is an attractive feature of this cultivar.

This is an upright-growing tree, gradually spreading at the top as it attains age. It tends to become quite twiggy inside but will retain leaves well on the small twigs. It makes a fine shaped specimen for landscaping since it attains a height of up to 7 meters and the top broadens to about 6 meters. As an accent tree, it offers size, good form, interesting seasonal foliage changes, and outstanding bark coloration for the Winter months.

Young plants grow quite fast the first few years and then take on a multi-branching and thickening habit of growth. Planted near the contrasting green-barked cultivar, 'Aoyagi', the color combination for Winter accent is very striking.

In some areas the name "Corallinum" has been applied to this maple because of the bark color. This name, however, belongs to an entirely different cultivar.

A. *palmatum* 'Seigai'
See: 'Akaji nishiki'

Nurserymen in Japan usually use the name 'Seigai.' This has had many unfortunate misnomers here in the United States. Often I find references equating it with 'Corallinum,' 'Crispum,' 'Chishio,' and 'Bonfire.' The very similar name 'Seigen' represents a separate cultivar.

A. *palmatum* 'Seigen'

This is another of the group of palmatums which develop bright crimson foliage in the Spring. The new leaves range into the bright "fire-red" tones which last for several weeks. It then develops light-green Summer foliage. Fall colors range from yellow to "persimmon."

The five-lobed leaves appear dainty. They are about 3 to 5 cm long and wide. Lobes are divided about half way to mid-leaf and margins are lightly toothed. The tips are not acutely sharp. Petioles are stiff and 2 to 3 cm long. Leaves are close together on the short branches.

This is a semi-dwarf type of plant similar to the 'Tamahime' and 'Kiyohime' types. It will form a small, rounded bush 1½ meters high.

A. *palmatum* 'Seigai'

Leaf color is a bright tone of green. The edges of the new leaves have a strong reddish tinge which fades as the leaves mature. This early red margin tone gives the entire tree a striking appearance during the Spring season. As Summer approaches, the foliage becomes typical palmatum green of the lighter range. The leaves have a rather thin texture. The Fall colors change to yellow golden tones with a strong blend of apricot and light red. Some Japanese writers have referred to this cultivar as dull in the Fall season, but here in the Pacific Northwest it is quite showy almost every Fall.

A. *palmatum* 'Sango kaku' in full Fall color.

'Seigen' is very popular for bonsai work in Japan because it is dwarf and multi-branched. The crimson Spring foliage gives added value to the bonsai plant.

A. palmatum 'Senkaki'
See: A. palmatum 'Sango kaku'

A. palmatum 'Sessilifolium'
See: A. palmatum 'Hagoromo'

A. palmatum 'Shindeshōjō'

The cultivar name means "new deshōjō", indicating it is a later selection of 'Deshōjō.'

In the Spring, this is one of the most brilliant foliage plants in our collection. Some people refer to it as "fire-engine red." Flaming scarlet, or crimson scarlet, is a better description. The new foliage retains this color during the first month or more of Spring. As mid-Summer arrives, the color turns to a pleasant reddish-green. Occasionally leaves are found with minute flecking of light cream or white. However, it is not strongly marked. In the Fall, the colors become blends of reds and orange.

The leaves are small, palmate, and usually 7 (5) lobed. The two base lobes are quite small. Lobes are strongly ovate, bluntly tapering to a point. Margins are serrate with minute, sharp tips on each serration. Lobes unite half way to the center of the leaf. Leaves are 3 to 4 cm long and wide on older, twiggy wood, but up to 6 cm long and 7 cm wide on vigorous, newer growth. Slender petioles are red-brown and 2 to 4 cm long. Young bark is also reddish brown.

This is not a tall palmatum but forms a shrub about as wide as high. As it matures it may reach 2 meters. Young plants will produce vigorous new shoots, but in later years the growth becomes more twiggy.

This is an excellent container plant for patio display. It is also popular as a bonsai plant. With proper care the rate of growth and the leaf size can be reduced without harming the plant.

In my opinion, this is a brighter foliage than found in such plants as 'Chishio,' 'Seigai,' ('Bonfire'), or 'Deshōjō.'

A. palmatum 'Shindeshōjō'. Summer foliage changes to a mottled green, followed by scarlet Fall colors.

A. palmatum 'Shishigashira'
(lion's head or lion's mane—mythical lion of Japanese drama)
Syn.: 'Ribescifolium' and 'Minus'
Misnomers: 'Crispa' , 'Crispum' , 'Cristata'

The compact, stubby growth of this cultivar makes it very popular for small landscape planting, container growing, and bonsai. The outstanding feature is the close-packed arrangement of the leaves on the twigs and the close arrangement of the twigs on the branches, giving the compact and "stubby" character to this cultivar. The twigs are thick and short.

The bright green foliage is quite crinkled, which adds to the effect. The leaf is from 3 to 5 cm wide and about as long. Petioles are short and stiff, from 1½ to 3 cm long. Each leaf is seven-lobed, with the two base lobes much smaller. The lobes divide almost to the center of the petiole attachment. Each lobe is elongate-ovate, tapering to a sharp point. The sides are curled upward, occasionally convoluted, and in most cases forming a v-shaped trough. In addition, most leaves are further crinkled along the edges of the lobes, and the margins are also strongly but irregularly incised. Most of the crinkled leaves display the veins prominently, providing an almost rugose-appearing surface. However, some leaves do retain a smooth appearance.

A. palmatum 'Shindeshōjō'. Brilliant Spring foliage.

A. palmatum 'Shishigashira'

Usually a slow-growing form, 'Shishigashira' can exceed 2 meters with age. I have seen old plants, 3 meters tall, on which shoots had made a strong growth for one season, thus adding considerable height. The plants then returned to the normal short, multi-branched habit.

Size of the plant can be easily controlled by the amount of fertility available. It should always have enough nutrients to keep the good green tones in the foliage. However, the plant will stay quite short and dense if not over-fertilized. In a very fertile location the tree can reach a large size in a few years. To emphasize the character of the plant, training and pruning will accentuate the shrubby tufts of growth on the branches for a more outstanding effect.

This unique cultivar always attracts attention. It has been in cultivation for over 100 years and is popular around the world. Japanese literature lists it before 1880 and indicates its wide use both in landscape and bonsai culture.

There are two forms of 'Shishigashira' in Japanese horticulture—'Mejishi' and 'Ōjishi'. Please refer to these.

A. palmatum 'Shishio improved'
    Alternate spelling: 'Chishio improved'

I have received this cultivar from various sources in the past few years and am holding it as a separate cultivar even though the name 'Chishio,' and 'Shishio' have been used as synonyms in different countries.

It is another of the small-leafed palmatum forms with extremely brilliant Spring foliage. This cultivar is as bright as 'Shindeshōjō,' but we find the color more of a crimson than crimson-scarlet. The color lasts well through the Spring and is followed by a good green in the Summer.

The deep green foliage is of heavy substance, firm to the touch. Color is maintained very well during the Summer season even in hot sun. There is very little sunburn on vigorous plants.

The Fall coloration is a striking combination of gold, suffused with rose and crimson tones. The entire plant takes on a different appearance during the seasonal change, making it quite prominent.

A. palmatum 'Shishio improved'

The leaves are small, 5 (7) lobed, and 4 to 6 cm long and 5 to 7 cm wide. The lobes are ovate, with a tapering, well-defined point. Margins are slightly round-toothed, ending in a sharp spine. Lobes radiate outward and join over half way to the center. Petioles are slender and 3½ to 4 cm. The bark of the young wood is quite red on the upper side.

This is a multi-branched, shrub-type plant (2–3 meters). New shoots are up to 1 meter long. However, as it becomes older, the rate of growth slows. This cultivar adapts well to container growing for patio display and bonsai culture. Shoots and leaves dwarf down with this type of care.

A. *palmatum* 'Tsuchigumo'
(ground spider)

This is a delightful semi-dwarf palmatum cultivar. When new growth first unfolds, the leaves are rust-red, soon changing to bright green. This color holds well all Summer and does not burn in full sun. Fall colors are bright, blending crimson edges into the gold leaves.

The interesting leaves are 7 (5) lobed, with each lobe separated to within 1 cm of the base. Leaves vary from small ones on old wood (2 to 4 cm long and wide) to larger ones on vigorous new growth (5 cm long and wide). On old plants the twigs are closely spaced. Petioles are stiff and 1 to 2 cm long.

Lobes are elongate, slightly ovate, tapering gradually to a sharp point. They radiate outward. Margins of lobes turn slightly upward. The ends of some lobes turn slightly downward, while others curl completely under and in. The margins are conspicuously serrate. These leaves compare with 'Shishigashira,' but are not quite as convoluted.

This is an excellent semi-dwarf which reaches 2 or 3 meters at maturity. It grows slightly faster than 'Shishigashira,' and although the stems are sturdy, they are not quite as stubby or thick.

One Japanese reference states, "This cultivar is not seen in Japan these days." Apparently it is one of those lost when horticulture was disrupted 30 or 40 years ago, which has been re-introduced.

A. *palmatum* 'Wabito'
(lonely person or man)
Syn.: 'Wabibito'

These very unusual leaves have three to five lobes, each a slightly different shape. When three-lobed, the other two rudimentary lobes remain only as tiny spurs at the leaf base. Lobes are shallowly to deeply incised. Each resulting portion is blunt or toothed, smooth or serrated, flat or twisted, slender or broad, short or elongate—any of these combinations can occur along the margin. The pattern will vary from one side of the lobe to the other as well as between lobes and leaves. The total effect is a pleasing "tattered" appearance.

Leaves vary from 3 to 5 cm long and wide. The petioles are 1 to 1½ cm.

The basic color is green. However, the margins are strongly edged with rose or rusty-red, especially on new foliage. Summer color remains green, changing to a good scarlet in the Fall.

This is a small, shrub-type plant which reaches 1 to 1½ meters with maturity. It tends to be a fastigiate. It is not a sturdy cultivar and is not easily propagated. It appears in maple lists of 1710.

A. *palmatum* 'Yu jishi'
See: A. *palmatum* 'Ō jishi'

A. *palmatum* 'Yūshide'
See: 'Momenshide'

A. palmatum 'Tsuchigumo'

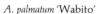

A. palmatum 'Wabito'

NEW HYBRIDS

The selection of "new" forms has been discussed in the section on propagation. I include in this chapter references to certain seedlings which I find of interest. These are still young plants and need to be observed for several years for evaluation of persistence and quality of character, growth habit, hardiness, and ease of propagation. These are values which should be established for each new seedling before selecting and naming. Also, as stressed before, a new selection should be noticeably different from other existing cultivars and have at least one desirable feature to separate it from other similar cultivars.

A. palmatum dissectum. A new selection.

A. palmatum. A most unusual form under observation.

The first seedling is a variegated red-leafed palmatum. The basic leaf color is a very uniform, strong maroon or black-red. However, markings of intense and strong crimson form different patterns. They occur as small flecks in a lobe, or an entire half-lobe may be crimson with the colors separated by the mid-vein. Occasionally an entire leaf may be the lighter color.

The leaf is separated entirely to the center by seven lobes. The two base lobes point back over the petiole. Each lobe is oblong-ovate with the base constricted to almost the mid-rib. The outer ends taper to a long, slender point. The margins are strongly double-serrate. The leaves measure 9 to 10 cm long and broad. The slender petioles are 5 cm long and also dark maroon.

The second selection is one of the most peculiar we have seen. We cannot class it as "beautiful", perhaps, but of interest because it is so unusual. The surface of the leaf is extremely rugose. The veins are raised and prominent. The leaf texture is rather thick but not leathery. It is of deep green color with contrasting red petioles. The twigs and branches are almost black.

The shape of the leaves is decidedly non-uniform. Most leaves consist of five lobes. However, on this five-year old plant there are leaves with as few as one full lobe with two rudimentary lobes. Other leaves have 3, 4, or 5 lobes, but none are the same size or shape. Some are almost strap-like, but many are broad-ovate. The base of the lobes narrows almost to the mid-rib, and they join only in the center of the leaf. The outer ends taper to a long, gradual tip. The margins of all lobes are deeply incised with serrations between and are often undulate.

A third selection has the typical rolled-edge leaves of 'Okushimo', but the leaf color is dark red. This will bear watching.

A. palmatum. A newly selected variegated form.

Cultivars and Selections of *Acer Japonicum*

This section includes the several cultivars and forms of the species *A. japonicum* which are commonly included in the "Japanese Maple" category of the commercial nursery trade.

This species is not quite as variable in foliage forms as *A. palmatum*. However, some extraordinary forms do occur, such as the delicately dissected, pendulous 'Green Cascade,' the fern-like foliage of 'Aconitifolium,' and the brilliant yellow leaves of 'Aureum.' Most of the other cultivars are variations in leaf size and lobe shape from the "type" leaf of the species.

A very important feature of all the japonicum selections is the brilliant Fall coloration. All the cultivars and seedling selections will display brilliant tones of yellow, orange, and red at the end of the growing season. This feature makes the japonicum group worthwhile as selections for landscape plantings. Most of them are sturdy, strong-growing trees, adaptable to most culture situations.

Some extraordinary forms may result from cross pollination. While *A. japonicum* does not seem to have as great a genetic variance as *A. palmatum*, seedling-produced hybrids may vary considerably. In a controlled cross which I made, the forms *aconitifolium* and *filicifolium* produced a generation of seedlings with great foliage variation. They ranged from small, cascading plants with multi-dissected leaves, to bold upright trees with exceptionally large orbicular foliage. There were all degrees of variation in between. I believe there is an opportunity in controlled hybridization to obtain additional interesting clones. It is a time-consuming procedure but could be rewarding. Inter-cultivar crosses within the japonicums should be tried as well as controlled hybridizing between *A. japonicum* cultivars and the better clones from other closely allied species of the Series *Palmata*.

Acer japonicum Thunberg 1784
   (Series *Palmata*)
   Fullmoon Maple
   Syn.: (Japanese nomenclature)
   'Hauchiwa kaede,' 'Meigetsu kaede'

This important species (in the Series *Palmata*) is second only to *A. palmatum* in contributing to the large number of cultivars in the "Japanese Maples" of the commercial nurseries.

The rich green leaves are generally orbicular in outline and normally have 11 (7–13) lobes. Each lobe is separated about 1/3 the distance to the center of the leaf. The lobe ends taper rapidly to a point, with margins lightly toothed to coarsely serrate. The leaves vary from 8 to 11 cm in diameter, occasionally as large as 14 cm.

Trees resulting from open-pollinated seed may show subtle variations from the leaf type of the species. This is particularly true when seed is collected in arboreta where cross pollination with other species in the Series is possible. In the native forests, some cross pollination is evident.

However, seed from large stands of *A. japonicum* are rather uniform. Arboreta-collected seed has produced some seedlings which I find vary greatly from the "type."

It may be assumed that this species is more genetically stable than *A. palmatum* since fewer cultivars have evolved over the past centuries of cultivation. *A. japonicum* is a desirable, sturdy tree of small stature. Plants may reach 10 meters in height at maturity. Ogata reports that the species grows to a height of 15 meters in the native forests. This maple is endemic to Japan.

Two native varieties should be noted here, as recorded by Ohwi: Var. *insulare* occurs on Honshu and is distinct in having the wings of the samaras spreading horizontally. The Japanese name for this variety is 'Shinano hauchiwa,' or 'Ō meigetsu.' Var. *kobakoense* occurs on the island of Hokkaido. It has leaves with the lobes simply and coarsely toothed. The Japanese name is 'Kobako hauchiwa.'

A. japonicum f. *aconitifolium*
   'Maiku jaku'   (dancing peacock)
   Syn.: 'Hau hiwa', 'Heyhachii', 'Parsonii',
   laciniatum, palmatifidium,
   Fern Leaf maple

This bold form of japonicum has leaves
which are multi-divided and deeply cut.
Each leaf separates into lobes which divide
almost to the center petiole attachment
point. Each lobe is again divided on each side
with numerous cuts which extend almost to
the midrib. These are irregularly dissected,
giving a "fern-like" appearance. It
approaches the leaf form of genus *Aconitum*,
hence the name.

The points of the dissected segments are
not sharp. The inner one-third of each lobe
narrows almost to the midrib, giving an open
form to the center of the leaf. The lobes hold
fairly close together as in a half-closed fan.
The leaf thus becomes longer than it is wide.

Each leaf usually contains 11 lobes, but
may vary on the same plant from 7 to 13
lobes. Leaf size depends upon the vigor and
age of the plant. The foliage on the younger
portions of the plant will always be larger.
Leaves will vary from 7 cm long and 6 cm
wide to an extreme of 17 cm long and 14 cm
wide. Petioles are strong, often curved, and
up to 7 cm long. They are usually reddish in
color.

The foliage is a deep green and has good
substance and texture. The underside has
inconspicuous tufts of minute hairs at some
of the junctions of the veins. When first
unfolding, the leaves show some
pubescence on the surface. Leaves of
vigorous plants tend to hold a horizontal
attitude, giving an "Oriental" appearance.

The white and maroon blossoms are quite
prominent on this cultivar and are more
striking than on most maples.

An additional desirable feature of this
cultivar is the intense Fall coloration. Brilliant
scarlet tones develop, shaded with carmine
and sometimes into the purple range. The
total appearance is flame red when viewed
from a distance. The leaves persist on the
plant thus giving a long Fall color period. The
prominent seeds, held in clusters of samaras,
color a maroon red in the Fall and add to the
attractiveness.

This is a strong-structured plant, never
weak or willowy. It is upright and
multi-branching in habit. The twigs are
sturdy and stiff. It forms a round-topped
small tree as it matures but does not grow
rampantly. It will ultimately reach a height of
5 meters depending upon the site and vigor.

This is one of the largest leafed types of *A.
japonicum*, exceeded only by cv. 'Vitifolium'
which is the undivided leaf form. Although
the foliage is large, 'Maiku jaku' is not a
coarse tree. The dissection of the leaves gives
it a lacy appearance. This is one of the most
desirable forms of *A. japonicum* for any size
landscape.

A. japonicum f. *aconitifolium* 'Maiku jaku'

A. japonicum f. *aconitifolium* 'Maiku jaku' has brilliant
Fall colors.   *A. palmatum* 'Ornatum' in the foreground.

A. japonicum 'Aureum'
The Golden Full Moon Maple
Syn.: 'Kinkakure,' 'Kakuregasa'

This "yellow-leafed" form of the species is a most spectacular cultivar and is highly prized in culture. Its popularity is constantly increasing, but of limited availability because it is rather difficult to propagate commercially in large quantities.

The Spring foliage is a pale yellow-green of a very distinct tone. As the season progresses, the leaves gradually become darker green. In partial shade, the foliage retains the yellow tones a little longer than in full sun. Direct hot sun will cause some leaf scorch in areas with hot climate.

The orbicular leaves form a dense cover on the plant rather than the open pattern found in other japonicum cultivars. The leaves have 11 (9-13) sharply-pointed lobes. Each lobe separates only $^1/_5$ the distance into the leaf. The leaf normally measures from 6 to 8 cm across but may vary from 5 to 11 cm on more mature trees.

The Fall colors are often spectacular, varying from orange through red and occasionally blended with a purple tone.

The growth habit is "stubby" as new shoots usually grow from 6 to 12 cm per season. Young plants will grow quite vigorously the first few years, but the plant becomes more bushy and multi-branched as it matures. In older plants the angular branching forms a most attractive branch scaffold which is attractive in the Winter.

The bark on the new shoots is an interesting bluish-green, almost glaucous. The seeds form in tight bunches of samaras and become bright red. These often stick up through the golden foliage and add one more attractive feature to this fine plant.

Large trees are not commonly seen. In fact, in Kobayashi's descriptions, he mentions that they do not grow very large and are mostly used as "container plants."

The most magnificent 'Aureum' I have seen grows in Boskoop, Holland. It is at the home of D.M. Van Gelderen and is over 110 years old. I remember the tree as about 5 meters high and 5 or 6 meters in the spread of branches. It forms an immense golden dome at the end of the main path in their nursery,

A. japonicum 'Aureum'. A mature specimen growing at Boskoop, Holland.

and is a sight I will never forget. Scions for grafting have been taken from this plant for several generations, so the progeny of this fine specimen are growing in many places around the world. I have not been able to find records of any larger *A. japonicum* 'Aureum' in any other country.

A. japonicum 'Aureum'. Brilliant Fall foliage.

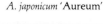

A. japonicum 'Ezono momiji'

The very large leaves of this japonicum form an orbicular outline, broken only by the sharp lobe tips. The 11 lobes separate into the leaf about ¼ the distance and abruptly terminate in a sharp point. The margins are only slightly serrate. The leaves are variable in size, but most remain in the 9 to 11 cm range. The stiff petioles hold the leaves out firmly.

Spring colors are light yellow-green, with inside foliage a darker green tone. This is not the same intense tone which is found in *A. japonicum* 'Aureum' but has a duller appearance due to the rougher surface foilage texture. The green darkens during the Summer but develops the strong blends of golden-red in the Fall.

This is a medium-size plant which matures at 4 meters. The twigs are thick and of a stubby growth pattern and form a multi-branched scaffold in older plants.

This is classed as medium-hardy, rather difficult to grow, and hard to propagate. The pithy scions do not heal rapidly in grafting.

A. japonicum 'Filicifolium'
Syn.: 'Parsonii'

There is some controversy over this nomenclature. It is often regarded as a synonym for *A. japonicum* f. *aconitifolium.* However, I find references and evidence that they were originally two separate clones.

Koidzumi and other authors separate them in early literature. In his letters, Henry Hohman always made a distinction between the two. Plants from his old collection, grown side by side, do show slight differences.

Basically the leaf and plant descriptions will be found very similar to 'aconitifolium.' The leaf size of 'Filicifolium' is slightly smaller, and the foliage tends to have two fewer lobes in many leaves. The two plants vary greatly in the number of leaf lobes which range from 7 to 11. The width of the incised lobes is not as great in 'Filicifolium,' and the texture of the leaves is not as substantial.

Admittedly, the two cultivars are very similar. Perhaps only the most devoted "maple fancier" is concerned with the differences. Certainly in the commercial nursery trade the question may be only academic.

A. japonicum 'Green Cascade'

This cultivar is one of the excellent japonicums developed recently in the United States. The selection, naming, and propagation were done by Art Wright, a nurseryman of Canby, Oregon.

The unique selection is a weeping or pendulous form of japonicum. The growth habit is much like the true dissectum types of palmatum. I saw the "mother" plant located on a raised portion of the landscape. It cascaded down the bank, forming a green mantle. Young plants should be staked to form a center stem from which the limbs can cascade.

The individual leaf is a rich green with 9 (11) divisions. Each division is up to 8 or 10 cm long, radiating out from the central attachments, and separated entirely to the center of the leaf. The base of each section is very little wider than the mid-vein (1 mm). From this extremely narrow base, which continues about 1/3 the length, the section of the leaf becomes broad but is deeply dissected into narrow sections so that the entire effect of the double division of the leaf is lace-like.

The Fall colors are quite brilliant and range through the yellow-orange-crimson tones of the japonicums.

A. japonicum 'Green Cascade'

A. japonicum 'Heyhachii'
See *A. japonicum* f. *aconitifolium*

A. japonicum 'Itaya'
Alternate spelling: 'Itayo'

This is one of the large-leafed forms of japonicum. The light green leaves can be 15 cm or more long and broad. The general leaf outline is round. The 9 (7-11) lobes are broadly ovate, tapering to a point with shallowly-toothed edges. Lobes rarely separate more than 1/3 the way to the center. The strong petioles (3 to 4 cm) have a heavy base. This foliage is of heavy substance, slightly rugose, often slightly folded upward between radiating main veins. Leaves usually are not as large as the cultivar 'Vitifolium.'

This is a stocky, sturdy, small tree with short, angular twigs. These form an inner-structure which is picturesque during the Winter. It becomes a round-headed tree up to 6 meters at maturity.

As with most japonicums, the Fall color is worth waiting for. Bright tones of yellow, orange, and red blend in various combinations.

The name Itaya can be confusing. It is widely used as the cultivar name of the japonicum as described here. However, I also find the name used in older Japanese literature as the name of other maples. For instance, "Itaya," or "Itaya meigetsu" is a Japanese name for *Acer Siebolidanum*, a closely related species. Also, references show *Acer pictum* (*Acer mono*, and in some cases *Acer truncatum*) as "Itayo," "Itayi," or "Itaya kaede." It is also used by some authors in describing *Acer pictum*, var. *mono*, and var. *Mayri*, as well as one form of *Acer shirasawanum*.

A. japonicum 'Junihitoye'
Alternate spelling: 'Junihitoe,' 'Jyunihitoe'

This cultivar has the smallest leaves of the japonicums. They measure from 5 to 7 cm long and broad, with a circular outline. Each of the 11 lobes is very short, separating about 1/3 or less into the center of the leaf. The lobe forms a short, rounded point which is slightly toothed on the margins. The short, stiff petioles hold the leaves out horizontally in contrast to those of *A. japonicum microphyllum* which extend at various angles.

Fall colors are brilliant orange tones. The seeds, in tight bunches of samaras, also turn orange and add to the beauty.

A. japonicum 'Junihitōye'

Twig growth is very short and stubby, often only two bud nodes in length. Each year the new growth is more angular, making the structure intricate and dense. New bark is a grey-green changing to grey-brown in older wood.

This is a stubby-growing, short tree which matures at about 5 meters. I have seen 30-year old trees only 3 meters high.

The name 'Junihitoye' is retained here as a cultivar name. It is listed as such in old catalogs from Japanese nurseries. Henry Hohman of Kingsville Nursery carried it in his early listings. I do find, however, references in old literature where it is given as a Japanese term for the "type" species. Koidzumi, in 1911, shows it in his synonym list for the form *typicum*. Some authors make it synonymous with 'Ogurayama.'

A. japonicum 'Kakure gasa'
See *A. japonicum* 'Aureum'

A. japoncium 'Kasagiyama'
Alternate spelling: 'Kagagiyama'

This cultivar name has been attached to three entirely different clones which I have received in recent years. Each plant is from a different source. One is a japonicum; the other two are palmatums.

I am quite sure that the japonicum is mislabeled. However, there is an obscure reference to a cultivar of this name in this species. Since our reference plant is in question, I will omit any description.

See *A. palmatum* 'Kasagiyama'

A. japonicum 'Kinkakure'
See *A. japonicum* 'Aureum'

A. japonicum 'Kinugasayama'

This cultivar is sometimes designated as an *A. japonicum*. Other references place it in *A. Sieboldianum*. Because of the structural characteristics and the strong pubescence of foliage, petioles and twigs, I describe this under the latter.

See *A. Sieboldianum* 'Kinugasayama'

A. japonicum 'Kokonoe'

I have not grown this cultivar. One Japanese authority states that it is lost to cultivation. We describe it here in hopes it still remains in some collection and can be brought forward again.

Both Koidzumi and Kobayashi describe it as a japonicum with orbicular leaves of 11 lobes. They are light or yellow-green with whitish petioles.

Another author places it in the species *A. palmatum*.

A. japonicum 'Kujaku nishiki'

This is a very rare form of japonicum. The leaves are almost identical in shape to *A. japonicum* f. *aconitifolium*. However, the foliage is variegated. The variegation is the Haki komi Fu (brushed-in) type of marking. The white variegation occupies a large part of the deeply dissected leaves.

It is tender and very difficult to propagate.

A. japonicum 'Maiku jaku'
See *A. japonicum* f. *aconitifolium*

A. japonicum 'Meigetsu'

In searching through old literature, I find this name used both as a cultivar designation and as a synonym for the species.

Imported grafts, carrying the cultivar label 'Meigetsu,' have the typical orbicular leaf of "type" japonicums. They have 9 to 11 lobes—also typical of the species. The lobes separate one-third the distance to the center, with the outer end ovate, terminating in a sharp point. The outer margins of the lobes are sharply toothed.

The leaves vary from 6 or 8 cm across to 10 cm long. The stiff petioles are usually 3 cm long.

The foliage is bright green and glabrous, and the petioles are smooth. The leaves have good texture and take full sun very well. The Fall colors are blends of gold and red.

This is a sturdy, strong, multi-branched tree. It will grow to 6 to 8 meters and form a round-topped canopy as it matures.

A. japonicum microphyllum
Syn.: 'Yezo meigetsu kaede'

The leaves of this plant have a round outline and are slightly cupped at the attachment of the petiole. The 11 (9) lobes are short and ovate-triangular, coming to a sharp point. The margins are shallowly double-serrate. Leaves are 6 to 8 cm long and 8 to 10 cm wide. The lobes separate only about ⅓ the distance to the center.

A. japonicum 'Meigetsu'

The basal lobes overlap, and with the upturn of the leaf form a shallow cup. The color is dark green, and the leaf texture is substantial, forming a durable type leaf. The underleaf is glaucous and lighter green. The red-green petioles are sturdy and about 7 cm long.

The Fall foliage is a typically bright japonicum blend of yellow and orange. The leaves remain firmly attached into late Fall, thus extending the color period.

The growth seems less vigorous than the type speices, although the plant will form a small tree up to 6 meters high. The twigs and branches are sturdy and form an interesting branch structure which adds to the Winter beauty.

This is a sturdy and hardy form of japonicum.

A. japonicum 'Mikasayama'

This is one of the smaller-leafed forms of A. japonicum. The outline of the leaf is orbicular, but the seven (9) lobes cut half way into the center. The lobe sides remain close together except for the outer ends, which rapidly taper to a sharp point. The margin of this outer taper is sharply-toothed.

The new foliage is a light green with a light pubescence covering the entire surface. This imparts a silvery sheen to the leaves. The pubescence disappears later in the season. The 2 to 3-cm petioles also are covered with these minute hairs. Fall colors are golden, occasionally tinged with crimson. The average leaves measure 4 to 7 cm, both long and wide, although larger leaves sometimes occur.

This is a sturdy plant of medium height for japonicums. It is not widely known because it is not very spectacular.

Kobayashi gives this cultivar status in A. japonicum, and descriptions vary somewhat in other references. An Eastern United States maple list places it in the A. palmatum species. After close study of the bud scales, pubescence of foliage and twigs, and other characteristics, I feel it may rightfully belong in A. Sieboldianum.

A. japonicum 'Ō isami'
Alternate spelling: 'Ohisami'
Syn.: 'Taiyu'

The large, orbicular leaves measure 10 to 12 cm, and the 9 to 11 lobes are elongate-ovate, separating about half way into the leaf. The tapering ends of the lobes are deeply notched. The petiole is 4 to 5 cm long and fairly sturdy.

The new leaves are light green, especially the outer ends of the lobes. The older leaves become a rich green which persists well into the Fall without sunburning. The upper suface of the newer leaves has a scattered amount of very fine silvery hair. There is also pubescence on the petioles.

The Fall coloration is an outstanding combination of reds and yellows blending with deeper tones of scarlet.

The twigs and limbs are sturdy and rather thick on this vigorous plant. It forms a round-topped, small tree which reaches up to 4 to 5 meters at maturity.

A. japonicum 'Ō taki'
Alternate spelling: 'Ohtaki,' 'Odaki'

The leaves of this cultivar are circular in general outline and have 11 (9-13) lobes. The lobes lie close together but are divided about half the distance to the center. Leaves range from 6 to 8 cm in diameter but are occasionally larger on vigorous, new growth. Petioles are stiff and relatively short—about 2 to 3 cm. The lobe margins on the outer end are deeply toothed, giving a feather-edge appearance.

Coloration is a deep rich green, almost a blue-green in partial shade. They are thick leaves of good substance and texture which will take full sun. The surface is sometimes sparingly covered with fine, silvery hairs.

The Fall coloration is an outstanding feature of this cultivar. The blended red, crimson, gold, and orange colors are brilliant.

The twigs and small branches are thick, sturdy, and short. It will form a small tree, up to 3 or 4 meters at maturity.

A. japonicum 'Ogurayama'

This is one of my favorite cultivars in the medium-sized japonicums. Every Fall the brilliant display of colors persists for several weeks. The attractive display of rich orange blended with scarlet dominates its portion of the garden.

Spring foliage is a light yellow-green. The leaves soon change to a purer green with a silvery overcast due to a covering of extremely fine pubescence. In mid-Summer this disappears, and the leaves darken further. Fall brings forth the dependable brilliant coloration.

The circular leaves have nine (7-11) lobes. These lobes are separated half way to the center. However, the edges remain adjacent, even overlapping slightly, making the leaf appear solid. Only the tapering, sharp points are separated, with each margin noticeably toothed. The

A. japonicum 'Ō taki'

smaller lobes on more mature leaves have a strong tendency to cup upward.

The outer leaves measure 6 to 8 cm. Throughout the inner areas of the tree, smaller leaves of 4 to 5 cm dominate. The petioles are stiff, pubescent, and 3 to 4 cm long.

This cultivar has formed a round-topped bush 2 to 3 meters high in 12 years. The growth becomes more multi-branched and twiggy each year. It should reach 4 meters in height. It is a sturdy plant and quite hardy.

Some authors have placed this cultivar in *A. Sieboldianum*. Perhaps the bud scale formation and the pubescence would lend weight to this taxonomy.

'Ogurayama' is also given as a synonym for *A. japonicum* 'Junihitoye.'

A. japonicum 'Sayo shigure'

This cultivar is little known and not particularly outstanding. The foliage is a dull green, appearing to have a dusty sheen. The leaves are 9-lobed with margins lightly toothed. The lobes are ovate-acuminate and divide half way to the center of the leaf. Leaves measure 5 to 7 cm long and wide.

The Fall colors become gold, blended with orange. It is a medium-size, tall shrub or small tree of the species. Japanese writers indicate that this form is not planted widely in landscaping in modern times.

A. japonicum 'Taiyu'
See *A. japonicum* 'Ō isami'

A. japonicum 'Takinogawa'

The name of this cultivar remains in doubt with me. Several references in Japanese literature place this cultivar name in *A. palmatum*.(See *A. palmatum* cv. 'Takinogawa.') Several nursery sources in the United States and Europe place it in the *A. japonicum* species.

In addition, we have received japonicum forms from Eastern United States sources which were completely different from those from European sources bearing the same label, 'Takinogawa.'

The European-source plant has very large leaves (11 to 14 cm) with seven large lobes. These separate half way into the leaf and are oblong-ovate, terminating in a sharp point. The margins are deeply incised. The glabrous foliage is a deep, rich green in the Spring and Summer months.

In contrast, plants from Eastern United States sources have much smaller foliage

which is orbicular. The nine lobes separate beyond the center of the leaf and hold very closely together, with only the outer half of the lobe being separate, acuminate, and strongly incised. Leaf color is a lighter shade of green with a silvery overtone due to a covering of minute pubescence. The petioles are also pubescent and very short (1 cm).

At this time, I am unable to determine the true status of the cultivar name as it relates to the species *A. japonicum*. There is little doubt in my mind as to the veracity of the *A. palmatum* assignment. Whether or not there is valid application in *A. japonicum* is open to doubt.

A. japonicum 'Veitchii'

This is a selected seedling from *A. japonicum* f.*aconitifolium* and is virtually identical to the parent.

See *A. japonicum* f. *aconitifolium*

A. japonicum 'Vitifolium'

As the name implies, the very large leaves resemble the grape or *Vitis*. They are deep green and of good texture with stiff petioles which are 4 to 7 cm long. The leaves are from 10 to 12 cm long and 12 to 16 cm wide. The lobes number 9 to 11. Each lobe is separated almost half way to the center of the leaf. The lobe bases are close together, making the outer ends of the lobes appear ovate. They terminate in a sharp point. The margins are toothed and prominent. The main veins show distinctly as a lighter green.

This is a strong-growing tree with thick, sturdy twigs and branches. It is upright and becomes broad and round-topped with age. 'Vitifolium' is large for the species and will probably reach 7 to 9 meters.

The Fall colors are magnificent. The golds predominate, with strong tones of crimson and scarlet.

A. japonicum 'Yezo meigetsu kaede'
See *A. japonicum microphyllum*

A. japonicum 'Vitifolium'

A. japonicum 'Ogurayama' in Fall foliage.

A. buergerianum 'Iwao kaede' (rock maple)

This is a form of the species whose leaves are slightly larger than "type." The leaf measures 6 to 8 cm long and 7 to 9 cm wide on a 3 cm petiole. The appearance is very broad, since the two side lobes extend sharply at right angles. The base of the leaf is broadly sub-cordate. All three lobes are triangular, tapering rapidly to a blunt tip. The three typical main veins are prominent.

New foliage is a dark green-red to a bright red (depending upon the amount of shade). It later becomes a very shiny dark green with a leathery texture.

The plants we have are only a few years old and are developing a very twiggy nature.

A. buergerianum 'Jakō kaede'
See *A. buergerianum* "Musk Scented"

A. buergerianum 'Kyū den'

A. buergerianum 'Mino yatsubusa'

A. buergerianum 'Kyū den'

'Kyū den' is a very dwarf form of the species. The internodes on the twigs are very close together, making the dense leaf pattern.

The foliage is also small, measuring 3 to 3½ cm long and 2 to 3 cm wide. The base of the leaf is cordate, and the leaf outline is ovate to triangular-ovate. The side lobes may be totally absent or very small and blunt tipped. The leaf terminal is also very blunt.

The leaf color is a very shiny, deep green above and glaucous beneath. It has a heavy texture for its size.

This is a rather rare cultivar and is not easily propagated.

A. buergerianum 'Mino yatsubusa'

The very odd leaves of this cultivar are most "un-maple-like!" They are three-lobed, with the center lobe long and narrow. The side lobes are quite short and extend at right angles. They are situated about ⅓ the distance from the leaf base. The leaf mainly consists of the long, narrow, gradually-tapering center lobe. This lobe ends in a very sharp point, while the side lobes end in rather blunt points. The margins are plain or are very indistinctly notched. There are only three main veins—one in the center of each lobe. The sides of the lobes tend to curl upward. Leaves vary in size. The foliage on new growth is 7 to 8 cm long and 5 cm wide, while leaves on mature wood are only 4 to 5 cm long.

The foliage is a very rich, shiny green, and the substance is firm. The Fall coloration is a brilliant combination of scarlet and orange. The shiny leaves have the appearance of being "lacquered" as the Autumn colors develop.

This is a dwarf, shrubby-growing plant. Frequent re-branching makes for a dense, rounded, small shrub. New shoots are rarely over 15 to 25 cm long. Leaf nodes are closely spaced on the shoots. Secondary buds occur at the primary leaf base and produce either tiny new side shoots or a small leaf cluster.

It is hardy in our plantings, but it is very difficult to propagate and remains one of the rarer forms in collections.

I place this cultivar in the species *A. buergerianum*. In many old references it is included with the *A. palmatum* cultivars. This may have been for convenience in grouping it with the "Japanese Maples." The bud structure, bark characteristics, leaf venation, and growth habit firm my opinion for buergerianum placement. It is most interesting, however, that I have had much difficulty grafting it on *A. buergerianum* understock. It also will graft on *A. palmatum* (but with difficulty), which in itself is rather unusual.

A. buergerianum 'Mitsuba kaede'

This form of the species produces a multi-branched type of growth because the leaf nodes are placed very close together. The resulting leaf cover is very dense.

The foliage is bright green and is a lighter or thinner texture than the species. Shade-grown foliage is quite shiny.

The leaf forms a distinct "T" shape; the long center lobe is twice as long as the two side lobes which extend at right angles at the base. The leaf base is truncate, forming a flat top to the "T". The two base lobes measure 4 to 6 cm across, and the leaf is 3 to 6 cm long. The margins are notched or lobulate at times.

This does not appear to be a tall-growing form. However, I have grown this cultivar only a short time and have not seen it in maturity.

A. buergerianum 'Miyasama kaede yatsubusa'

This plant is almost identical to 'Miyasama' except for size. The plant is short and stubby, and the rate of growth is only a few cm per year. It forms a very dense foliage pattern because the distance between the leaf nodes is only 1 to 1½ cm. Since it is also multi-branched, the result is a very dense plant.

The leaves are very similar to 'Miyasama' and measure 3 to 5 cm long and wide. The side lobes are prominent, forming at right angles at about the center of the leaf sides. The three main veins are prominent—one in the center of each lobe. The stiff petioles are 2 or 3 cm long.

The leaves are a bright reddish color as the new foliage develops. As the leaf attains full size, it becomes the typical bright green. The texture is rather firm, almost leathery. The undersurface is bluish-green. Fall colors develop in the yellow-gold tones, with shadings of rose.

This delightful dwarf is rather rare in collections and slightly difficult to propagate.

A. buergerianum "Musk Scented"
'Jakō kaede'

The outstanding character of this plant is the scented leaf. When touched, or rubbed between the fingers, it gives off an unusual "musk-like" odor. It is not strong enough to be objectionable.

The second valuable character is its dwarf shrubbiness. This plant makes a most desirable addition to the collection of "interestiing and unusual plants."

The very deep green, small leaves have a general outline of elongate-triangulate, but with two small, rounded lobes extending from each side. The tips of the lobes are blunt. The leaves normally measure 1½ to 2½ cm long and 1½ cm wide. New shoots may produce leaves up to 3½ cm long. The base of the leaves is cuneate, sometimes broadly so.

Fall colors are of the gold tones, shaded lightly with red or crimson. New shoots are very slender and up to 15 or 20 cm long. Multi-branching develops strongly on most stems. At the main leaf nodes, buds either shoot additional small leaves or small side twigs. Foliage on the side twigs develops on a horizontal plane.

This is a rounded, dense, small shrub and is hardy but not rugged. The branch texture is a little thin.

This most interesting "cultivar" has caused me much amusement, and I feel will also amuse the reader. For many decades it has been included in the Japanese Maple lists as the "Musk Scented Buergerianum" and regarded as a rare form of this maple. Many very early references place it in the "maple" group.

During his research studies last year, Thomas Delendick of the New York Botanical Gardens included some of this plant specimen with other plant material assembled by Dr. Herman F. Becker (a paleobotanist) for venation studies. The material was submitted to Dr. Toshimasa Tanai of Hokkaido University, a noted authority on leaf venation, particularly on paleobotanical determination. Dr. Tanai made the determination that 'Jako kaede' was not an *Acer* but belonged to the *Vebenacea*, and was identified as the species *Premna japonica*.

Little wonder I was having no success grafting onto *A. buergerianum* understock, but found cuttings rooted easily! If we ever have a plant mature and bloom, the floral structure will remove all doubt about taxonomy.

A. buergerianum 'Miyasama kaede yatsubusa'

A. buergerianum "Musk Scented"

A. buergerianum 'Nusitoriyama'

A. buergerianum 'Naruto kaede'

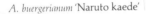

A. *buergerianum* 'Naruto kaede'

This interesting cultivar is notable for its surprising foliage. Each leaf appears to form a sharp-pointed "T". The center lobe is a long triangle, and the side lobes extend at right angles, all being sharply pointed. All three lobes have margins which are strongly involute, making the lobes appear much narrower. The incurled margins are almost smooth or very slightly toothed. The "T" shape of the leaf is accentuated by these rolled margins and sharp points. The leaves are 3 to 5 cm long and measure the same across the side points. The petioles are strong and 4 cm long.

The heavy-textured leaves are a deep, rich green. The top surface is shiny, but the under surface is glaucous. This gives a two-toned effect to the foliage. Fall colors are rich gold, blended with red.

This cultivar is a sturdy-growing, tall shrub, and in the early years may grow as much as 1 meter a year. It soon forms a rather dense, twiggy plant. This is a little-known but most interesting form of the species.

A. *buergerianum* 'Nusitoriyama'

The leaves of this delicate plant are almost entirely white. As they first emerge in the Spring, they have a strong pinkish overtone, which will soon turn white or cream. The foliage will vary according to the conditions under which this sensitive plant is grown. Usually leaves will be 2 to 3 cm long and wide. Leaves twice this size will form under optimum conditions.

The shape of the leaf is the triangular form of buergerianum but side lobes are often suppressed into small, rounded portions. Occasionally the side lobes are entirely lacking, resulting in an ovate leaf. The texture of the foliage is rather thin and delicate. All margins are smooth. The petioles are short (1 cm or less) and sturdy.

This is considered a very slow-growing plant. It rarely forms a long shoot or very strong growth. All twigs and branches are thin.

This cultivar is extremely difficult to maintain in a planting. It is also very difficult to propagate. The grafts will heal, but to culture the new graft on into a two- or three-year old plant takes special care and attention. Since the foliage is almost totally lacking in chlorophyll or food-producing tissue, it is necessary to leave a small amount of the understock. This should produce the normal green foliage which will help sustain the cultivar graft, through photosynthetic support.

This is not a particularly beautiful or attractive plant but is of considerable interest to the collector of rare plants. It should be grown in full shade to prevent complete leaf scorch from the direct sun. It also seems quite sensitive to mold or fungi which destroy the buds and leaf tissue.

A. *buergerianum* 'Tanchō'

This cultivar is much like 'Naruto kaede' in foliage but is a more dwarf form.

The leaves measure 2½ to 3 cm long and wide. Each leaf is strongly 3-lobed. The margins of the lobes roll tightly involute. In some cases, they are almost tube-shaped. The rolled margins are slightly incised, but this is hidden. As the center lobe and the two side lobes are tightly rolled, the leaf appears to be a "T". The leaf cups upward from the petiole, which is thin and 3 cm long.

The leaves are deep, rich green above, with the lower surface glaucous. Since both sides show on each leaf, because of the curling, the foliage appears bi-toned. The leaves are set closely on the twigs, forming a dense pattern. There is also much side-branching at the nodes of the main shoots.

This is a dwarf type which may grow 8 to 12 cm per season. Since it is multi-branched, it becomes rather dense and shrubby. It is a most unusual and little-known form of *A. buergerianum*, is not easily propagated, and remains rare in collections.

A. buergerianum 'Wakō nishiki'

The tiny variegated leaves of this cultivar set it apart from all others. The very small ones on older wood are only 2 cm long and 1 cm wide. On younger wood, they are as much as 4 cm long and 3 or 4 cm between side tips. The leaf is oblong-ovate, rapidly tapering to a very sharp tip on the center lobe. The ovate outline is broken by the two very small, sharp side lobes which extend almost at right angles. The stiff petiole is about 1 cm long.

The new foliage may appear almost totally white in some growth, but most of it is a very light green, heavily to almost completely shaded white. This white color is due to the concentration of very tiny dots which merge together and become almost solid. In the leaves with the most white, the three main veins are a distinct, contrasting green.

This is a very slow-growing, compact, shrub form of the species. It is not easy to propagate and requires extra care in cultivation.

Acer capillipes Maximowicz 1867
Series *Tegmentosa*
'Hosoe kaede', 'Ashiboso urinoki'

This is one of the desirable forms of "striped-bark" maples. It will become a big tree, up to 25 meters high at maturity. The bark of the trunk is green with dark lengthwise stripes. Very old bark becomes grayish-brown and fissured.

The new foliage unfolds with a bright red color. As the leaves mature, they become a bright green and are thick-chartaceous in texture. The leaf is broadly ovate with 3 or 5 small, sharp side lobes. Occasionally lobes are totally absent. The base is cordate to rounded. The margins are irregularly serrulate. Leaves vary in size from 8 to 13 cm long and 4 to 8 cm wide.

While this tree is endemic to Japan and distributed through the Honshu and Shikoku regions, it is almost completely concentrated in a fairly small area of Central Honshu.

This is a bold, beautiful tree which is useful in overstory plantings in landscape.

Acer carpinifolium Sieb. & Zucc. 1845
Series *Carpinifolia*
'Chidorinoki', 'Yamashiba kaede'

A. buergerianum 'Wakō nishiki'

A. carpinifolium

A most unmaple-like maple! The leaves are quite distinct among *Acers* but closely resemble those of the genus *Carpinus* (the "Hornbeam" tree).

The leaf is ovate-oblong, acuminate, but slightly cordate at the base. The texture is a little thin. The margins are regularly and sharply double-serrate, often with long persistent hairs on the veins underneath. The 18 to 23 pairs of lateral nerves are prominent, are ascending parallel, and form a noticeable feature of the foliage. The pairs of leaves are openly spaced along the twigs, lying horizontally. Each leaf is from 8 to 15 cm long but 3 to 7 cm wide. The short petioles are 1 to 1½ cm long.

This is a small tree, maturing at 7 to 10 meters. It is upright in habit, and the top canopy is not very spreading. It is hardy, durable, and makes an outstanding specimen plant for landscaping.

This species is common in the ravines of the mountains of Honshu, Shikoku, and Kyushu areas of Japan, where it occurs at elevations of 200 to 1300 meters.

A. circinatum Pursh 1814 Series *Palmata*
"Vine Maple"

Knowing full well that this is not a "Japanese Maple," I include *Acer circinatum* for comparative purposes. This is the only species in the Series *Palmata* which occurs outside the Asian area in which all the other species are closely grouped. This lends credence to the theory of some authors that there was once a land bridge between the Pacific Northwest and Asia (over which plants and animals migrated and exchanged) during the development of present-day species. *A. circinatum* is native in the Pacific Northwest America, while all the other closely allied species are indigenous to Japan, China, and adjacent areas.

The close affinity of species is further demonstrated by success in cross hybridizing and interspecific grafting of *A. circinatum* on *A. japonicum* and *A. palmatum*. It is also possible to make the reverse grafts successfully, although *A. circinatum* heals too slowly to be a more desirable understock than *A. palmatum*.

A. circinatum apparently is genetically more stable than the other species in the Series. There are not the large numbers of variations from "type" as in other *Palmata*. However, a "Fern leafed" variety has been discovered. (See *A. circ.* 'Monroe') Also, I have under observation a "yellow leafed" form and a dwarf form (reportedly a "Witch's Broom").

The "Vine Maple" is a tall shrub or small tree. In horticultural plantings it often makes a multi-stemmed tall shrub up to 5 or 6 meters tall. In its native habitat, and when under an over-story of large conifers, it will become a tall, viney-stemmed, slender tree, winding its way up toward the sunlight, ultimately reaching a height of 10 or 12 meters. This winding vine-like growth gives rise to the common name.

It is most appreciated in the Pacific Northwest for its beautiful Fall colors which turn the mountainside to "Flame." Most colors are brilliant scarlet, although many tones of orange and yellow blend throughout the foliage. Unfortunately, these intense colors do not always develop under landscape conditions where abundant moisture and fertility prevent the plant from being under any stress.

In the Spring the foliage is a bright green. The orbicular leaves have 7 to 9 lobes, shallowly separated, and tapering sharply to the tip. The margins are lightly toothed. The leaves measure 4 to 7 cm in diameter, but can vary tremendously in size (up to 10 cm) depending upon the site in which the tree is grown.

A. circinatum. Fall foliage

A. circinatum 'Little Gem' (Photo by Ken Hixson)

This is an excellent, trouble-free small tree for landscaping as a companion plant for many types of perennials and shrubs. Its popularity is increasing in the nursery trade.

A. circinatum 'Little Gem'

This beautiful dwarf originated from a "Witch's Broom" on a normal plant. The leaf is orbicular in general outline with (5) 7 to 9 points. The lobes are very shallow, separating about ¼ the distance into the leaf center, and are ovate-triangular with lightly incised margins. On the small leaves the lobes are hardly more than a toothed margin.

Many leaves measure only about 1 cm in diameter. Others vary from 2½ to 3 cm. Occasionally on strong new growth the foliage is 3½ cm long and 4 cm wide. The following year, however, as the wood matures the leaves will be much smaller.

The foliage is a light shade of green with the surface very lightly rugose. Plants growing in our collection have colored very nicely in the Fall in the orange and crimson tones.

The leaf nodes are very close together, forming a dense foliage pattern. The growth is multi-branched and forms a compact plant. New growth may be as little as 2 or 3 cm long and up to 6 or 8 cm. Occasionally on young plants a new shoot will develop up to 15 or 20 cm long. However, this produces the very short typical growth the following year.

The original plant material was sent to me by Mr. Alleyne Cook of North Vancouver, B.C. , Canada. It was from a "Witch's Broom" growth on an *A. circinatum* in Stanley Park in Vancouver, B.C. It is a very good dwarf form but has had a limited distribution among plant collectors.

There are several other "Witch's Broom" Vine Maples on record. In fact, Mr. Cook has supplied me with two other forms. One seemed to die-back considerably, and the other was a much more coarse-growing type which, in my opinion, is not as desirable. I feel this particular clone is of sufficient worth to register in order to prevent confusion with other similar forms.

A. circinatum var. Monroe
Mulligan 1974 Series *Palmata*
"Monroe's Vine Maple"

This is the first known true variant of *A. circinatum* to be described for multi-dissected foliage. There is one other clone named 'Elegant' which has deeply indented margins and good Fall coloration.

The foliage ranges in size from 6 to 10 cm long and 7 to 13 cm wide. The petioles are 4 to 5 cm long. The leaf divides into 5 to 7 lobes, each separated entirely to the center of the leaf. The sides of each lobe are deeply incised pinnately, almost to the midrib. These sublobes are further incised or serrated, forming very irregular margins. The inner ⅓ of the lobe restricts almost to the width of the main vein. The two basal lobes are very small, at times only sub-lobes, but otherwise completely separate from the other lobes and clasping the petiiole. The leaves are reminiscent of, and intermediate between, the *A. japonicum aconitifolium* and *A. palmatum dissectum*.

This is a sturdy plant under cultivation and will form a tall bush, becoming broad with age. The branches are stiff and upright and occasionally multi-branching. It has not been in cultivation long enough to give mature heights, but one can assume from the rate of growth that it will ultimately reach at least 4 meters.

This plant was discovered by Dr. Warner Monroe, a philosophy professor at Warner Pacific College, Portland, Oregon. It is fortunate for horticulture that Dr. Monroe is an observant and persistent person. While conducting a nature study hike with a group of young people, he noted a plant which "looked different." It was in the deep conifer forests on the headwaters of the McKenzie River high in the Cascade Mountains. The ten years following discovery (in 1960) were spent in trying to get identification of this plant. Meanwhile, Dr. Monroe layered a side branch, in situ, and successfully moved the resulting plant to his home. In 1965 he successfully layered another side branch which was later given to the author in 1970. The original plant remains in the dense conifer forest almost smothered under low-growing native plants. When I last visited it, it was still a very small, weak plant—only 50 cm tall.

I gathered material and made structural studies and photographic studies of leaves, buds, and blossoms. These were submitted to Brian Mulligan, Director Emeritus of the University of Washington Arboretum. The original descriptions and taxonomic determinations were subsequently published by Mr. Mulligan in BAILEYA, 1974.

Acer cissifolium Sieb. & Zucc. 1864
  Series *Cissifolia*
  'Mitsude kaede', 'Ammakko kaede', 'Amakuki'

The foliage of this maple resembles the North American "Box Elder" (*Acer negundo*). *A. cissifolium* has leaves which are three-foliate, with all leaflets uniform in size.

(*A. negundo* leaves are composed of 3 to 7 (9) leaflets). *A. Henryi* is also similar in foliage pattern.

The individual leaflet is ovate-elliptic, 5 to 8 cm long and 2 to 4 cm wide, cuneate at the base. The tip is elongately tapered. The foliage is an olive green color and of rather thin texture.

This is a strong-growing, upright tree which tends to remain rather narrow. It will mature at about 25 meters. In its native areas it grows in rather moist situations and seems to enjoy plenty of moisture under landscape conditions. This maple occurs throughout the main islands of Japan at elevations of 200 to 1300 meters.

A. circinatum var. Monroe

A. crataegifolium Sieb. & Zucc. 1845
  Series *Crataegifolia*
  "Hawthorn Maple"
  Syn.: 'Uri kaede,'
  'Me urinoki,' 'Shirahashinoki,'
  'Hana kaede,' 'Yama kaede,'
  'Shira kaede,' 'Ao uri,' 'Hon uri'

An excellent tree for landscaping and as a companion plant for flowering shrubs and perennials. It does not become too large (6 to 7 meters) and is not overly aggressive in root competition with other plants. It is hardy, holds foliage color very well, and stands full sun.

The 3-lobed leaves are typically "ginnala" (long triangular shape) with the elongate center lobe and abbreviated side lobes. Leaves are smaller than the species, measuring about 4 cm long and 2 or 3 cm wide.

The foliage during the growing season is light green, changing to a brilliant crimson in the Fall. This color is uniform over the entire plant. It is, indeed, a "burning bush!" It makes a spectacular accent plant.

Acer griseum Pax 1902
Section *Trifoliata*
"Paper Bark Maple"

The remarkable feature of this *Acer* is the excoriating bark. As the mature outer layer flakes or peels off, the underbark is exposed and is a rather bright copperish color. This very attractive feature has engendered the popularity of this species as a landscape plant or specimen tree.

Another outstanding feature is the brilliant scarlet Fall foliage. The leaves are somewhat persistent in late season and give a long period of bright color. The Spring and Summer foliage is a rich green.

The leaf is composed of three leaflets. Each is attached on a short stalk and is elliptic, or ovate-oblong, and 3 to 8 cm long. The margins are lobulate or coarsely toothed. The leaf is glaucous and pubescent underneath. The petioles are densely hairy. The nutlets have very thick, hard coatings and are tomentose.

This is an upright, small tree. It matures at 8 to 12 meters. The branching is sturdy and stiff and with age becomes twiggy inside, having many small spurs bearing few leaves.

This is a very hardy tree, originating in China. It is quite difficult to propagate vegetatively as compared with other *Acer*. Production from seed is also undependable. Usually a large percentage of the heavy nutlets are well-formed but hollow, lacking viability. Those seed which are complete are very slow to germinate. The usual methods of stratification to induce germination are of little aid. Seed quite often takes two or three years to germinate even after any one of several seed treatments.

A. griseum showing the peeling bark characteristic.

A. micranthum

Acer micranthum Sieb & Zucc. 1845
Series *Micrantha*
'Komine kaede'

This is another of the delicate-appearing species of *Micrantha*, but it is not delicate in structure. It is hardy and adaptable. The shape of the leaves and the light limb structure contribute to the delicate, attractive appearance. This is one of my favorite trees in the Series, along with *Acer Maximowiczii* from China, and *A. Tschonoskii*.

The leaf measures 5 to 8 cm long and about as wide. It is strongly divided into five lobes. The two base lobes are very small and almost ovate. The two side lobes are elongate-lanceolate and acuminate. The center lobe dominates the leaf and is long-ovate, acuminate, tapering to a very long, slender tip. The margins are incised and doubly serrate.

The foliage is bright rusty-red when it first unfolds, as are the new stems and shoots. The new growth makes a bright contrasting combination in the landscape. It matures as a bright tone of green, often with the center vein of each lobe a contrasting light yellow-green.

This species will form a tall shrub or small tree, maturing up to 10 meters. It occurs throughout the Honshu, Shikoku, and Kyushu areas of Japan. It is found in sunny places in the forests at elevations of 700 to 1800 meters. Ogata reports that it will be found as high as 2300 meters.

A. Miyabei Maximowicz 1888
Series *Campestria*
'Kurobi itaya' 'Shibata kaede'

A large tree which may reach 15 to 20 meters at maturity. It is sturdy, strong-branching, and forms a broad canopy.

The leaves consist of five lobes, separated over half way to the center. Each lobe is caudate-acuminate with a blunt tip and a small obtuse lobule on each side. The leaves are 8 to 15 cm across with long petioles, 4 to 10 cm long. The young leaves are lightly pubescent on both surfaces, heavier along the veins. The mature leaves are olive-green and of rather heavy texture.

A. Miyabei is endemic to Japan in Hokkaido and parts of Honshu Island. It grows in very moist and somewhat swampy places along streams. It is not widely found in cultivation and is considered rather rare.

A. mono Maximowicz 1857 (*Acer pictum*)
Series *Platanoidea*
"Painted Maple"
Syn.: 'Tsuta momiji', 'Shiraki kaede', 'Tokiwa kaede', 'Itagi kaede', 'Itaya', 'Ao kaede', 'Yorokko kaede', and others

A fast-growing large tree which develops a rounded, spreading canopy as it matures. It is quite hardy, and I find it surprisingly free of insect and disease problems. This is a fine selection for over-story shade in perennials and shrubbery plantings. It reaches at least 14 meters when mature.

The leaves measure up to 10 cm long and 14 cm wide. There are 5 to 7 lobes which are very short and triangular. However, some leaves have deep separations between the lobes. Foliage varies from plant to plant. Each lobe is sharply pointed.

Throughout the year the foliage is a very bright green and is resistant to sunburn. In the Fall, the trees become quite brilliant gold with crimson blending and shading through the leaf. So the notable color gives rise to the common English name of "Painted Maple".

There are many subspecies and varieties of *A. mono*. The large list of Japanese names indicates the variation in type, appearance, and leaf shape to be found in different localities throughout the natural range of the plant. *A. mono* var. *ambiguum*, 'Oni itaya' is one of the selections widely planted in Japan. The leaves of the variety *Mayrii* ('Aka itayo', 'Beni itayo') are reddish when they first emerge.

Ogata has excellent descriptions and discussions in his writing on the *Acer* in Japan. For detailed information, the serious *Acer* student would be advised to read his published material.

Some taxonomists place *A. mono* as a subspecies of *A. truncatum*.

For reference purposes, I list the following sub-division of *A. mono*.

> f. *glabrum* "Ezo itaya"
> f. *magnificum* "O ezo itaya"
> f. *marmorata* "Enko kaede"
> f. *piliferum* "Ke enko kaede"
> f. *connivens* "Urage enko kaede"
> f. *puberulum* "Ke urage enko kaede"
> var. *Taishkuense* "Taishaku itaya"
> var. *glaucum* "Urajiro itaya"
> var. *Mayrii* "Aka itaya"
> var. *trichobasis* "Itomaki itaya"
> var. *ambiguum* "Oni itaya"
> f. *pulvigerum* "Miyama oni itaya"

A. mono 'Asahi kaede'
  See *A. mono*, var. *dissectum* (Koidzumi)

A. mono 'Hoshiyadori'

This remarkable foliage has variegation of both the "Hoshi fu" type (star-like) which consists of tiny scattered flecks or specks of color and the "Sunago fu" type (scattered sand). The cream colored, or white markings boldly cover the deep green basic leaf color in varying amounts. In some leaves, the light tone markings predominate (in some cases completely masking the green), while in other foliage, the green is dominant. There are all gradations of patterns from light dots to bold color slashes. The color varies according to the light intensity. In full shade, the markings will be almost pure white. In full sun, they will be light yellow to gold. Full exposure to hot sun, however, will cause leaf damage.

The leaves are 5 to 7-lobed, with each lobe broadly triangular and not deeply cut into the leaf. However, foliage varies greatly, depending upon the degree of variegation. Some leaves will exhibit only 3 lobes. The leaves will be very dissimilar in shape. They will measure up to 9 or 10 cm in diameter.

This is a semi-dwarf shrub type, not exceeding 3 or 4 meters as it matures. It is multi-branching, and the plant is rather compact and broadens with age. I like to have it near a path so that the unique foliage can be easily seen and appreciated.

A. mono 'Hoshizukiyo'
  Alternate spelling: 'Hoshi tsukiyo'

This cultivar is almost identical to *A. mono* 'Hoshiyadori'. The variegations are very similar but usually are more intense in color and cover the leaf area more fully. At times, the variegations are so concentrated that the colors coalesce and become solid. It is possible to find all degrees of variations, however, on both the cultivars so descriptions overlap.

The leaf shape, growth habits, and other characteristics are identical. Literature on the subject indicates that this was originally a bud-sport of *A. mono* 'Hoshiyadori.' It is not widely propagated because the two cultivars are difficult to differentiate.

A. mono. Fall coloration.

A. mono 'Hoshiyadori'

A. mono var. *marmorata,* form *dissectum*

A. nikoense

A. mono var. *marmorata*, form *dissectum*
  Syn.: 'Akikaze', 'Enko kaede',
  'Asahi kaede'

The leaves of this form of *A. mono* contrast with the type species by being deeply cut. The five lobes are separated half way to the center of the leaf with the ends tapering to a sharp point. The lobes arrange in a radiating pattern. The foliage is a deep green color and turns golden in the Fall. The leaf is about 7 or 8 cm long and broad.

This tree is not widely planted in Japan. It is normally a shorter tree than the type species of *A. mono*. It will reach about 10 or 12 meters as it matures.

This is not to be confused with 'Akikaze nishiki' which is the variegated form.

Ken Ogata points out in his discussion that the form *dissectum* of the variety *marmorata* is the juvenile type of foliage. His research indicates that this should be delineated as *A. mono*, var. *marmorata*, form *marmorata*.

A. mono 'Tōkiwa nishiki'
  (Probably the variegated form of
  A. mono var. *marmorata*)

This cultivar has the typical leaf shape of the species—broad leaves with 5 to 7 lobes. The lobes are very shallow, and the ends form a short triangle. The leaves are 7 to 10 cm long and broad, with smooth margins. The petioles are 5 to 6 cm long.

The leaves are a strong green tone. The variegations within the leaf are quite heavy and occasionally occupy the entire area. The markings vary from white to light cream or yellow. Occasionally the white area fills one-half the leaf, divided by the center vein, and the other half is green.

This hardy, small tree is a favorite for landscaping in Japan, and it should be better known and more widely used elsewhere.

This is a bolder variegation than found in the similar cultivars of *A. mono*, such as 'Hoshiyadori', and 'Hoshizukiyo'.

A. mono 'Usugumo'
  Syn.: 'Usugumori'

This most unusual leaf form has been likened to a bat's wing. However, the leaf is more beautiful than this term would indicate. The "fabric" appears to be stretched between the sharp-pointed lobe ends and the prominent main vein in each lobe. Each of the 7 to 9 lobes is triangular, but very short and terminates in a sharp point. This results in a large, undivided leaf surface. The tissue extending between each lobe is slightly folded so that the leaf surface is not flat.

The leaves are 8 to 11 cm long and broad, with a long slender petiole of 6 to 8 cm. The green leaves are thickly speckled with very fine dots of white, usually rather scattered, but occasionally concentrated, making the leaf appear white-green. A narrow strip which is almost pure white runs along both sides of the center vein of each lobe. The vein is a contrasting strong green.

This is an upright-growing plant (not a strong grower) which reaches 3 or 4 meter height rather slowly. It is difficult to propagate and not widely known in collections.

A. nikoense Maximowicz 1867
  (*A. Maximowiczianum* Miquel 1867)
  Section *Trifoliata*
  Nikko Maple
  Japanese names: 'Megusurinoki',
  'Chyojanocki', 'Chojanoki', 'Meguro',
  'Kochōnoki', 'Seminoki', 'Ohmitsude
  kaede'

This is a sturdy, large, but slender-growing tree which will mature at about 18 to 25 meters. It is native to the central and southern regions of Japan and also recorded from China.

The large leaves are trifoliate. Each leaflet is narrowly ovate to narrowly elliptic and measures from 5 to 12 cm long and 2 to 6 cm wide, with an obtuse tip. The margins are bluntly serrate to subentire. The mature leaves are dark green, glabrous above and glaucescent beneath. The young twigs, pedicels, and petioles are hirsute. The nutlets are pilose, and the pericarp is very hard and thick which makes germination of this species rather difficult. Germination often takes two or more years to occur, even with stratification and other seed treatments.

A. nipponicum Hara 1938
  Series *Parviflora*
  'Tetsu kaede'

This tree has large, bold foliage which is shallowly 5-lobed, each lobe deltoid, acuminate, and with margins sharply double-serrate. The leaves measure 10 to 15 cm long and 10 to 20 cm wide. They are a pleasing green, but rather thin in texture, cordate at the base, and glabrous on the upper side. Underneath there is a rusty-brown pubescence, especially persistent along the veins.

A mature plant will probably grow to 18 or 20 meters. An excellent specimen plant in the Zuiderpark, The Hague, Holland, was most impressive when I saw it in full bloom. The bold racemes were large and quite beautiful.

This is considered a rather rare plant in arboreta and nurseries. It occurs in the high mountainous regions of Honshu and Kyushu, Japan, but the distribution is irregular.

A. nipponicum

A. pentaphyllum Hu & Cheng 1948
  Series *Pentaphylla*
  (monotypic)

The beauty of this tree is the unusual foliage which is unlike any other species of *Acer*.

The leaves are usually divided into five lobes or leaflets (rarely 3 or 7). The oblong-lanceolate lobes are palmately or digitately arranged, separated entirely to the petiole attachment. Each lobe restricts at the base to the width of the main vein. The margins are sub-entire to serrate and slightly revolute. The outer end tapers gradually to a very sharp tip. The individual lobe measures 7 to 10 cm long but only 5 or 7 mm wide, rarely to 1 cm. The leaf extends to 8 to 12 cm long and 16 cm wide. The long, slender petioles are 6 to 8 cm.

The foliage is bright green above and glaucous underneath. These are durable leaves which resist sunburn very well. The Fall coloration is quite spectacular, ranging through the spectrum of yellow, gold, orange and crimson—occasionally all shading together.

The tree is upright in habit and forms an open structure. The twigs and branches are not coarse. I am not sure of the hardiness of this plant, but regard it as "tender" in cold winters. The plants in my collection have withstood −8° to 0° (18° to 32°F). Without special Winter protection, I doubt that it would stand temperatures much lower than this, especially specimen plants grown in large containers.

This is a very rare species of *Acer* and not widely grown even though it is a most

A. pentaphyllum

desirable plant. It is native to a very small area in S.W. China. The seeds were first collected by J. Rock (Rock #17819) in the Szechuan Province along the Yalung River. I have been told that there are only about 200 to 300 trees existing in the native habitat. A plant from Rock's seed is growing at the Strybing Arboretum in San Francisco, California. All plants in cultivation in the United States have originated from that tree.

A. pseudosieboldianum (Pax) Komarov 1904
Series *Palmata*
Syn.: *A. Sieboldianum* var. *mandshuricum* (Maxim)

This delightful little tree occurs in Manchuria and Korea. I include it here as a closely related species of the Series, and also because it is growing in popularity in horticulture. As a small tree, it will mature at about 7 or 8 meters. It is not aggressive and so is a good companion plant. The interesting foliage makes it a very desirable addition to the garden.

The leaves are a bluish-green, contrasting with the other species of *Palmata*. New foliage is lightly covered with minute pubescence which gradually disappears in mid-Summer. The petioles are also pubescent when young. The Fall colors are excellent and are brilliant yellow and scarlet tones.

The leaf is 7 to 9-lobed, palmately divided half way to the middle. Each lobe is short ovate, tapering rapidly to a sharp point. The margins are unevenly serrate but smooth on the inner half of the lobe. Leaves are 4 to 5 cm long and wide. These are noticeably smaller than the close relative, *A. shirasawanum*, *A. Sieboldianum*, or *A. circinatum*.

Young twigs are dark and change to grey-purple in older branches.

Acer pycnanthum K. Koch 1863
Series *Rubra* 'Hananoki', 'Hana kaede'

This species is considered quite rare and is closely related to *Acer rubrum* of Eastern North America which is quite common. Ogata mentions that it is restricted in its distribution to a radius of about 60 km, centering around Mt. Ena, in Honshu. It was found later in another locality about 120 km further north. However, it is not common even within its range. Usually it is found growing in very moist situations at elevations of 400 to 500 meters.

It blooms in April before any leaves appear. When in full flower, every twig has numerous small red blossoms. After the bloom period, the foliage begins to develop. The leaves are sub-orbicular, **3-lobed**, 4 to 7 cm long and 3 to 6 cm wide. The lobes are ovate-triangular, acuminate, and irregularly serrate. The foliage is deep green—glabrous above and glaucous beneath. The nodes are rusty brown and slightly pubescent when young.

The seeds mature very early, compared to other *Acers*. They ripen in mid-May and soon spiral to the ground. The seed is very short-lived. I have had difficulty in storing seed of this species.

This tree grows to about 25 meters with maturity. It is a valuable tree for overstory shade in mixed landscapes.

Ogata mentions that certain large trees, both wild and cultivated, have been designated as "natural monuments" by the Japanese government.

A. rufinerve Sieb. & Zucc. 1845
Series *Tegmentosa* 'Uriha kaede'
Syn.: 'Urihada kaede', 'Iizuku', 'Komori kaede', 'Ao kaede'

A strong, upright tree of medium height, reaching 15 or 18 meters at maturity. On occasion it tends to grow almost fastigiate, but generally broadens only slightly in the mature canopy.

The bark is unusually attractive with dark, narrow lengthwise stripes running up the lustrous green surface, which gradually becomes greyer as it matures.

The leaves are of heavy texture and appear almost rugose. They are three-lobed, with the two side lobes comparatively small. The strong center lobe is triangular, and the side lobes point forward. Leaves measure from 10 to 15 cm long and 12 to 15 cm across. The base of the leaf is cordate, and the margins are bluntly and doubly serrate. The stiff petioles are 5 cm long.

The deep green foliage changes to exceptionally bright tones in the Fall. The leaves become rich yellow and gold, heavily and brightly suffused with crimson.

In Japan, the native stands grow in the drier locations from the middle to the upper part of the forest slopes. It adapts well in landscape use, accepting dry to moist situations but does not tolerate saturated soils.

A. pseudosieboldianum

A. rufinerve. Fall coloration.

A. rufinerve 'Beni uri'
Syn.: 'Kyō nishiki'

This bright cultivar has a large leaf which measures 8 to 14 cm long and occasionally slightly wider, depending upon the amount of variegation. The leaves are not as regularly triangulate as the type leaves of the species. This is due to the altered shape where the strong variegations occur in the blade. The 3 to 5 lobes are short and triangular, serrate, and terminate in a sharp point.

The basic leaf color is a deep green, strongly variegated with yellow. This is "Kiri fu" (cut in) type of marking which occupies half the lobe, dividing color at the main vein. There are other lesser forms of markings which form only slender yellow streaks in the green. These are mainly bold and diversified variegations.

In the Fall, the light colored portions change to a bright crimson, hence the name "Beni" or red.

This plant is not as strong-growing as the species and is rather capricious in cultivation. It is also difficult to propagate and is rather rare in collections.

The name "Beni uri" is being used on cultivars of two different species of *Acer*. In the United States it has been applied to a variegated form of *A. crataegifolium*. The name rightfully belongs on the variegated cultivar of *A. rufinerve*.

A. rufinerve 'Hatsuyuki'
Syn.: 'Fuiri urihada kaede', 'Uriha nishiki', albo limbatum

The leaves are typical "rufinerve" in shape, rather thick and of good substance. They are rounded at the base, and the two side lobes are very short compared with the long center lobe. The size varies from 7 to 15 cm long and 5 to 9 cm wide, forming an ovate-triangular shape. The margins are lightly double-serrate.

This cultivar varies widely in the amount of white variegation in its deep green foliage. The edges are normally tinged with white, but on some leaves the markings are scattered and extend over the entire surface. There will also be some leaves which are

entirely free of white mottling. I feel that high levels of fertility and the resultant rapid growth will mask the tendency to variegated marking. As the trees slow in growth rate, the variegation becomes more marked.

This is an upright tree but usually it will not reach the heights of the species.

A. rufinerve 'Shirayuki'
(*luteo variegatum*)

This variegated form of *A. rufinerve* is almost identical to 'Hatsuyuki' in all aspects except leaf color. The variegations are yellow rather than the white color found in 'Hatsuyuki'.

A. shirasawanum Koidzumi 1911
Series *Palmata* 'Ō itaya meigetsu'

This tree adds a delicate foliage pattern to mixed plantings. Its foliage is a different texture than others in the Series *Palmata*. The leaves have the feeling of rather stiff paper (chartaceous) and are a little thin, almost translucent. Sunlight through the foliage dramatizes the difference from other closely related species.

Also, the color is a light tone of green that sets it apart. Though appearing delicate, the foliage resists sunburn. Autumn coloration ranges into the gold tones with a blending of crimson. The total effect of the foliage texture and color makes it a desirable choice as a companion tree for shrubbery plantings.

The orbicular leaves have 11 (9) short lobes which separate only ⅓ the distance to the center. The lobe ends are ovate, terminating in a short tip. The margins are prominently serrated. The young leaves are lightly white-pubescent, soon becoming glabrous. The new twigs are bright green and sometimes glaucous.

As the tree matures, the growth is slender and multi-branched and forms an interesting scaffold pattern. Very old trees may reach 20 meters in height, but this is rarely seen in cultivation.

This species is native to Central and Southern Honshu and Shikoku, Japan. Since it was first described, its popularity has increased for large landscape plantings.

A. rufinerve 'Hatsuyuki'

A. shirasawanum

A. shirasawanum palmatifolium

A very beautiful selection of *shirasawanum*, not yet widely distributed in many countries. The distinct foliage is most attractive in all seasons.

The bright green leaves will take full sun without burning and have an almost translucent appearance. The Fall colors are very spectacular and persist for a long period. The colors are bright blends of yellow and gold which are mottled and shaded with crimson.

The leaf has 11 lobes which are long, lanceolate-acuminate, with a sharp narrow tip. They separate distinctly over half way to the center and radiate openly. The margins are prominently toothed and roll slightly downward making the separation between lobes more distinct. The veins on the underleaf stand out prominently. The leaves measure 10 cm in diameter.

The bark of the twigs and young branches is a dusty green with prominent white striations. The older wood assumes a darker grey-green.

This is a sturdy upright type of small tree. It forms a rounded canopy and matures at about 8 meters. It is hardy and accepts a wide range of culture conditions.

A. Sieboldianum Miquel 1865
Series *Palmata* "Siebold's Maple"
Syn.: 'Itaya meigetsu', 'Kibana uchiwa kaede', 'Ko hauchiwa kaede'

The bright green leaves are 9-lobed (rarely 7 to 11). The leaf surface has a minute pubescence when first unfolding, but this is soon lost as the leaf matures. The petioles are pubescent when young, as well as the main veins on the undersurface of the leaf.

These are large leaves for *Palmata*—up to 7 or 8 cm long and 8 or 9 cm wide. They are orbicular, with the ovate-oblong lobes separating half way to the center. Each lobe terminates in a sharp point, and the margins are sharply toothed.

The Fall coloration is an outstanding feature of this species. It becomes a brilliant scarlet with some orange leaves. It is a dependable plant for coloration—more so that *A. circinatum* under landscape culture. I find that *A. circinatum* will usually color poorly when grown in mixed shrubbery plantings, while *A. Sieboldianum* displays color very well under these conditions of moisture and fertility.

It forms a tall, multi-stemmed shrub up to 3 meters. If trained as a single-stemmed tree, it will reach 9 or 10 meters at maturity. It is a very hardy, trouble-free plant for mixed landscapes.

This is one of the most common species in the mountain woods and thickets of Japan. It is widely used in horticulture, and there are several popular named cultivars.

Also, there are several important varieties of this species:
var. *albiflorum* "Shirobana itaya meigetsu"
var. *Tsusimense* "Koha itaya meigetsu"
var. *microphyllum* "Hime uchiwa kaede", "Ko uchiwa kaede"

A. Sieboldianum 'Kasatoriama'

The leaves of this cultivar are circular in outline and have 9 to 1 [1]lobes, rarely 13. Each lobe separates about ⅓ the distance into the leaf. Lobe ends taper rapidly to a sharp point with margins toothed.

The foliage is a pale or yellowish green and rather thin in texture. The Fall coloration is in strong combinations of yellow and orange.

It is a stocky, small tree, not growing as tall as the "type" species. It will become twiggy as it matures and the multi-branching replaces the longer growth of the juvenile shoots. The tree will mature at 4 to 5 meters.

A. Sieboldianum 'Kinugasayama' (silk canopy or umbrella)

The foliage is a distinct bluish-green color and is heavily covered with a silvery pubescence. These minute hairs are longer and more pronounced than those usually found on foliage of other cultivars of this species. The petioles are also strongly pubescent. This pubescence gives rise to part of the name, "kinu" (silk)-like hairs. The Fall colors are blends of brilliant orange and red which vary on different portions of the tree.

The medium-size leaves range from 4 by 6 cm to as large as 8 by 10 cm. The petioles are 2 to 3 cm long. Each leaf has 7 lobes which separate at least half way to the center. The lobes are ovate, with sharp tips, and the margins have prominent serrations.

A. shirasawanum palmatifolium. Fall coloration.

A. Sieboldianum 'Kinugasayama'

It is a stocky, small tree which is strongly branched and makes a round-topped plant. It matures at 6 or 7 meters and is not difficult to grow.

A. Sieboldianum microphyllum
'Hime uchiwa kaede'

This is a small-leafed variety of the species. The leaves measure 5 to 6 cm in diameter with petioles 2 cm long. The orbicular outline is separated by 9 or 11 lobes with ovate-acuminate terminals. The margins are serrate.

New leaves are yellowish green, darkening to deep green as they mature. The Fall color is spectacular in tones of gold and red.

This is a sturdy plant which grows like the type species but not as tall. It may reach 10 meters at full maturity.

A. Sieboldianum 'Momijigasa'

The foliage has a light or whitish-green appearance. This is partly due to the dense covering of silvery pubescence over the light green color base. The undersides of the leaves, as well as the petiole, are also covered with pubescence. The Fall colors develop brilliant gold tones, blended with red.

The leaves have 9 lobes which separate deeply into the leaf. The lobes hold closely together on the inner half. The outer half is ovate, tapering to a long, narrow point. The margins have strong serrations. The leaf is 5 to 7 cm and 7 to 8 cm wide, with 4 cm petioles.

The twigs and branches are sturdy, and the plant forms a tall shrub or small tree. Like the species, it is a hardy plant for landscaping.

I find conflicting taxonomy on this cultivar. Some authors place it in this species, while others place it in *A. japonicum*.

A. Sieboldianum 'Sode no uchi'

This is the smallest-leafed form of the species. The foliage is a bright, light green which holds well through the season. The Fall colors are predominately bright yellow, with red tones blended in most leaves.

The leaf size varies from 2½ to 4 cm long and 3 to 5 cm across. On the old wood of the plant, the leaves will be half this size. There are nine lobes which radiate evenly from the center but are separated only half way to the base. The lobes are ovate, terminating in a blunt point. The margins are only lightly toothed. The stiff petioles are only 1 cm long.

This is a dwarf-growing little plant and tends to form a rounded bush. The annual growth is only about 10 to 20 cm on young shoots and much less on older wood.

This attractive little plant fits in well in many types of planting, particularly in alpine gardens and in containers on patios. It is also popular for bonsai in Japan, forming a tight shape with little pruning.

A. tenuifolium Koidzumi 1911
Series *Palmata*
'Hino uchiwa kaede'

The light green foliage of this small tree is thin in texture—almost papery. The Fall colors are yellow tones. Leaves have nine (7) lobes separated into the leaf ⅓ distance. Each lobe is broadly lanceolate, tapering to a sharp terminal. The margins are strongly incised and are double serrate.

The leaves are 4 to 6 cm long and 6 to 7 cm wide. The slender petioles are 2½ to 4 cm long and often glabrous.

This is a smaller and more delicate-appearing tree than the close relative, *A. shirasawanum*. The twigs and branches are thin, but not weak, and form an interesting scaffold pattern as the tree ages. Ogata reports that it will reach 8 meters in native stands in Central and Southern Japan.

I find this a delightful little tree, rather "different" from the other species in the Series *Palmata*. It makes an interesting contrast.

A. truncatum Bunge 1833
Series *Platanoidea*

This species is quite similar to *A. mono* and is native to Northern China, Manchuria, and the Amur River region. It is very cold-hardy, forms a large tree up to 18 meters, and makes an excellent over-story tree in the landscape. I include it with *Acers* from Japan because of its close relationship with *A. mono* and its popularity in horticulture in Japan.

The green leaves are 5 to 7-lobed and from 7 to 12 cm long and wide. The lobes are more deeply divided than in typical *A. mono*, separating about half way to the center. The lobes are triangular-ovate, terminating in a sharp tip. The margins are only slightly irregular. The Fall colors are bright gold, blended with scarlet.

A. Sieboldianum 'Sode no uchi'

A. tenuifolium with dew-wet leaves

A. truncatum 'Akikaze nishiki'

A. truncatum 'Akikaze nishiki' (Cv. of *A. mono*, of some authors)
Syn.: 'Shūfū nishiki', 'Shūhū nishiki', 'Shūen nishiki'

The desirable feature of this plant is the white-on-green color pattern of the foliage. The basic color is a rich green, but each leaf is marked differently, varying from all-white leaves to those with hardly any flecks of white. The main pattern is white or cream cut in (Kiri fu) a portion of the green leaf. In these leaves, the variegated portion is curved or sickle-shaped, usually quite strongly so. Often the green leaf is stippled with tiny specks of white, forming a solid pattern with the green showing through from beneath.

The leaf is usually deeply divided with five lobes. However, the foliage varies from 2, 3, 5, to even 7 lobes, depending upon the intensity of the variegation. The normal lobe is triangular-ovate, but all lobes with white areas are irregular and curved. Leaves vary greatly on each plant, but the average size is 6 to 8 cm long and 5 to 6 cm wide.

As the new foliage first appears, it has a definite pink tone which soon changes and becomes the white or cream marking in the variegation.

This cultivar forms a tall shrub, reaching up to 5 meters as it matures. It is multi-branching which means the plant thickens as it grows older. It is not a rapid grower, especially after the first few years. As with most variegated *Acers*, this cultivar should have some protection from hot afternoon sun which will burn the light-colored leaf portions.

A. truncatum albovitatum
See *A. truncatum* 'Akikaze nishiki'

A. truncatum 'Shūfū nishiki'
Alternate spelling: 'Shūhū nishiki', 'Shūen nishiki'
See *A. truncatum* 'Akikaze nishiki'

Acer Tschonoskii Maximowicz 1886
Series *Micrantha*
'Minekaede', 'Hime ogurabana', 'Hakusan momiji'

The delicacy of its foliage makes this cultivar a very pleasant choice for mixed landscapes. It will form a shrub-like plant or small tree, maturing at 5 (rarely 7) meters. It never looks "coarse" in mixed plantings.

The leaf is orbicular in outline but with five lobes. Leaves measure 5 to 9 cm long and slightly wider to 10 cm. The five lobes are rhombic-ovate, with long tapering tips. There is often a very short lobe on each side of the base. The margins are incised and double-serrate.

The bright green foliage has a rusty-brown pubescence underneath when new. Fall colors become golden, often tinged with red.

The branching is not coarse, although it is sturdy. It soon becomes multi-branched but not objectionably twiggy.

This species ranges from the North in Hokkaido, down through Central Honshu in Japan. There is a variety *australe*, ('Nangoku mine kaede') which ranges on down into Southern Japan. Another variety, *rubripes*, occurs in Manchuria and Northern Korea.

Acer ukurunduense Trautv. & Meyer 1856
Series *Spicata* 'Ōgarabana', 'Hozaki kaede'
(*A. caudatum* subsp. *ukurunduense* Murray)

A variable-growing plant, this will form a shrub or small tree from 3 to 10 meters high, often multi-stemmed. Occasionally it will form a tall tree up to 17 or 18 meters at maturity. The bark of older trunks is light greyish-brown and peels off in thin flakes. Bark on young twigs is yellowish-brown and pubescent.

The leaves are orbicular in shape but lightly five-angled. They measure 8 to 13 cm long and 8 to 15 cm wide and are cordate at the base. The green leaf has a light whitish tone above with a dull yellowish pubescence underneath. The lobes are ovate-triangular, acuminate, with margins sharply serrate and incised.

This tree is widely distributed, occuring in Japan, The Kuriles, Manchuria, S.E.Siberia, and Korea. It is closely related to *A. spicatum*, the "Mountain Maple" of eastern North America.

APPENDICES

Japanese Names and their Meanings

The following list of Japanese words and their English equivalents represent words used in the Japanese names for many of the cultivars. In many cases the translations are direct applications of meaning. In others, they are portions or combinations of interpretations which cannot be applied literally. Many of the cultivar names are only abbreviated references to a more complex meaning, such as in the case of 'Shigitatsu sawa' and 'Tanabata'. The latter is the "Festival of the Stars" (July 7th), but has a delightful "fairy tale" behind the name, as told to me:

In the skies of Japan there are two constellations related to this Festival. One is called Kengyū (the young boy who cared for the cows), and the other is Syokūjō (the girl who was a weaver at the loom).

"Once upon a time there were two diligent young people, Kengyū and Syokūjō. When they met the first time, they fell in love at once. After this happened, they didn't work very hard any more but spent all their time walking together. When the gods noticed this, they got very angry and separated the two young people by a great river (The Milky Way). After this, the young people couldn't be together any more. But, the gods said if they worked very hard they could see each other again once a year. So, they worked very hard and could see each other once a year on July 7th." Thus the "Festival of the Stars", "Festival of the Weaver"—Tanabata.

The terms described in the following list will enable the reader to understand more of the names which have combined terms such as: beni = red; shidare = drooping or cascading—"The red, cascading variety."

Aka — red
Ao — green
Aoba — green leaves
Aocha — yellow green
Araka wa — rough bark
Asahi — rising sun
Beni — red
Chirimen — Japanese crepe paper
Gasane — piling one thing on another

Gasumi or Kasumi — a mist or haze
Goshiki — multicolored
Hime — dwarf, princess
Ito — fine strings or thread
Iwato — rock
Kaede — one of the terms for maple, often applied to foreign maple species
Kagami — mirror
Kaku — tower
Kakure — shade or shelter
Kamagata — falcate (hort.)
Kara — Ancient Chin or Chinese
Kashi — filament (hort.)
Kin — gold
Komachi — beautiful girl; dwarf (hort.)
Koto — an old harp
Koto no ito — harp of string
Kujaku — peacock
Kumo no su — a spider's web
Kyō — Ancient capital, Kyoto city; beautiful dress, variegated leaf (hort.)
Mai — dancing
Maruba — round leaves
Masu — wooden "box" used to drink Saki
Mejishi — mythical female lion
Miyama — remote high mountain
Miyasama kaede — Prince's maple; early plant of this grown at Prince Fushima's garden
Nishiki — variegated (actually means brocade or tapestry); "fine dress"
Nishiki or Nishikisho — rough bark, like on a pine (hort.)
No — of
Nomura — beautiful
Ōjishi — mythical male lion
Ryū — dragon
Saku — fence
Sango — coral
Sarasa — a type of fabric with beautiful figures
Sei — green
Sekka — dwarf (from witch's broom)
Shidare — cascading or willowy
Shigure — soft drizzle
Shime — a decoration used on New Year's Day
Shime no uchi — "within New Year's Day"
Shin — new
Shira — white
Shishigashira — lion's head (mythical lion)
Shōjō — red-faced monkey. This applies to a fictional monkey of Japanese drama. Can also mean a young girl. Can also be read Syojo.
Tama — ball or gem
Tana — "shelves" or layers
Tanabata — Festival of the Stars (July 7)
Ten nyō — "angel"
Toyama — name of a place
Tsuchi — earth
Tsuma — nail
Uchi — within
Yama — mountain
Yatsubusa — compact, dwarf (hort.)
Yezo nishiki — Yezo, northern island of Japan
Yū — evening
Yuki — snow

Cultivar Names Not Elsewhere Described

The names included in the following list are not described elsewhere in this book. They are recorded here for reference purposes. This is an indication of the vast number of names which have been applied to this one small group of plants over the past 300 years. The names included fall into at least one of the following categories:

1. Names used in very early literature which may have been discontinued
2. Cultivars propagated in very early times which may no longer be in cultivation
3. Names which may be synonyms but are not presently verified
4. Modern-day plant selections not yet widely known or distributed
5. Early European nomenclature later found to be synonymous or invalid
6. Cultivars which I have not grown long enough to describe or evaluate and for which I lack adequate written descriptions
7. Names which are alternate interpretations of the Kanji written forms

Adlerschwanz (diss.)
Akashigata
Akitsushima
Akitsuta
Amatum (diss.)
Amelopsifolium (laciniatum?)
Arashiyama
Arimayama
Asagiri
Asanoha
Asatsuyu
Asu kagawa
Aya nishiki
Ayai
Ayai gasa (Sieboldianum)
Azumasato
Baldsmith (diss.)
Barrie Bergman (diss.)
Beni goromo
Beni nomi
Bonnie Bergman
Carane brokat (laciniatum?)
Carneum (Palm. atropurpureum)
Chikumano
Chizome
Compactum
Crippsii
Cuneatum
Cupreum
diss. atrosanguineum (Nigrum?)
diss. polychromum (diss. variegatum?)
Euchlorum
Ezo nishiki
Fichtenast (Matsugae?)
Furusato
Futagoyama
Genji gurama
Genjiyama
Goshozome
Hana asobi

Hane ogi
Hatsu seyama
Hatsushigure (diss.)
Hikaru genji momiji
Hino tsukasa
Hira no uchi
Hitoshio
Hitosome
Ho o nishiki
Horinji
Howzan (diss.)
Idenosato
Illustre (Heptalobum?)
Ima deshōjō
Ino brokat
Ito shidare (Ao shidare)
Iwado kagami
Iwateyama
Izayoi
Jedo nishiki (Yezo nishiki)
Jiman zome momiji
Kamegaya
Kan nazuke
Kara aya
Karukaya
Kasado
Kayoi
Kihatsijo (Ki hachijo?)
Killarny
Kimigayo
Kinshojo
Kogane sunago
Kogasayama
Komadome
Kondeshōjō
Kumogasumi
Kureha
Kushimiyano
Lovett (selection jap. aconitifolium?)
Luteum

Marmoratum (Shigitatsu sawa?)
Matsu yoi
Me ho nishiki
Meikets
Mimuruyama
Mino kasayama
Mioun, diss
Miyadono
Mon nishiki
Morris (diss.)
Murasaki daka
Murasaki taka
Narihirabeni
Niho beni
Nimura (Nomura?)
Noki bata
Nou nishiki (Wou nishiki?)
Oboku (Kigi)
Obtusum
Ochikochibito
Okima
Okotoi
Okustanea (Okushimo?)
Ominato
Otome zakura
Pinnatifidium (diss.)
Pixie
Plumosum
Pulchrum
Red Head
Rhodophyllum (diss. atro.?)
Roscoe Red (Novum?)
Roseum
Rubellum (diss. tinctum?)
Rubricaule
Rubrinerve (Rubricaule?)
Ruth Murray (diss.)
Sahoyama
Saintpaulianum (Nishiki gasane)
Sangotsu

Sawagani
Sayoginu
Seicha nishiki
Seminohane
Senri
Sensunagasi
Shigara jama
Shika momiji
Shikainami
Shioname (Shinoname?)
Shishi yatsubusa
Shokune nishiki
Spring Fire (Van Gelderen?)
Sumieda shidare
Sumizome
Surizume
Taiyo nishiki
Tatsuta teuka
Thread leaf (dissectums)
Tinctum (diss.)
Tobikawa nishiki
Toi mire nike
Tokonatsu uchiwa nagashi
Tonariya
Tsuka mano
Tsuten
Uchiwanagashi
Unicolor
Uzuranoha
Verkade's Witch's Broom
Wakamidori
Wakana
Wasure gatami
Yamashigi
Yashio
Yodo gawa
Yog saku (Hog yoku?)
Yoshino gawa
Yubae

Guide to Use and Character

These charts are provided to assist in the selection of plants for individual situations considering color, size, and special cultural needs and conditions. They tabulate in summary fashion the most important landscaping characteristics of many of the cultivars and species included in this book. Before making selections from these tables I urge you to turn back to the cultivar descriptions to double check the suitability of a specific cultivar in terms of the specific location or use the reader has in mind. The classifications are not rigid criteria but are designed to suggest uses and qualities of the plants described. Each classification must be interpreted for the reader's specific needs and locality. Symbols and explanation of categories are as follows:

Height of plant, approaching maturity:

    a = under 1 meter (up to 3 feet)

    b = 1 to 2 meters (3 to 7 feet)

    c = 2 to 4 meters (7 to 13 feet)

    d = 4 to 6 meters (13 to 20 feet)

    e = 6 to 12 meters (20 to 40 feet)

    f = over 12 meters (over 40 feet)

Form of maturing plant:

    U = upright tree

    W = spreading, pendulous, or weeping branches

    S = upright shrub

    M = mound-shaped shrub

Container = Plants suitable for containers on patios, etc. All cultivars will adapt to container culture, but those so designated are more commonly used.

Bonsai = Those designated are popular for bonsai culture due to the nature of the cultivar. However, all the cultivars will adapt to bonsai training.

Dwarf = These are cultivars which fit in particularly well with rockeries and alpine gardens.

Companion plants = These cultivars fit in very well with most other shrubbery, perennials, and mixed plantings. Not overly aggressive and keep their shape well.

Light requirements

    SH = partial shade. This classification does not imply that the plant will only grow in shade, but rather that it benefits from partial shade.

    SU = full sun. This indicates that the plant will grow well in exposed situations although some foliage may tip-burn under extreme conditions.

Garden *Effects*

    S = Indicates that the plant is notable for the color and effect of the Spring foliage and shoots.

    F = Indicates that the plant is notable for the outstanding Fall colors.

    D = Indicates that the plant is noteworthy for dramatic foliage, bark, or growth habit.

Cultivars listed alphabetically.

Cultivar	Height	Form	Container	Bonsai	Dwarf	Companion	Light	Effects
Aconitifolium	d	U					Su	F
Aka shigitatsu sawa	c	U	×	×		×	Sh	S
Akaji nishiki	c	U	×	×		×		S
Akegarasu	c	U						
Akikaze nishiki	d	U	×			×		D
Ao shidare	b	M	×			×		
Aoyagi	c	U				×		
Asahi zuru	d	U				×		
Atrolineare	c	S				×		D
Atropurpureum	e	U						
Atropurpureum, dissectum	c	M	×			×		
Aureo variegatum	d	U	×					

Cultivar	Height	Form	Container	Bonsai	Dwarf	Companion	Light	Effects
Aureum, japonicum	d	U	×			×		S
Aureum, palmatum	d	U	×			×		S
Azuma muresaki	d	U						
Beni kagami	c	W				×		
Beni komachi	b	S	×	×	×		Sh	D
Beni maiko	b	S	×	×		×		D
Beni schichihenge	c	U	×			×		S
Beni shidare	c	M	×			×		
Beni shidare variegated	b	M	×			×	Sh	S
Beni tsukasa	c	S	×	×		×		S
Beni uri	e	U						D
Bloodgood	e	U						
Bonfire	d	U	×	×				S
Brocade, diss.	b	M	×			×		
Burgundy Lace	d	W						
Butterfly	c	S	×	×		×		D
Chirimen nishiki	b	S	×	×		×	Su	S
Chishio	c	U	×	×				S
Chitoseyama	c	W	×					S
Coonara Pygmy	b	S	×	×	×			
Corallinum	c	S	×			×		S
Crimson Queen	c	M	×			×		
Deshojo	d	U				×	Su	
Elegans	d	W					Su	
Ever Red	c	M	×			×		
Filigree	c	M	×			×		D
Flavescens	c	M	×			×		
Garnet	c	M	×			×		
Garyu	a	M	×	×	×	×		D
Goshiki kotohime	a	S	×	×	×	×		D
Goshiki kaede	c	U	×			×	Sh	S
Goshiki shidare	b	M	×	×	×	×	Sh	S
Green Cascade	c	M	×			×	Su	D
Hagoromo	d	U				×	Su	D
Hamaotome	c	U				×		
Hanami nishiki	b	S	×	×		×		S
Hanazono nishiki	d	U					Sh	
Harusame	d	U						
Hatsuyuki	e	U						D
Hazeroino	c	U				×		D
Heptalobum	e	U					Su	F
Hessei	d	W	×					
Higasayama	d	U	×	×				D
Hogyoku	d	U				×	Su	F
Hoshiyadori	c	U	×			×		D
Ichigyoji	d	U					Su	F
Iijima sunago	d	U						D
Inaba shidare	c	M	×			×		D
Inazuma	c	U				×		
Iso chidori	b	S	×	×		×	Su	
Itayo	e	U					Su	F
Jiro shidare	c	W	×					
Junihitoye	c	U	×	×		×	Su	

Cultivar	Height	Form	Container	Bonsai	Dwarf	Companion	Light	Effects
Kagero	d	U	×					S
Kagiri nishiki	c	U	×	×		×	Sh	S
Kamagata	b	S	×	×	×	×	Su	D
Karaori	d	U	×					
Karasugawa	d	U	×			×	Sh	S
Kasen nishiki	d	U	×			×		S
Kashima	b	S	×	×	×	×		
Katsura	b	S	×	×	×	×		
Ki hachijo	c	W				×	Su	
Kinugasayama	e	U					Su	F
Kinran	d	W	×			×		F
Kiri nishiki	c	M	×			×	Su	
Kiyohime	a	S	×	×	×	×	Su	
Komon nishiki	d	U	×			×		
Komurasaki	d	U						S
Koreanum	e	U					Su	
Koshibori nishiki	b	S	×	×		×		S
Koshimino	d	U	×				Su	D
Koto ito komachi	a	M	×	×	×	×		D
Koto no ito	c	U	×	×		×	Su	
Kotohime	a	S	×	×	×	×		D
Kurabeyama	c	W	×			×	Su	
Kurui jishi	b	S	×	×			Su	D
Kyuden	a	S	×	×	×	×		
Linearilobum	c	U	×			×	Su	D
Little Gem	a	S	×	×	×	×	Su	
Lutescens	d	W				×	Su	
Maiko	c	S	×			×		D
Mama	c	S	×			×		D
Marakumo	c	U				×	Sh	
Maruba tokaede	d	U					Su	
Masukagami	d	U	×				Sh	S
Masumurasaki	c	U	×			×	Su	S
Matsukaze	d	W						S
Matsugae	c	U	×					S
Meigetsu	e	U					Su	F
Mejishi	c	U	×	×		×		D
Meuri ko fuba	c	U	×			×		
Meuri o fuba	c	U						D
Microphyllum, japonicum	d	U	×				Su	F
Microphyllum, Sieboldianum	e	U	×				Su	F
Mikawa yatsubusa	a	M	×	×	×	×		
Mino yatsubusa	b	M	×	×	×			D
Miyagino	d	U					Su	F
Miyasama kaede	d	U	×			×	Su	
Mizu kaguri	c	U	×				Sh	
Momenshide	c	U	×			×		D
Monroe	d	U	×			×		D
Monzukushi	d	U					Su	F
Moonfire	d	U				×		S
Murasaki hime	b	U	×	×	×			
Murasaki kiyohime	b	U	×	×	×			
Mure hibari	d	W				×		
Murogawa	d	W						S
Musashino	d	U				×		S
Musk scented	b	M	×		×	×		D
Nana segawa	d	W						
Naruto kaede	c	U	×				Su	D

Cultivar	Height	Form	Container	Bonsai	Dwarf	Companion	Light	Effects
Nicholsonii	d	W						F
Nigrum	d	U						S
Nigrum, dissectum	b	M	×			×		S
Nishiki gasane	c	U	×			×	Sh	d
Nishiki momiji	e	U					Su	
Nomura nishiki	c	W	×					
Novum	d	U						S
Nuresagi	c	U	×			×		
Nusitoriyama	b	S	×		×		Sh	D
O isami	e	U					Su	F
O jishi	a	M	×	×	×			D
O kagami	c	W	×					
Ogan sarasa	d	W				×	Su	
Okushimo	e	U	×	×				D
Omato	d	U					Su	F
Omurayama	d	W				×	Su	F
Orido nishiki	c	U	×				Sh	S
Ornatum, dissectum	c	W	×			×		
Osakazuki	d	U	×				Su	F
Oshio beni	e	U						
Oshu beni	d	U						
Oshu shidare	c	W						
O taki	e	U					Su	F
Palmatifidium, dissectum	c	W	×			×	Su	F
Palmatifolium, shirasawanum	d	U					Su	F
Pendula Julian, diss	c	M	×			×		
Pend. angust. atro. diss.	c	M	×			×		
Pine Bark Maple	b	U	×	×		×	Su	D
Red Filigree Lace, diss.	b	M	×		×	×		D
Red Pygmy	c	M	×	×		×		D
Roseo marginatum, diss.	c	M	×			×		
Rough Bark Maple	d	U					Su	D
Rubrifolium, diss	c	M	×			×		S
Rubrum	d	U						
Rufescens	d	U						F
Ryumon nishiki	c	U	×			×	Sh	
Ryuzu	a	M	×	×	×	×		D
Sagara nishiki	c	U	×	×		×	Sh	D
Samidare	d	U					Su	F
Sango kaku	d	U	×	×		×	Su	D
Saoshika	c	S	×			×		
Saotome	b	S	×	×				
Sazanami	b	S	×					
Scolopendrifolium	d	U	×			×	Su	D
Seigen	b	S	×	×		×		S
Seiryu, diss.	c	U	×			×	Su	
Sekimori, diss.	c	M	×				Su	F
Sekka yatsubusa	a	S	×	×	×			
Sherwood Flame	d	W				×		
Shigarami	d	U					Su	S
Shigitatsu sawa	c	U	×			×	Sh	D
Shigure bato	b	W	×			×		
Shigurezome	c	U				×		
Shime no uchi	c	U	×	×		×	Su	
Shindeshojo	c	W	×	×		×	Su	S
Shino buga oka	c	U	×	×		×	Su	
Shino nome	d	W				×		S

Cultivar	Height	Form	Container	Bonsai	Dwarf	Companion	Light	Effects
Shishigashira	c	U	×	×		×	Su	D
Shishio improved	c	W	×	×		×	Su	S
Shishio improved	c	W	×	×		×	Su	S
Shojo	d	U						S
Shojo nomura	c	U	×					
Sode no uchi	b	S	×	×		×	Su	
Suminagashi	d	W						
Taimin nishiki	b	U	×				Sh	
Takao	d	U					Su	F
Tama nishiki	c	U	×			×	Sh	S
Tamahime	a	S	×	×	×			
Tamukeyama, diss	c	M	×			×		
Tana	d	U				×	Su	
Tana bata	d	U						
Tancho	a	M	×	×	×			D
Tatsuta	c	W	×			×		
Toyama nishiki	b	M				×	Sh	D
Trompenburg	c	U	×			×		D
Tsuchigumo	b	S	×	×		×	Su	
Tsukomo	a	S	×	×	×			
Tsukubani	c	U						
Tsukushigata	c	U	×			×		D
Tsuma beni	c	W	×			×		S
Tsuma gaki	c	W	×			×		S
Tsuri nishiki	d	W						F
Ukegumo	c	U	×			×	Sh	S
Ukon	c	U				×		
Umegae	b	S	×	×				S
Usugumo	c	U						D
Utsu semi	c	U						
Variegatum, dissectum	b	M	×			×	Sh	D
Veitchii	e	U						D
Versicolor	d	U					Su	
Villa Taranto	c	W	×			×		D
Viridis, dissect.	c	M	×			×		
Vitifolium	e	U						F
Volubile	d	U					Su	
Wabito	b	S	×	×	×	×		D
Wako nishiki	a	S	×	×	×			D
Waterfall, diss.	c	M	×			×		
Wou nishiki	c	U				×		
Yatsubusa	b	S	×	×	×	×		
Yezo nishiki	d	U					Su	S
Yugure	d	U						

SPECIES	HEIGHT	FORM	FEATURE
Argutum	6–12 m	Spreading	Fall color
Buergerianum	6–12 m	Spreading	Fall color
Capillipes	Over 12 m	Upright	Striped bark
Carpinifolium	6–12 m	Upright	Foliage
Circinatum	6–12 m	Spreading	Fall color
Cissifolium	Over 12 m	Upright	Foliage
Crataegifolium	6–12 m	Upright	Foliage
Diabolicum	Over 12 m	Upright	Fall color
Distylum	6–12 m	Upright	Foliage
Ginnala	4–6 m	Spreading	Fall color
Griseum	6–12m	Upright	Peeling bark
Japonicum	6–12 m	Spreading	Fall color
Micranthum	6–12 m	Upright	Foliage
Miyabei	Over 12 m	Upright	Fall color
Mono	Over 12 m	Upright	Fall color
Nikoense	Over 12 m	Upright	Foliage
Nipponicum	Over 12 m	Upright	Foliage
Palmatum	6–12 m	Upright	Fall color
Pentaphyllum	6–12 m	Upright	Foliage
Pseudosieboldianum	6–12 m	Spreading	Fall color
Pycnanthum	6–12 m	Upright	Fall color
Rufinerve	Over 12 m	Upright	Fall color
Shirasawanum	6–12 m	Spreading	Fall color
Sieboldianum	6–12 m	Spreading	Fall color
Tenuifolium	6–12 m	Upright	Fall color
Truncatum	Over 12 m	Upright	Fall color
Tschonoskii	6–12 m	Upright	Foliage
Ukurunduense	6–12 m	Spreading	Fall color

BIBLIOGRAPHY

Angyo Maple Nursery Catalog, 1930. Japan

Anstey, Miss J. M. (Kent, England) "*Acers* from Cuttings." Inter. Plant Prop. Soc. Proceedings Vol. 19, 1969

Baker, Kenneth F., Editor, *The U.C. System for Producing Healthy Container-grown Plants*. Univ. of Calif. Divisions of Agricultural Sciences, Manual 23. Berkeley, Calif. 1957

Bean, W. J. *Trees & Shrubs Hardy in the British Isles*. 3rd. ed. England 1950

Carey, Dennis P. (Worcester, England) "Production of Japanese Maples by Cuttings." Inter. Plant Prop. Soc. Proceedings Vol. 24, 1974

Carville, Lawrence L. (Middletown, R.I.) "Propagation of *Acer palmatum* Cultivars from Hardwood Cuttings." Inter. Plant Prop. Soc. Proceedings Vol. 25, 1975

Chugai Shokubutsu Yen (Nursery Catalog) 1931–32; 1938–39; 1940–41. Yamamoto, Kawabegun, Kobe, Japan

Coggeshall, R. G. "Asiatic Maples, their Propagation from Softwood Cuttings" Arnoldia, Vol. 17, July 1957

Curtis, William J. (Sherwood, Oregon) "Seed Germination and Culture of *Acer palmatum*." Inter. Plant Prop. Soc. Proceedings Vol. 19, 1969

de Jong, P. C. *Flowering and Sex Expression in Acer*. (thesis) Agricultural University Wageningen, The Netherlands. 1976

Essig, Prof. E. O. *Insects of Western North America*. The MacMillan Co. New York 1929

Fang, Wen-pei *A Monograph of Chinese Aceracea*. Contr. Biol. Lab. of the Science Society of China, Vol. 11, Nanking, China. 1939

Fordham, Alfred (Jamaica Plains, Mass.) "*Acer griseum* and its Propagation." Inter. Plant Prop. Soc. Proceedings Vol. 19, 1969

Forest Service, U.S.D.A. *Woody-plant Seed Manual*. Misc. Pub. No. 654, G.P.O., Washington, D.C. 1948

Garner, R. J. *The Grafter's Handbook*. East Malling Research Station, Oxford Univ. Press, 3rd ed. 1967

Hanado, San-nojo *Kadan Chikinsho* 6 vol. 1965

Harris, D. C. (Exbury, England) "Propagation of Japanese Maples by Grafting" Inter. Plant Prop. Soc. Proceedings Vol. 26, 1976

Harris, J. Gordon (Somerset, England) "Maples from Japan." Journal Royal Hort. Soc. 1975

Harris, J. Gordon "Growing Maples from Seed." from "The Garden" of the Journal Royal Hort. Soc., Oct. 1976

Harris, J. G. S. "Propagation of *Acers*." Inter. Dendrology Society Yearbook 1973

Hartmann, Hudson T. and Dale E. Kester. *Plant Propagation*, 3rd ed. Prentice-Hall New Jersey 1975

Hillier, Harold G. *Hillier's Manual of Trees and Shrubs*, 2nd ed. Winchester, England 1970

Hitchcock, C. Leo and Arthur Cronquist *Flora of the Pacific Northwest*. U. of Washington Press, Seattle, Wash. 1973

Hohman, Henry J. *List of plants in Collection*. Kingsville, Md. 1968

Hohman, Henry J. Personal Correspondence & Cultivar Descriptions 1966–74

Hutchinson, Peter A. (Leicestershire, England) "Propagation of *Acers* from Seed." Int. Plant Prop. Soc. Proceedings Vol. 21, 1971

Iconographia Cormophytorum Sinicorum, Vol. 2. Botanical Institute of the Univ. of Peking, China 1972

International Code of Nomenclature of Cultivated Plants. 1969. Published by The International Bureau for Plant Taxonomy and Nomenclature, Utrecht, Netherlands.

Ishii, Yugi *Gen Shoku Engei Shokobutsu Zukan*, Vol. 4. Sebundo, Tokyo 1932

Ito, Ibei *Zoho Chikinsho*, Vol. 4 Japan 1710

Ito, Ibei *Koeki Chikinsho*, Vol. 3 Japan 1719

Ito, Ibei *Shikinsho Furoku* Japan 1733

Itoh, Jirozaemon (Matsu Zakaya) *Momiji*. (hand illus. in color, 200 illus; notes by Kokoh) Geichikudo Corp. Tokyo 1911

Kobayashi, Jiro *Maples for Beginners*. Nihon Bungei Sha, Ltd., Tokyo 1975

Kaede Rui Zuko, 3 vol. Japan 1891

Kobayashi Nursery Catalog. Angyo, Japan 1967

Koidzumi, G. *Revisio Aceracearum Japonicarum*. Journ. College of Science,Imperial Univ. of Tokyo, Vol. XXXII, 1911

Lamb, J. G. D. (Dublin, Ireland) "Vegetative Propagation of Japanese Maples at Kinsealy." Inter. Plant Prop. Soc. Proceedings Vol. 22, 1972

Lancaster, Roy *Trees for Your Garden*. Scribner New York 1974

Lancaster, Roy "Maples of the Himalaya." from "The Garden" of the Journal Royal Hort. Soc., Dec. 1976

Matsumura, Y. "Maples of Japan." in Arboretum Bulletin, U. of Washington Arboretum, Seattle, Wash., No. XVII, Winter 1954

McMinn, Howard E. and Evelyn Maino *Illustrated Manual of Pacific Coast Trees*. U. of Calif. Press, Berkeley, Calif. 1967

Mulligan, Brian O. "*Acer circinatum* 'Monroe' " Baileya, Vol, 19, no.3, Cornell Univ., Ithaca, N.Y. 1974

Mulligan, Brian O. *Maples Cultivated in the United States and Canada*. Amer. Assoc. of Botanical Gardens and Arboretums 1958

Mulloy, M. S. (Waterbury, Conn.) "Variability in Japanese Maples." Amer. Rock Garden Soc. Bull., Vol. 24, Winter 1976

Murray, A. Edward, Jr. *A Monograph of the Aceraceae*. (thesis) June 1970 Penn. State University

Murray, A. Edward, Jr. "Acer Notes" Kalmia, Nos. 1 & 2, 1969–1970 Philadelphia, Penn.

Nakamura, Tsuneo et al. *Momiji & Kaede*. Seibundo Shinkosha, Tokyo 1974

Ogata, Ken "On *Acer pycnanthum*." Jour. Geobotany, Univ. Tokyo, Vol. XIII, No. 4, March 1965

Ogata, Ken "On the Varieties of *Acer mono*, Found in Japan." Jour. Geobotany, Univ. Tokyo, Vol. XII, No. 4, 1964

Ogata, Ken "A Dendrological Study on the Japanese *Aceraceae*, with Special Reference to Geographical Distribuion." Bulletin of the Tokyo Univ. Forests, No. 60, June 1965

Ogata, Ken "A Systematic Study of the Genus *Acer*." Reprint from the Misc. Information, Tokyo Univ. Forests, Bulletin No. 63, 1967

Ohwi, Jisaburo *Flora of Japan*. Pub. by Smithsonian Institute, Washington, D.C. 1965

Oka, Seigura, Isaoburo Ito and Gosaburo Ito. *Kaede Binran* Japan 1882

Pax, Ferdinand *"Aceraceae"* in A. Engler, *Das Pflanzenreich*, Vol. IV.163, Verlag von Wilhelm Englemann, Leipzig 1902

Pringle, James S. "The Concept of the Cultivar," Journal Pacific Hort. Foundation, Vol. 37, Nos. 3, 4; Vol. 38, Nos. 1, 2 (Reprint from Bulletin of the Royal Botanical Gardens, Ontario, Canada Vol. 27, No.3)

Rapley, B. A. (New Plymouth, New Zealand) "Grafting Maples from Imported Scions." Inter. Plant Prop. Soc. Proceedings Vol. 24, 1974

Rehder, Alfred *Manual of Cultivated Trees & Shrubs*. New York 1929

Rehder, Alfred "New Species, Varieties . . . of the Arnold Arboretum," Journal of the Arnold Arboretum, Vol. XIX 1938

Savella, Leonard (Exeter, R. I.) "Top Grafting of Japanese Maples and Dogwood." Inter. Plant Prop. Soc. Proceedings Vol. 21, 1971

Shurtleff, Malcolm C. *Plant Diseases in Home and Garden*. Iowa State Univ. Press, Ames, Iowa 1966

Tominari & Hayashi *Nihon no ka boku* (Ornamental Trees and Shrubs of Japan) Kodansha, Pub. 1971

Townsend, M. Alden and Winand K. Hock. "Tolerance of Half-sib Families of Red Maple to Verticillium Wilt," Phytopathology, Vol. 63, No. 6, 1973

Uehara, Dr. Keiji *Jyuboku Daiju Setsu*, 3 vol. Pub. Ariake Shobo. Bunkyo-ku, Tokyo, Japan 1961

Van Gelderen, D. M. "Japanese Maples." Dendriflora, No. 6, 1969, Royal Soc. Nurs. & Dutch Dendrology Soc.

Suzuki, Hideo Personal Correspondence and Translations 1972–77. Kumagaya, Saitama-ken, Japan

Van Klaveren, Richard (Seattle, Wash.) "Growing *Acer palmatum* from Cuttings," Inter. Plant Prop. Soc. Proceedings Vol. 19, 1969

Vertrees, J. D. "Observations on Propagation of Asiatic Maples." Inter. Plant Prop. Soc. Proceedings Vol. 22, 1972

Vertrees, J. D. "Maples of Japan," American Horticulturist, Vol. 52, No. 2, 1973

Vertrees, J. D. "Maples." American Horticulturist, Vol. 53, No. 3, 1974

Vertrees, J. D. "Japanese Maples Gain Recognition," American Nurseryman, Vol. CXLII, No. 2, 1975

Vrugtman, F. (Hamilton, Ontario, Canada) "Notes of the *Acer* Collection of the Botanical Gardens and the Belmonte Arboretum," Misc. Paper No. 6, Landbouwhogeschool, Wageningen, The Netherlands, 1970

Wada, K. (Hakoneya Nursery) Nursery Catalog 1938

Weaver, Richard E., Jr. "Selected Maples for Shade and Ornamental Planting," Arnoldia, Vol. XXXVI, No. 4, 1976

Wells, James S. *Plant Propagation Practices*. Macmillan New York 1955

Wolff, Richard P. (Media, Penn.) "Success and Failures in Grafting Japanese Maples." Inter. Plant Prop. Soc. Proceedings Vol. 23, 1973

Yokohama Nursery Co. Ltd. Illustrated Nursery Catalog 1898

Yokohama Nursery Co. Ltd. Nursery Catalog 1919

INDEX